Praise for
Love for No Reason

"Marci Shimoff once again touches the heart with her new book, *Love for No Reason* . . . a guide to creating a life of love and happiness that saturates your soul. Thank you, Marci, for this important and inspiring book."

—Mariel Hemingway, award-winning actress
and author of *Healthy Living from the Inside Out*

"What the world needs now is Marci Shimoff and her extraordinary handbook on how unconditional love can end heartache, feed the soul, and light the world."

—Lynne McTaggart, author of the bestsellers *The Field* and *The Intention Experiment*

"*Love for No Reason* is a book to read again and again. Engaging, wise, and profound, it will change your life for the better—no matter where you begin your journey to greater unconditional love."

—Kristine Carlson, author of *Don't Sweat the Small Stuff in Love*
and *An Hour to Live, An Hour to Love*

"In ways both profound and practical, this book shows you proven ways to open the gates of love. Grounded in brain science and illuminated by spirit, it helps you find the love that's already in you and around you. Funny, warm, and with lots of practical suggestions, Marci Shimoff's voice is with you on every page, like a good friend speaking from the heart."

—Rick Hanson, PhD, author of *Buddha's Brain: The Practical Neuroscience of Happiness, Love, and Wisdom*

"*Love for No Reason* takes a scientific approach to unconditional love, where emotion meets spirit. Every reader will find something that resonates and opens their heart!"

—Candace Pert, PhD, author of *Molecules of Emotions*
and *Everything You Need to Know to Feel Go(o)d*

"There are thousands of books that educate us on how to give and receive love. But this unique and powerful book does that and more—it shows us how to *BE* love, which is what we are at the most profound root of the Self."

—Michael Bernard Beckwith, founder of the Agape International Spiritual Center and author of *Spiritual Liberation: Fulfilling Your Soul's Potential*

"*Love for No Reason* is a brilliant how-to guide for expanding your capacity to love. Highly recommended."

—John Gray, #1 *New York Times* bestselling author of *Men Are from Mars, Women Are from Venus*

Love for No Reason

7 Steps to Creating a Life of Unconditional Love

Marci Shimoff

WITH CAROL KLINE

Free Press

New York   London   Toronto   Sydney   New Delhi

*f*P

Free Press
A Division of Simon & Schuster, Inc.
1230 Avenue of the Americas
New York, NY 10020

First Free Press trade paperback edition January 2012

FREE PRESS and colophon are trademarks of Simon & Schuster, Inc.

For information about special discounts for bulk purchases,
please contact Simon & Schuster Special Sales at
1-866-506-1949 or business@simonandschuster.com.

The Simon & Schuster Speakers Bureau can bring authors to your live event.
For more information or to book an event, contact the Simon & Schuster Speakers
Bureau at 1-866-248-3049 or visit our website at www.simonspeakers.com.

Manufactured in the United States of America

10 9 8 7 6 5 4 3 2 1

The Library of Congress has cataloged the hardcover edition as follows:

  Shimoff, Marci.
  Love for no reason : 7 steps to creating a life of unconditional love / Marci Shimoff
with Carol Kline.
      p.   cm.
  1. Love.   I. Kline, Carol, 1957–   II. Title.
  BF575.L8.S562   2010
  152.4'1—dc22   2010034732

ISBN 978-1-4391-6502-7
ISBN 978-1-4391-6503-4 (pbk)
ISBN 978-1-4391-6504-1 (ebook)

This book is dedicated to all those who hear the call of their heart to live in unconditional love.
And to Mom, I carry your love in my heart.

CONTENTS

Contents

FOREWORD

BY MARIANNE WILLIAMSON

*I*t might be a cliché at this point to quote the Beatles and say, "All you need is love," but it couldn't be truer. In the words of Martin Luther King Jr., "We have a power within us more powerful than bullets." Surely that power is love. Amen.

Yet how do we harness that power? How do we take the most profound philosophical realization, "Love is the answer," and make it operative in our everyday lives and in our world? How do we take the greatest spiritual injunction of all time, "Love one another," and actually *do* it? How do we apply love in situations where violence, both physical and emotional, violates that love at every turn? How do we keep from growing cynical and jaded at the thought that love could heal the world, when hatred has such a hold upon it?

There are no questions more important, and the book you're reading now has answers. Marci Shimoff has her finger on the pulse of the greatest evolutionary leap in the history of humanity—our leap out of fear into the attitudinal matrix of love. From philosophy to science, from theory to experience, this book covers the gamut and makes a very good case for not only the power but also the practicability of love.

Marci Shimoff is my friend. She is one of the most loving people I've ever known, and with this book she provides to the world what she provides to all who know her: a compelling case for the power of love.

When my book *A Return to Love* was first published in 1992, the idea of love as a mainstream conversation was kind of a new thing, as odd as that sounds today. We've come a long way since then in taking the conversation of love to an even broader, more socially relevant place, and *Love for No Reason* contributes mightily to the cause. Do not just read this book; practice it. If you do it and I do it and everyone else who reads it does it, then in our own small ways we will have helped turn the tide of history. Blocks to love will fall by the wayside, walls that separate us will begin to melt, wounds will heal, and the world will change.

Don't just take my word for it. Take Jesus'. And Buddha's. And John Lennon's. And Martin Luther King Jr.'s. And Gandhi's. And the word of everyone else who has ever seen through the veil of illusion that blocks love from our sight.

How do we *do* it, though? This book has answers. And Marci Shimoff is a worthy guide.

PART I

Love:
The Final Frontier

There is no difficulty that enough love will not conquer . . .

No door that enough love will not open

No gulf that enough love will not bridge,

No wall that enough love will not throw down . . .

It makes no difference how deeply seated may be the trouble,

how great the mistake,

sufficient realization of love will resolve it all.

If only you could love enough,

you would be the happiest and most powerful being in the universe.

—Emmet Fox, twentieth-century author and teacher

INTRODUCTION

What the World Needs Now Is Love, Sweet Love

Through the train window, she watched the villages and vineyards of the Italian countryside go by. It was 1942 and Sussi Penzias, a young Jewish woman who'd fled Nazi Germany, was traveling alone, hoping to remain unnoticed. Since she'd arrived in Italy three years earlier, she'd been moving from place to place, staying with friends and friends of friends, hiding from the authorities. Now she was on her way to yet another safe house in a new town.

Suddenly, the door at the end of the train car swung open and two police officers came in. Sussi's heart beat wildly. They were wearing the black uniform of the Fascisti, the government police. To Sussi's horror, the policemen began making their way down the aisle, stopping at every row to examine the papers of each passenger.

Sussi knew that as soon as the policemen discovered she had no papers, she would be arrested. She was terrified she'd end up in a concentration camp and would face unimaginable suffering and almost certain death.

The officers were getting closer, just a few rows away. There was no escape. It was only a matter of minutes before they would reach her seat. Sussi began to tremble uncontrollably, and tears slid down her cheeks.

The man sitting next to her noticed her distress and politely asked her why she was crying.

"I'm Jewish and I have no papers," she whispered, hardly able to speak.

To her surprise, a few seconds later the man began shouting at her, "You idiot! I can't believe how stupid you are! What an imbecile!"

The police officers, hearing the commotion, stopped what they were doing and came over. "What's going on here?" one of them asked. Sussi began crying even harder.

The man turned a disgusted face to the policemen and said, "Officers, take this woman away! I have my papers, but my wife has forgotten hers! She always forgets everything. I'm so sick of her. I don't ever want to see her again!"

The officers laughed, shaking their heads at the couple's marital spat, and moved on.

With a selfless act of caring, the stranger on the train had saved Sussi's life. Sussi never saw the man again. She never even knew his name.

♥   ♥   ♥

When Sussi's great niece, Shifra, told me this story, I was in awe. I wondered, *What is it that inspires someone to extend himself, even risk his life, for someone he doesn't know?* The man on the train didn't help Sussi because she'd made him a great breakfast that morning or had picked up his dry cleaning. He helped her because in that moment of heroism he was moved by an impulse of compassion and unconditional love.

What if you could live in that state of unconditional love all the time? The kind of love that allowed you not only to feel compassion for a stranger but that also let you bring the highest and best part of yourself to your family and friends, to your work, to your community, and even to the things that you find most challenging in your life. Imagine loving people, not because they fill your needs or because their opinions match your own, but because you're connected to a state of pure love within yourself. I'm talking not about a Hollywood or Hallmark-card kind of love, but about love as a state of being: the kind of love that is limitless and doesn't ask to be returned.

This inner state of love, one that doesn't depend on anything outside us—another person, situation, or romantic partner—is what I call Love for No Reason, and it's the subject of this book. By the time you finish reading, you'll know how to access that state of love more and more of the time, no matter what else is going on around you. And in doing so, you'll become the most powerful, peaceful, and loving person you can be.

Love from the Inside Out

As you'll see, this book is unlike any other book on love. Its goal is not to teach you how to get more love or be more loving in your relationships, even though it will do that. Instead, it will provide something even more important and fundamental: it will show you how to connect to that state of unconditional love inside you. From there, you'll naturally be more loving and draw more love into your life.

That's why this book could be considered the "prequel" to any other book about love—be it about relationships, parenting, or serving others. *Love for No Reason* contains the secret to fully loving anyone—including yourself. When you love and accept yourself completely, your old patterns of beating yourself up, criticizing and condemning yourself dissolve. Instead, your appreciation of others and your fulfillment in life grow.

When you experience Love for No Reason, you no longer need to look outside yourself to get love. You stop being a love beggar and become a love philanthropist, dispensing love, kindness, and goodwill wherever you go.

This simple but profound shift will create remarkable changes in every area of your life. It will improve your health, your relationships, and your success and satisfaction at work. Instead of feeling a little hungry all the time—for love, security, more stuff, more recognition, more everything—you'll feel full and complete. It will affect how you show up in every moment. In fact, though your life might not depend on making this shift, the *quality* of your life does.

Why We All Need This Now

The most important resource isn't time, or oil, money or gold; it's love. Without this, we may have everything, but life is nothing.

—Kute Blackson, inspirational speaker and life coach

If you look around, you'll see that most people's lives aren't overflowing with love. At my speeches and book signings, many people tell me that their relationships are filled with conflict, or they're unhappy at work, or they're worried about their children. They feel alone, mired in their judgments of themselves and others. Something fundamental is missing in their lives, and they're not sure how to fill the void.

Think about your own life. Do you ever

- reach for food, alcohol, or drugs to fill an emptiness inside?
- feel frustrated or unfulfilled with your work?
- get dragged down by negative thoughts, feelings, and criticisms of yourself and those around you?
- have tension and conflicts with your spouse or children?
- experience fatigue, boredom, or a sense of malaise?
- shut down your heart or push love away?
- grab on to love or try to please others to get love?
- feel isolated, separate, or disconnected from others and life?

As varied as these problems may seem, they all have one underlying root cause: *we're looking for love outside ourselves and have lost touch with the unconditional love at our core.*

Experiencing that state of pure love inside can be an uphill battle in today's world. Almost everyone I know is feeling stressed to the max and pulled away from inner love. We have email inboxes that are exploding. We're struggling to pay the mortgage or rent, we're juggling family and work commitments, we're eating empty, nutrient-depleted foods that zap our energy, and we're drained by environmental toxins that, oftentimes, we aren't even aware of. On top of all this, there's disharmony in our communities and intense polarization between nations, religions, and political parties.

Consider these unfortunate trends:

- The divorce rate in the United States, which remains around 50 percent, is the highest of any developed nation.
- One in five women in America is on antidepressants. And according to

the World Health Organization, 15 percent of the population of most developed countries suffer severe depression.

- Loneliness and social isolation, which lead to illness and a shorter life-span, are increasing.
- An estimated 90 percent of all disease is stress-related or induced.
- Global conflicts based on political, cultural, and religious divisions have reached epidemic proportions.

We couldn't have a more pressing need for greater love, personally and for the world as a whole. We are facing what Martin Luther King Jr. called "the fierce urgency of now," and finding the love inside ourselves is the only answer. Luckily, love is *right here*, waiting for us.

Love for No Reason: The Bonus Package

I know it may sound too good to be true, but cultivating an inner state of love that you can access at any time and in any circumstance really *is* a miracle cure-all. This isn't just wishful thinking. There's an emerging science of unconditional love that verifies its power in our lives. Here are some of the proven and practical perks of living in Love for No Reason:

You have more fulfilling relationships. When you bring love to everyone—including yourself—you don't continually seek approval and appreciation from others. You come to your relationships from fullness rather than lack and you don't need to control or manipulate others to get your needs met. In the midst of conflict, you don't shut down or attack others but stay present and compassionate.

You're comfortable in your own skin and you're able to be your authentic self in relationships. Research clearly demonstrates that when you love yourself, your relationships are more satisfying.

You're healthier and will live longer. Love is great medicine! When you experience love, the heart and the brain in concert with the endocrine and nervous systems release "love chemicals," including endorphins, oxytocin, and vasopressin, which strengthen the immune system and increase resilience.

Renowned physician Bernie Siegel, the author of *Love, Medicine and Miracles,* was one of the first doctors in America to talk about the effect of unconditional love on health. He writes, "If I told patients to raise their blood levels of immune globulins or killer T-cells, no one would know how. But if I can teach them to love themselves and others fully, the same changes happen automatically. The truth is: love heals."

Love brings our biochemistry into balance. Various research studies show that love can increase longevity, lower blood pressure, protect against dementia, and reduce the risk of depression. In one study conducted at Ohio State University, scientists found that couples in loving marriages are 35 percent less likely to get sick than couples in unhappy marriages.

You recover more quickly from stress. Negative emotions usually have a deep and lasting impact. You feel this in both your mind and body as a result of powerful neurochemicals released in your system under stress. However, as love grows, the biochemicals of love take over, and the mental and physical effects of stress aren't as strong and long-lasting.

You're more effective and creative. Studies show that being in a state of love increases your brain power and clarity through a physiological response called *cortical facilitation*. Blood and neurotransmitters flow to your cerebral cortex, activating the higher brain centers that govern creativity, intelligence, and problem solving.

You're a better parent. The benefits of experiencing more unconditional love on an ongoing basis are huge for both you and your children. Besides the increased patience, empathy, and appreciation you'll feel interacting with your kids, research suggests that you'll be instilling those traits in them by example.

A groundbreaking study conducted at Humboldt State University by Pearl and Samuel Oliner showed that children raised by compassionate parents tend to display more compassion and altruism themselves. The Oliners interviewed Germans who had helped rescue Jews from the Nazis during World War II, and they found that the strongest predictor of this compassionate and altruistic behavior was the person's experience of growing up in a family that prized and practiced those qualities. There's no better gift you can give your child than to be a model of unconditional love.

You magnetize more love. When you radiate love, the universe responds to your thoughts and feelings in kind. You attract more positive, loving people to you and you create a more loving atmosphere around you.

(If you're single and want to draw in a partner, living in unconditional love is absolutely the best strategy.)

Everyone can experience Love for No Reason. You don't need to have the right partner, the perfect body, the ideal child, or a great job. Love for No Reason is your natural state. Whatever your experience of love is right now—whether you're in pain or feeling great—you can learn to love at a higher level. And that is exactly what this book will help you do by giving you techniques and exercises specifically designed to increase your ability to be in a state of unconditional love more of the time.

Why I Wrote This Book

No one can resist the charm of love. Even happiness takes a back seat to love. A fact I discovered once I'd cracked the happiness code—and saw what lay beyond.

Just picture it: I'd been a best-selling author for fifteen years, first with the hugely successful *Chicken Soup for the Woman's Soul* series and then with my book *Happy for No Reason*, which became an instant best seller and was translated into thirty-one languages. In addition to selling more than 14 million books, I'd been featured in the hit film and book *The Secret* and had traveled around the world, speaking to audiences about success and happiness.

In the process, I'd learned to be happier. I knew about exercise, diet, gratitude, forgiveness, and how important they all are for supporting well-being. I practiced the Happiness Habits of the unconditionally happy people I'd interviewed and was finally experiencing a deeply satisfying state of contentment more and more of the time. And yet something still beckoned me on, whispering that there was more to learn. That I could go deeper.

It began when people started showing up in my life who were more than just happy. Traveling to speak about *Happy for No Reason*, I met them in unexpected places: the woman sitting next to me on the airplane to Kiev, the waiter in Peru, the man on the street in St. Louis. Each of them radiated a palpable quality of open-heartedness that was impossible to miss. I started doing what I love to do: asking them questions. "There's something special about you. What is it?" I'd say. They told me they were experiencing a sense of unity with those around them and the world in general that they described as being filled with love. Love—that word kept coming up over and over again.

And then I'd ask the most important question: "How did you get there?" In a small percentage of cases, the person had had some kind of spontaneous awakening, you might say a divine intervention. But in most cases, I was able to identify something specific that he or she had done to set up the conditions for full-time love. I was so excited: there was actually something I could do to experience more love in life. Even though I was fortunate to have had two great love role models in my mother and my father, I still had to find my own way.

So I set out to learn about love—not romantic love, but the expanded, more universal love that connects us all and gives meaning to life—and to write a book about it. I wanted to share my discoveries and my journey to this larger love, the same as I'd done with happiness.

But there's a warning among authors: Watch out! When you write a book on any topic, all of your issues about that subject will come up to be healed.

Sure enough, writing about unconditional, pure love forced me to look at all the ways it was present—and missing—in my life. No sooner had I signed the contract for *Love for No Reason* than my marriage, which was very happy on many levels, began to feel . . . well, *wrong* on the deepest level. I did a lot of soul-searching and talking with my husband, Sergio, and in the end we came to the realization that the most loving thing we could do for each other was to go our separate ways. Though it was a remarkably loving split based on our devotion to each other, it was painful nonetheless.

So there I was, writing about love and going through a divorce. Talk about on-the-job training!

Then, unexpectedly, my beloved eighty-eight-year-old mother died. She sat down one afternoon in her favorite chair to rest—and never got up. Though her passing was peaceful, it still left me reeling. My grief was compounded by what soon followed: the sale of my childhood home, which had been in my family for almost sixty years. Three of my biggest anchors of love and stability—Sergio, Mom, and my family home—were now gone.

All of this gave me the opportunity to put the principles of Love for No Reason to what many would consider the ultimate test. I was dealing with sadness, separation, and loss. Could I experience, maintain, even grow in love while in the midst of these challenges?

What happened next blew me away: when I started *looking* for that kind of unconditional love, I soon had glimpses of it everywhere. I would often see it in people I encountered and feel its presence in many situations; I could sometimes find it in my own heart. The truth is, *love is like a radio channel that's always broadcasting; to listen to LOVE FM, all you have to do is tune in to it.*

Unfortunately, it wasn't always that easy. There were many days I forgot there was a tuning knob. Or if I remembered, I couldn't find the station. At other times, the static on the line was so great that I couldn't hear a thing.

I soon invited my collaborator and dear friend Carol Kline to join me on my quest. She had written *Happy for No Reason* with me, and I knew she would be the perfect person to co-explore this more universal dimension of love. We'd been college roommates over thirty years ago, and we'd seen each other through thick and thin (literally!). I trusted that she would keep us digging for the deepest truth possible.

We began consciously looking for role models, people who consistently radiated that kind of Higher Love. (Hat's off to singer-songwriter Steve Winwood for his great song with that title!) We ended up interviewing over 150 of what we called our "Love Luminaries." Some were famous spiritual leaders and teachers. Some were scientists versed in the neurophysiology of love, while others were experts in understanding the psychological facets of love. Then there were the ones I call the "heart people," those who simply live a life rich in the gifts of the heart. We found their stories, insights, and recommendations profound and eye-opening.

In addition, we conducted a survey of the people visiting my website by posting this question: What do you do to experience more unconditional love in your life? The hundreds of responses we received reinforced the ideas we'd heard in our interviews. Finally, we delved into the most modern scientific research as well as the most ancient spiritual traditions to uncover their revelations about love. The wisdom we gleaned from all this investigation forms the basis of this book.

Encouraged and inspired, I put many of the tools and suggestions I received to the test. And they worked! It's clear to me that love is a practice, not something that just happens to you or that you get from others. As I've used these stepping stones to love on a regular basis, the easier it's become to hear the LOVE FM channel all the time.

I've also discovered through my research that in this field of energy we call the universe, love actually vibrates at a higher rate than happiness. It's said that love is more powerful than happiness because it's a higher spiritual frequency. What I experienced is that love contains happiness within itself. An idea mirrored in the last line of Emmet Fox's quote that begins this book: "If only you could love enough, you would be the happiest and most powerful being in the universe." If you master love, you've also got happiness by the tail—*and* the power to transform your inner world as well as the world around you!

Which is why I'm passing all that I learned on to you. In these pages, you'll find a guide to take you deeper and deeper into the love present in your own heart—and to live a more dazzling, love-filled life starting today.

What You'll Find in This Book

Consider this book your manual for learning to Love for No Reason. It's divided into three sections that will help guide your journey. Throughout the book, you'll find many practical and powerful tools that you can use immediately to experience greater love from the inside out. You'll also find inspiring, true stories from the Love Luminaries that illustrate their transformation to living in a state of Love for No Reason.

I know from my experience with *Chicken Soup for the Soul* and *Happy for No Reason* that stories grab your heart and stay with you long after you close a book. That's why I'm passionate about sharing the remarkable stories I heard from a wide array of people, including a Grammy award–winning singer, a former priest, and a grieving mother.

You'll meet Geneen, who gained and lost more than a thousand pounds over the last thirty years before finding the key to loving herself. And Rosemary, the wife of a former senator who went through a harrowing trauma that brought her to a higher experience of love. You'll hear Johnny's story about how his daily acts of love have made him a national icon.

To satisfy the skeptics and scientifically minded readers, I've also included supporting scientific documentation of the effects of unconditional love in all areas of our lives. Until recently, most of the research on love focused exclusively on relationships or the biochemistry of romantic love. But we're living in an exciting time as the study of unconditional love—expressed as compassion, forgiveness, empathy, altruism, and so on—gains steam in the scientific community. I'll share with you findings from various organizations, including the Fetzer Institute, the Templeton Foundation, and the Institute of HeartMath, that have pioneered research on the heart's role in our personal health and well-being as well as the effect of love on the planet.

Part I lays out a new paradigm of love. Here I'll define Love for No Reason and show you how it differs from the other kinds of love. You'll learn about the "love set point," examine what your own limits to Higher Love may be, and complete a self-assessment to see how much Love for No Reason you're already experiencing in your life. You'll be introduced to an amazing new concept: the love-body, which is the accumulated energy of all your past experiences of unconditional love. When strengthened and enlivened, your love-body magnetizes more love into your life.

Part II is the how-to of Love for No Reason. It contains the revolutionary seven-step Love for No Reason program that will increase your capacity to love and propel you into the state of Higher Love.

There are plenty of plans out there to help us lose weight or make more money, but we don't realize that love is actually a skill we can develop. That's what the seven steps will help you do, which is why I consider this the ultimate love fitness program.

Each chapter in this section presents a doorway to Love for No Reason and gives two Love Keys—two distinct approaches for unlocking that specific doorway. Each chapter also includes two inspirational true stories—one for each Love Key—and, perhaps most important, practical tools and techniques that you can use to experience more Love for No Reason right away.

In Part III you'll find guidelines for keeping Higher Love alive in your everyday life, along with a resource section. We'll also take a look at the powerful impact you can have on the world when you live from that expanded state of love. There's strong scientific evidence that when we raise our own level of love, we radiate a coherence that affects our families, our communities, and ultimately, the planet. Finally, I'll offer a vision of what's possible for our world when enough people are living with awakened hearts.

Love for No Reason may grow a little each day, like a well-tended plant, and blossom in due time. Or it may arrive full-blown, like a beautiful bouquet of roses delivered to your door. No matter how Higher Love shows up in your life, the important thing is that you invite it to stay.

You do this by first recognizing that this state of pure unconditional love exists, then by valuing its importance, and finally, by making its presence a priority in your life.

Here's a little caution: there are things that simply can't be explained or understood by the intellect alone. Love is one of them. Language, a left-brain function, can only point to Higher Love. Nonlinear experiences of wholeness like love are primarily processed in the right brain, and felt in the heart.

So I invite you to read this book in a new way—with an open heart. Ask your intellect to take the copilot's seat and let your heart work the controls for a while. Read with an openness and anticipation that these pages will change your life.

My deepest wish is that this book transforms your experience of love and that you become a conduit for Love for No Reason to flow in the world.

CHAPTER 1

An Invitation to Higher Love

*When one has once fully entered the realm of love, the world—
no matter how imperfect—becomes rich and beautiful;
it consists solely of opportunities for love.*

—Søren Kierkegaard, nineteenth-century philosopher

In medieval Japan, the fierce samurai warriors were revered as kings. They carried large swords and were highly skilled at using them.

One day, a famous samurai set out to find an aged monk who was known to be very wise. When he arrived at the monastery, he flung open the door and demanded of the old man, "Tell me, you are learned in these matters. What is heaven and what is hell?"

The monk sat still for a moment on the tatami-matted floor. Then he turned and looked up at the warrior. "You call yourself a samurai warrior," he said. "Why, look at you. You're nothing but a mere sliver of a man! I doubt you could cut off the head of a fly with your sword."

For a moment, the samurai stood gaping. No one talked to a samurai like that! Then, as if someone had waved a red cloth in front of a bull, the samurai's face contorted in rage. He bellowed, "How dare you! I won't let you get away with such an insult." Pulling his huge sword from its sheath, he raised it high above his head, ready to kill the old monk.

Unperturbed, the monk looked directly into the eyes of the furious warrior and said, "You asked what hell is? This is hell."

The samurai froze, his sword still raised, as the hatred and anger that had consumed him drained away. He looked at the old monk in amazement, realizing that this small, stooped man had risked his life to answer his question.

Lowering his weapon, the samurai bowed to the monk, as tears of gratitude appeared in his eyes. "Thank you for your teaching," the samurai said humbly, his heart filled with love for the monk's gift.

The monk smiled at the samurai and said, "And this, my friend, is heaven."

The book you hold in your hands is your passport to experiencing heaven right here on earth—no matter what your idea of heaven is. Because in the end, heaven on earth is about love—the biggest, most powerful, all-encompassing love you can imagine.

We All Want Love

Love.

What a small word for such an enormous, expansive, exalted experience!

Since the dawn of civilization, humans have been engaged in the pursuit of love. Monuments have been constructed, fortunes made, and treasuries emptied—all in the name of love. Whatever we think we want—more clothes, more friends, more money, more status, more power, more anything—in the end, it boils down to love.

When love flows in our lives, it opens our hearts, our arms, our eyes. We blossom, like a flower in the springtime sun. When love is missing, we wither and close, protecting ourselves against the harshness of life.

Imagine being so full of love that no matter how much you gave, there was always more than enough, and any love you received was just icing on the cake.

Every spiritual tradition tells us to love one another, and we'd all like to do just that. So, what's the problem?

In a nutshell, we're handicapped in the love department—both giving and receiving—because we're disconnected from the state of Love for No Reason, the source of love inside us.

When you learn how to access that huge internal reservoir of love, instead of looking for love outside yourself, you're able to *bring* love to every situation. And that's when your life becomes magical—a whole lot juicier and more fulfilling.

Living in Love

This isn't just a nice idea. As I discovered in my research, some people are actually living this way. After each interview with a Love Luminary, I would shake my head in wonder. The accounts of living in Love for No Reason were far better than any fairy tale—because they were true. For some the experience of this expansive state came on dramatically and suddenly—in a moment of grace—while for others it was a more subtle and gradual process.

One beautiful example of someone who experienced a moment of grace that changed her life came from Love Luminary Mirabai Devi, an international spiritual teacher from South Africa I interviewed while she was teaching in California.

Her experience of this pure state of love first happened almost twenty years ago, when as a young woman traveling through Europe on her own, Mirabai had an awakening:

> It was as if a dam burst in my heart, and the waters overflowed. The love that came forth was unlike anything I'd ever experienced before. Like a flood, it was all-consuming and all-encompassing; I could hardly contain it. I felt electrified; my body was tingling all over. I was so in love with the whole creation that I wanted to hug everyone I met. I knew that I couldn't do that because people would think I was crazy. Still, people could feel it. Everywhere I went they would just come up to me and say, "What can I do for you?" "Can I help you?" "Can I give you a ride?" "Can I get you some food?" "Can I . . . ?" They just wanted to be around me.

All I wanted to do was make humanity feel how loved it was. To let them know that this love was everywhere, and available to everyone. Nonstop I just sent it out to all people, all beings, and all life forms. I sent it to all those who were suffering.

Traveling through Holland one afternoon, I stopped on the side of the road and looked at a field of cabbages. All the cabbages were filled with this iridescent, luminous light. My heart was bursting with love for the cabbages.

I felt union with the whole creation. Everything was the creation of love. Everything was pulsing with love. It was everywhere, in everything. It was in the walls and in the trees. It was as though it was coming through the sky.

I saw that everything is connected and everything is one. And everything is radiant with this exquisite, ecstatic love.

That was the beginning of Mirabai's experience of living in an ongoing state of Love for No Reason. Today she travels around the world, speaking and teaching others about love.

In interview after interview, I heard more than a hundred variations on this theme. I thought, *If so many people, from all different backgrounds and all different walks of life, experience this, it must be possible for me and anyone else.*

My question became: How did this awakening of love happen for Mirabai and the others? And what are the conditions that you and I can set up to invite this experience of love into our own lives?

The Three Love for No Reason Themes

~⌒∞⌒~

We are made by love, we are made of love, and we are made for love!
Everything is love anyway. Our hate is love turned sour, jealousy
is love turned bitter, our fears are love standing upside down,
greed is love gone overboard, attachment is love gone sticky.

—Khurshed Batliwala, blogger

The starting place for inviting more love into your life is to understand the perspective of people who are already living this way. After listening to more than 150 hours of interviews with my Love Luminaries and reading through six thousand pages of transcripts, I saw three main themes that stood out in neon lights.

Love Theme #1: Love Is Who We Are

All the Love Luminaries told me that love isn't just something we feel for others, it's who we are. Love is actually the substance, the building blocks, the essence of everything in our lives. We're made up of love. Our molecules are formed from love. We *are* love.

I know that when I first heard this, I rolled my eyes, thinking, *I've heard this all before.* But at the same time I realized, *I have no idea what that really means.*

We think of love as a stream of emotion flowing between two points—between us and whatever we love. But in fact, love is more like an ocean that's inside and all around us.

We walk around with our little cups, begging for a few drops of love from others, when actually we're the huge ocean of love. This is why I say that when you experience Love for No Reason on an ongoing basis, *you stop being a "love beggar" and become a "love philanthropist."* Instead of looking at every interaction as a potential *source* of love—something to fill you up and make you feel good—you come to every interaction *radiating* love. You're overflowing with love because *you* are the source!

Having great relationships doesn't depend on finding the right person or circumstance; it depends completely on your capacity to love. Unconditional love for others is based on "being the ocean of love."

Experiencing that you *are* love is the ultimate form of self-love. It's not love of your small self—your personality. It's not about loving yourself because you look good or you did a great job or because you've gained a certain status. It's the love of your big Self—your essence. It's the love that comes from waking up to who you truly are.

Love Theme #2: The Purpose of Life Is to Expand in Love

Why are you alive? The Love Luminaries say that our ultimate purpose is to grow in our ability to give and receive love. In other words, love is our job here on earth!

So if love is your job description, the most important thing you can do is to find that ocean of love within you and bring it to the world—to yourself, to your loved ones, to strangers you pass in the street, to *everyone and everything*.

Now that doesn't mean standing on a street corner with a sign that says *Free Hugs* (although that might be fun!). What it means is that you live your life in a context of love, seeing that everything that happens to you is to help you expand your ability to love. It's easy to love things that are charming and attractive, but the real challenge is to experience love in difficult situations and with people you don't even like. To maintain an open heart when your spouse is being difficult, your child is throwing a tantrum, or your boss is making what seem like unreasonable demands requires a commitment to love as the number one priority in your life.

In fact, all the accounts I've read about near-death experiences point to the importance of focusing on love. Many people say that at the end of our lives there's a life review during which our souls are asked only two questions: How well did you learn your life lessons? And how much did you love?

If that's going to be our life's final exam, maybe it's a good idea to prepare now to answer those questions well. I don't think this is the kind of test you can cram for at the end!

Love Theme #3: The Heart Is the Portal to Love

The Love Luminaries all agreed that the heart is the central access point for our experience of Love for No Reason. Not our flesh-and-blood heart but our spiritual heart—the place in the middle of our chest we point to when we indicate who we are. In all cultures throughout history, the heart has been considered the seat of love.

The ocean of Higher Love flows into your life through this portal, and the more open you keep your heart, the healthier, happier, and more loving you are. It's the key to succeeding at your life's job: expanding your ability to love.

That's why keeping the heart open is the goal of all the practices, tools, and techniques in the Love for No Reason program that you'll learn in Part II.

These three themes are the bottom line—the CliffsNotes of the information I discovered in my research—and the foundation upon which this book is built. Keep them in mind as you continue to read. They are the mantras of Love for No Reason.

A New Paradigm of Love

I know all this can sound kind of airy-fairy. What does all this really mean for your day-to-day life? You may be thinking, *My heart is aching because my child is ill. I'm incredibly angry because my husband had an affair. I just lost my job and I'm scared I can't pay my bills. I'm eating all the time because I'm feeling so depressed. How can Love for No Reason help me with all that?*

It can, because Love for No Reason allows you to come to all types of situations with more centeredness, flexibility, and peace. You'll see more clearly how to respond to conflict, handle emotional upsets, and most important, feel compassion for yourself in the midst of your daily challenges.

Living with an open heart helps you cope—even thrive—as you deal with the frustrations and disappointments you face in everyday life.

Experiencing Love for No Reason doesn't mean you never feel sadness, anger, or hurt; what it does mean is that you also feel the comfort of the pure love that underlies those painful feelings. That pure love acts as a cushion, allowing the painful feelings to dissipate more quickly.

Love also helps you handle your difficulties more effectively. We're used to dealing with our problems on the level of the problem, but as Einstein said, "You can never solve a problem on the level on which it was created." Introducing Higher Love to any of your problems is like turning on the light in a dark room; it helps dispel the difficulty with grace and speed. You gain perspective and free yourself from old negative feedback loops. This approach to handling your everyday issues requires a new paradigm of love, a new way of considering what it means to "love."

Though we talk about love in so many ways—*I love my family. I love my pets. I love to shop. I love to eat. I love to help others. I love to watch television or read a book*—all our experiences of love can be divided into four distinct categories along what I call the Love Continuum. The following diagram illustrates the complete spectrum of love:

The Love Continuum

No Love	Love for Bad Reason	Love for Good Reason	Love for No Reason
Hate, fear resistance	Using others to fill a void inside	Healthy, mutually beneficial relationships	An inner state of pure, unconditional love
	CONDITIONAL		**UNCONDITIONAL**

No Love: In this state our hearts are shut down; we're in pain or feel angry or sad or may experience profound exhaustion. Feelings of fear and anxiety, which are hallmarks of No Love, often trigger the fight-or-flight response. We may feel empty, bored, disengaged, disconnected, or alone. We may want to lash out at the people around us, especially those we think are causing our pain. The state of No Love is the absence of everything that makes life worth living.

Note: People may find themselves in this state when dealing with serious grief, depression, and trauma. In these situations professional treatment may be necessary to help them come out of the deep well of sadness they're experiencing.

Love for Bad Reason: This type of love isn't actually love at all. It's really just No Love on painkillers. Love for Bad Reason is primarily concerned with "being loved" to fill a void inside ourselves. It isn't about appreciation or true caring; it's about trying to escape or ease our emptiness. We see this in the obsessed lover intent on getting his or her "love fix."

The state of Love for Bad Reason is the basis of all addictions and in the long run erodes our health on all levels—body, mind, and spirit.

Codependency falls into this category. People who are co-dependent get swallowed up in the lives of others in an effort to fill the vacuum inside themselves. They want to please the other person—in order to get love back. You can't tell from the outside whether someone is acting from Love for Bad Reason, as it depends on his or her internal motivation. But you can become aware of when *you're* loving for bad reason. Watch for any time you're feeling or doing the following.

- Giving love to get love
- Pleasing others to be accepted
- Feeling addicted to the object of your love
- Trying to fill a void inside yourself with something outside
- Feeling needy, hungry, or desperate for love
- Controlling those you love (trying to "fix" your partner or children so you'll look or feel better)

Love for Good Reason: This is what most people understand as love. It's when you deeply appreciate or feel connected to certain people, situations, or even material objects. Whatever you love in this way becomes special and valuable to you. When you love for good reason, you feel inspired to contribute to others and are able to both give and receive. This type of love is healthy and strengthens you.

Having many good reasons to love is a wonderful thing; my life coach, Bill Levacy, calls this having "multiple streams of emotional income." It makes you feel truly rich.

But this kind of love does have some limitations. The main problem is that it's linked to reasons, and if those reasons change, your love usually changes too. For example, if you love your spouse because he or she is wonderful to be with and then your spouse disappoints or betrays you, where does your love go?

Love for Good Reason has some other major drawbacks: you may feel attached, jealous, afraid of losing the object of your love, or you may feel satisfied but still sense there's something missing. Love that depends on any reason can come and go.

I don't know about you, but I've spent too much of my life at the mercy of "reasons to love" and they didn't bring me what I was really looking for. Fortunately, there's another level of love beyond this.

Love for No Reason: This is Higher Love, an inner state of pure love that doesn't depend on other people, external conditions, or circumstances. It's a love we experience from the inside out. When you're in a state of Love for No Reason you experience freedom, peace, joy, openness, and deep fulfillment. When you "Love for No Reason," you don't need a *reason*—you love *just because*.

When you love for no reason, you *bring* love *to* your outer experiences, rather than try to *extract* love *from* them.

Love for No Reason is entirely different from our old, limited concept of love. Even science points to this. According to the latest research, unconditional love appears to have its own unique state of brain functioning.

In a study conducted at the University of Montreal, researchers found that the brain scans of people consciously experiencing unconditional love showed a pattern of activation in areas of the brain different from the areas activated in people experiencing romantic or maternal love. A distinct neural network, including the insula, superior parietal lobe, and right caudate nucleus lit up when people were experiencing unconditional love.

When we live from this state, we create a radically different physiology. One of my first *Love for No Reason* interviews was with Love Luminary Eva Selhub, MD, a recognized authority on the physiology of love and an instructor at Harvard Medical School. She told me, "Love sets off a set of physiological events in the body: peptides and hormones are released, including endorphins, oxytocin, dopamine, vasopressin, and nitric oxide. These help turn off the fear response, evoke the relaxation response, and create a positive physiology."

Dr. Selhub calls this your body's "Love Response" and says it allows you to adapt to life's challenges, stop and even reverse disease, and maintain health. "The Love Response makes it easier for your body to improve rather than deteriorate with age." A very important ingredient in the body's love response is oxytocin. It's known as the "love hormone" because it stimulates feelings of bonding, safety, and trust, and reduces fear and anxiety. Activated by warmth, touch, movement, orgasm, and breastfeeding, oxytocin is also involved in what's called "tend and befriend" activities, such as taking care of children and pets, or talking to a close friend. When oxytocin is flowing, you feel full of love.

Living in a state of love transforms our experience of life, as the Love Luminaries demonstrated time and again. While they have a wide range of personalities, they all embody similar qualities that reflect this new way of being:

- Being fully present in the moment
- Feeling oneness and a sense of connection to all people and nature
- Trusting that they are supported by a friendly universe
- Living in the flow of their feelings and having great physical vitality
- Owning their power without ego
- Being equally comfortable giving and receiving love
- Speaking and listening from the heart
- Being compassionate and nonjudgmental toward themselves and others
- Feeling full and content and being able to love life as it is
- Feeling universal love flowing through them

My guess is that you've had glimpses of this state—I call them "peak love experiences"—when your heart was open and flowing, when you didn't need anyone or anything to be different, when you felt a strong sense of well-being and that all was well. These peak love experiences leave their mark; we never forget them. Growing in Love for No Reason means experiencing these qualities—from the inside out—more of the time.

My colleague and Love Luminary Morty Lefkoe, developer of the Lefkoe Method, a system for eliminating limiting beliefs, told me a beautiful experience of his that illustrates what it feels like to love for no reason in relationships:

> When I married my wife, Shelly, almost twenty-nine years ago, she asked me why I loved her. I answered, "Just because I do."
> She didn't like this answer. She wanted to know which qualities

about her made me love her. But I kept insisting that I simply loved her, not for any particular reason.

I explained. "If I love you for specific reasons, then my love is conditioned on your being a certain way. If you stop being that way or if you aren't that way at a given time, I may not love you. But if I love you 'just because,' then my love is unconditional and I can and will love you no matter what you do or don't do."

If I don't feel love toward Shelly at any given moment, I realize that I'm not experiencing love inside myself and that it's up to me to figure out why and to start experiencing it again. I'm not blaming her for anything and I'm not waiting for her to change in some way. This gives me complete control over the way I feel about her. In other words, there's nothing she has to do to make me love her, and there's nothing she can do that will lead me to not love her.

This experience has spilled over into my other relationships. I was recently with a group of colleagues and I noticed that I was also loving them for no reason. It was as if I was filled with love and directed it toward whoever showed up in my space. I could tell you what I liked and admired about each of the people, but the love I felt had nothing to do with those qualities.

And my love was independent of the response I got from the other person. I didn't feel more love for people who loved me back than I did for people who didn't express love for me.

Now that I know where that wonderful experience comes from (namely, me), I am committed to learning how to experience it consistently in my life.

When who I really am sees who you really are, all there is, is love.

Feel the Love (for No Reason)

Enough explanation. Now it's time to get a taste of Love for No Reason and experience how it differs from Love for Good Reason. Try this simple exercise:

Exercise

*The Difference Between Love
for* Good *Reason and Love for* No *Reason*

1. Close your eyes and think of someone or something you love. It can be a person, a pet, a place, or an experience.

2. What do you love about him, her, or it? Appreciate all the wonderful qualities you love about that person or thing. Let yourself savor the object of your love.

3. Ask yourself an unusual question, one that most people never consider: Where does this love come from? What's causing me to have this wonderful experience? The vast majority of people will answer that the love they feel is directly caused by the object of love they're thinking about. This is the experience of Love for Good Reason.

4. Now try something different. Switch your focus from the beloved to *the experience of love itself.* Put your attention on your heart and feel your appreciation independent of your thoughts about the object of your love. Instead of thinking of the qualities of the person or thing, let yourself really feel the love you have *inside* for whatever it is that you chose.

5. Be with that inner experience of love. You may feel warmth in the center of your chest and/or find yourself smiling.

The difference between these two experiences of love is that the second one is linked to your heart and doesn't depend on the object of your love. This is Love for No Reason. The following diagrams illustrate what you just experienced:

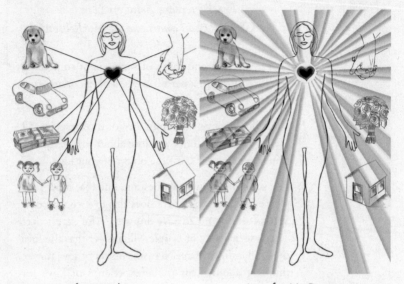

Love for Good Reason   Love for No Reason

In the first diagram, our love is directly linked to the object. In the second, the objects are secondary, and our primary experience is the love we feel in our own hearts. When we focus on the heart and its radiance rather than the objects the rays point to—that's the inner state of love we're talking about, which you'll learn to strengthen in the Love for No Reason program.

For many people, it may be hard to grasp that love can be a stand-alone experience. We think "it takes two to tango." We love *something*; we don't just *love*. We consider love as something that happens between two people.

Embracing this new idea of love as an independent state and learning how to experience it on a continuing basis is the key to living a life of unconditional love. You fill your own love tank and bring that love to everything in your life.

Then, as Mirabai experienced, you still love things outside yourself (in her case, love even extended to cabbages), but the difference is your love doesn't *depend* on things—people, jobs, relationships, cars, clothes . . . or cabbages.

Don't be fooled by the simplicity of this experience. This pure state of love is the most powerful force on the planet. When you develop and strengthen unconditional love and make it your default state of being, your life will switch from black-and-white to Technicolor.

Love for No Reason in Practice

Not long after writing this section, I put this new way of looking at love to the test, using it in a difficult emotional situation with my ex-husband, Sergio. Even though I was no longer living with him, I still loved him dearly, and I deeply missed his presence in my life.

One day, hanging up the phone after a conversation with him, I felt the pain and loss of not being together anymore. Even though I knew our parting was best for both of us, I was feeling enormous love for him and my heart was aching with longing for him. I felt as if I had to shut down the feeling of love because it hurt too much.

Okay, I thought, *I'm writing this book about Love for No Reason. Everyone I've interviewed has told me that love is who we are and that I can experience that love inside myself whenever I want. Let me give it a whirl.*

Closing my eyes, I told myself, *This feeling I have for Sergio—it's my love. It's coming from me. So I'm going to just sit here and feel it.*

And I did. I really let my love flow, savoring the sweetness of that experience in my own heart. If my attention started focusing on Sergio and the fact that we weren't together, I'd gently bring it back to my experience of love. That love was coming from me; it was mine. I could feel it regardless of who was with me or not with me. And it actually helped a lot. Normally, the pangs of loss and sadness would have stayed with me for hours, but within five minutes of just letting myself feel my own love *for no reason*, I felt better.

This experience reminded me of something a spiritual teacher of mine used to say: "I love you and it's no concern of yours." When I first heard the phrase at age seventeen, I was puzzled by it, but now I appreciate its profound message. The love that we think is for anyone or anything outside ourselves is really just our own love.

Feeling it is not the same as sharing that love with another person: that's a whole different kind of thrill. But I've found that experiencing that inner state of love truly has a charm of its own. It's filled me with a peace and sweetness that feels like home.

The Sun Is Always Shining

Look at the diagram of Love for No Reason again, and notice how the heart looks like a sun. This is a particularly apt metaphor, because when we stop connecting love to reasons—to external objects of love—and feel the sensation of pure love within, the radiant energy of love streams out from us like a sun.

That sun of Love for No Reason is always shining inside us. You don't have to "create love." It's already there. Love is your essence, your true nature. (Remember Love Theme #1.) Author and spiritual teacher Eckhart Tolle's description of this Higher Love is spot on:

> Something inside you emerges . . . an innate, indwelling peace, stillness, aliveness. It is the unconditioned, who you are in your essence. It is what you had been looking for in the love object. It is yourself.

All the world's spiritual traditions speak of this larger, more expanded kind of love, though each has its own terminology for it.

In Christianity, the term that's used for this highest and purest form of love is *agape*, a word borrowed from the Greeks. In the New Testament, *agape* is the love that God has for man and that He commands us to have for each other. It is selfless, generous, and healing—the foundation for a good life.

In Hebrew, the word for love is *ahavah*, and for Love for No Reason, *ahavat chinam,* literally "groundless love." In my interview with Love Luminary Rabbi David Thomas, he described *ahavat chinam* as "the love we show to a fellow human being without regard to our own interest, simply because we are human and we see the humanity of another."

The Buddhists call this love *metta* or lovingkindness, love that makes one want to help and to give of oneself for the welfare and well-being of humanity. They consider this love the ultimate source of strength and power.

Hinduism uses the Sanskrit phrase *parama prema* (supreme love) to describe a state of love that is full, with no conditions, and that brings a person to the truth of life. And in the sect of Islam called Sufism, the word *ishq* expresses this quality of unconditional and Divine love.

What is present in all traditions is the certainty that God is love and that each one of us has access to that love inside. It's only clouds of stress, negative habits, ego, and fear that block this pure state of love and prevent us from experiencing it.

The Love-Body

Those clouds of negativity that block the sun, preventing us from experiencing Love for No Reason, make up what Eckhart Tolle calls our "pain-body." In his best-selling book *The Power of Now*, he describes the pain-body as a negative energy field of painful emotional memories that we all carry around with us. This emotional energy body is triggered when an event or remark or even a random thought resonates with a past experience of pain. The pain-body survives by feeding on more pain, and it's always on the lookout for a chance to suffer. When you get into a fight with someone, it's your pain-body that pounces, ready for a good meal. It's the part of you that seems to go out of its way to stir up conflict, hurt, and sadness.

Remarkably, what hasn't been written about yet is that we also have a "love-body." This is a breakthrough discovery! It's an idea that came to me out of the blue. I thought, *If there's a pain-body that magnetizes pain to you, there must also be a love-body that magnetizes love to you!* I began asking the Love Luminaries about it and many of them verified its existence. The love body is a positive energy field formed from our experiences of unconditional love—the pain-body's opposite.

In the same way that the pain-body feeds on pain, the love-body develops by feeding on more love. The more you experience Love for No Reason, the stronger and healthier your love-body becomes. And the more developed your love-body, the more love you radiate. You become like a tuning fork of love; everything around you begins to resonate with the vibration of love you're sending out.

But for most of us, becoming a "tuning fork of love" requires creating new habits. We all have familiar grooves that our lives run in—ways of thinking, feeling, and behaving that feed either the love-body or the pain-body. If you want to develop a stronger love-body, you have to change your groove. You do this through practice.

Because as it turns out, practice really does make perfect! We know this from the many exciting scientific studies in the field of neuroplasticity. For years scientists believed that the brain developed only up until early adulthood and then hardened like cement, putting an end to further growth. However, numerous studies have recently shown that the brain makes new connections and dissolves old ones in response to our thoughts and actions even up until we die. When we repeat a thought or action, the neural pathways associated with it become wider: neurons that fire together, wire together. So *what we focus on repeatedly affects our neural circuits*, which means that we can change our wiring, even as adults.

Fortunately, the experience and expression of love are actually hardwired into our brains—a fact borne out by research. According to Dr. Dacher Keltner, professor of psychology at the University of California, Berkeley and the director of the Greater Good Science Center, "Compassion and benevolence are . . . rooted in our brain and biology, and ready to be cultivated."

A study conducted at the University of Wisconsin–Madison supports this idea. In this study the subjects were asked to concentrate on loving-kindness toward their families, and then to extend that feeling of love to include strangers. The results showed an activation of the brain regions that relate to empathy.

When you consciously and repeatedly connect to the state of Love for No Reason, it eventually becomes your groove. And as your love-body becomes more vibrant and powerful, it exerts a greater influence in your life and the lives of everyone you touch. The Love for No Reason program is designed to strengthen your love-body and allow you to keep your heart open more of the time. We'll explore the love-body more thoroughly in chapter 3.

How Strong Is Your Love-Body?
The Love for No Reason Self-Assessment

We all experience love in our lives, but how much of it is pure, unconditional love? The following self-assessment will show you how strong your love-body is and to what degree you're already living in the state of Love for No Reason.

This questionnaire is not concerned with measuring how much you love the external circumstances of your life, including your relationships with others: that's Love for Good Reason. Instead, it measures the qualities associated with that pure inner state of love that forms the basis of healthy relationships and a magnificent life.

As you answer these questions, be honest with yourself. No one will see your score but you.

The Love for No Reason Self-Assessment

Rate each question on a scale of 1 to 10, where 1 is "Not at all True" and 10 is "Absolutely True."

1	2	3	4	5	6	7	8	9	10
Not at all True				Moderately True				Absolutely True	

1. I move through my day feeling grounded—aware, awake, and appreciative of what is happening in the present moment.

   1 2 3 4 5 6 7 8 9 10

2. I feel connected to the natural world, including animals, plants, water, mountains, etc.

   1 2 3 4 5 6 7 8 9 10

3. I feel supported—by my friends and family, and by a friendly universe.

   1 2 3 4 5 6 7 8 9 10

4. I have a lot of physical energy and am able to feel my feelings without resisting or suppressing them.

1   2   3   4   5   6   7   8   9   10

5. I feel deserving of love and am able to be assertive without being aggressive.

1   2   3   4   5   6   7   8   9   10

6. I feel an abundance of love in my heart—I give and receive from a sense of fullness.

1   2   3   4   5   6   7   8   9   10

7. I am a good communicator. I express how I really feel and listen without being defensive.

1   2   3   4   5   6   7   8   9   10

8. I am intuitive and see the beauty all around me.

1   2   3   4   5   6   7   8   9   10

9. I experience periods of acceptance and/or peace on a daily basis.

1   2   3   4   5   6   7   8   9   10

10. I feel connected to a power larger than myself and feel higher love flowing through me.

1   2   3   4   5   6   7   8   9   10

Scoring:

If your score is 80–100: Congratulations, you could be one of my Love Luminaries!

If your score is 60–79: You're well on your way to Love for No Reason.

If your score is 40–59: You're having glimpses of Love for No Reason.

If your score is under 40: It's great that you're reading this book. Love for No Reason is waiting for you.

Once you've completed the Love for No Reason program laid out in Part II, you can take this self-assessment on a regular basis to chart your progress toward living a life of unconditional love.

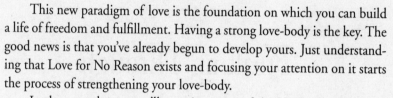

This new paradigm of love is the foundation on which you can build a life of freedom and fulfillment. Having a strong love-body is the key. The good news is that you've already begun to develop yours. Just understanding that Love for No Reason exists and focusing your attention on it starts the process of strengthening your love-body.

In the next chapter, we'll examine some of the blocks that limit our love and prevent us from living the most extraordinary lives we can.

CHAPTER 2

Breaking Through
Your Love Limits

∾

Don't settle for love of this or that, he or she;
that is all so, so small. Stubbornly hold
out for love itself—beyond everything.
—Bruce Allen, spiritual counselor

Every once in a while a fabulous email lands in my inbox that makes me laugh out loud but also carries a good amount of truth. When the following one appeared, I knew it was perfect to introduce the concept of our love limits.

Installing Love on the Human Computer

Technical Support: Yes, how can I help you?

Customer: Well, after much consideration, I've decided to install Love. Can you guide me through the process?

Tech Support: Yes. I can help you. Are you ready to proceed?

Customer: Well, I'm not very technical, but I think I'm ready. What do I do first?

Tech Support: The first step is to open your Heart. Have you located your Heart?

Customer: Yes, but there are several other programs running now. Is it okay to install Love while they are running?

Tech Support: What programs are running?

Customer: Let's see, I have Past Hurt, Low Self-Esteem, Grudge, and Resentment running right now.

Tech Support: No problem, Love will gradually erase Past Hurt from your current operating system. It may remain in your permanent memory but it will no longer disrupt other programs. Love will eventually override Low Self-Esteem with a module of its own called High Self-Esteem. However, you have to completely turn off Grudge and Resentment. Those programs prevent Love from being properly installed. Can you turn those off?

Customer: I don't know how to turn them off. Can you tell me how?

Tech Support: With pleasure. Go to your start menu and select Forgiveness. Do this as many times as necessary until Grudge and Resentment have been completely erased.

Customer: Okay, done! Love has started installing itself. Oops! I have an error message already. It says, "Error—

*Program not run on external components." What should
I do?*

Tech Support: *Don't worry. In nontechnical terms, it simply means you have to Love yourself before you can Love
others. Pull down Self-Acceptance; then click on the following files: Forgive Self, Realize Your Worth, and Acknowledge Your Limitations.*

Customer: *Got it. Hey! My heart is filling up with new
files. Smile is playing on my monitor and Peace and Contentment are copying themselves all over my Heart. Is this
normal?*

Tech Support: *Yes, that means Love is installed and running. One more thing before we hang up. This Love program is freeware. You're welcome to share it with others.
Please pass it along!*

What programs are *you* running that interfere with your ability to
experience Love for No Reason?

Your Love Set Point

Is there an invisible ceiling limiting your ability to experience love?
Scientists in the field of positive psychology have discovered that we each
have a happiness set point, a fixed level of happiness we hover around, no
matter what happens to us. Although there haven't been any scientific studies yet confirming the existence of a love set point, I've observed a similar
phenomenon.

Like happiness, your ability to experience love is based on an internal
set point rather than on your external circumstances. Positive or negative
situations and events cause dips or spikes in your experience of love, but
eventually you return to your love comfort zone, that old familiar range of
love experiences you're used to. The love set point works to your advantage

on the downside, helping you bounce back after challenges, but acts as a brake on the top end, limiting the amount of love you can give and receive.

My brilliant colleagues the authors and psychologists Gay and Katie Hendricks, who are also two of my Love Luminaries, use the term "upper limits" to describe how we unconsciously sabotage ourselves when we start to experience more good coming into our lives than we're accustomed to. It's as if that flood of positivity sets off a silent alarm when we go past a certain setting. In order to shut off that alarm, our subconscious finds ways to diminish our own joy, love, and success, bringing us back to a more comfortable, if less exhilarating, level.

We have these upper limits in all areas of our life. I once heard about a study done at IBM in the nineties showing that when salespeople started producing significantly more sales than usual, they tended to return to their accustomed level fairly quickly. On some level, people simply aren't comfortable with more wealth and success than they're used to. It's the same with love. When you start to feel a lot of love, do you inevitably mess it up? If so, without being aware of it, you've placed a cap on how much love you can feel.

Opening your heart and strengthening your love-body will help you break through your upper limits and raise your love set point. Let's explore the ways you can do this, starting with identifying and overcoming the top three myths about love.

The Top Three Myths about Love

～∞～

People . . . are so hungry for love that they are accepting substitutes.

—Morrie Schwartz, as told to Mitch Albom, author of *Tuesdays with Morrie*

Some of our love limits come from the outside, from societal myths and beliefs that are so widespread, we never think to question them. From the moment we're first able to understand, most of us are fed a steady diet of misinformation about love that's fueled by movies, magazines, and popular songs. You could call these our collective upper limits. These myths misdirect us, leaving us "looking for love in all the wrong places."

It's time to debunk the old myths about love and wake up to a new experience of love on the planet.

Myth #1: The Myth of Romantic Love

Whenever I told people I was writing a book called *Love for No Reason*, they'd invariably smile and say, "Oh, a relationship book." People automatically equate love with romantic relationships.

It's no surprise that romantic love steals the show. It's part of our survival wiring, necessary for humans to continue as a species.

Romantic love has long been humanity's favorite drug. It triggers the brain to serve up a powerful hormonal cocktail including dopamine, norepinephrine, adrenaline, and oxytocin guaranteed to send us soaring. World-renowned biological anthropologist Dr. Helen Fisher has spent over thirty years studying the physiological basis of romantic love. She's concluded that romantic love is "one of the most addictive substances on earth," with the same characteristics of any other type of addiction, including obsession, craving, and distortion of reality.

Her research shows that when we fall in love, primitive parts of the brain associated with euphoria, craving, and obsessive thinking become active, including the ventral tegmental area (VTA) at the base of the brain, which is a part of the brain's reward system. In fact, it's the same brain region that lights up when a person feels the high of cocaine. No wonder we're addicted to the rush that comes with romance. This addiction has created a collective preoccupation with romance and everything connected to it—our ability to attract a mate, the ups and downs of courtship, and, of course, sex.

If you're a love junkie, it's because you're addicted to that love high and are craving that amphetamine-like rush of love chemicals. When your body builds up a tolerance to these chemicals, you begin to require more and more of them to get that same high. You may go through relationship after relationship to get your fix.

While romance is certainly part of the whole love equation, our obsession with it has taken our attention off a bigger, more fulfilling love, the real brass ring. Many of the Love Luminaries told me that while they enjoy romantic love, it pales in comparison to the state of Higher Love they live in.

We look outside ourselves thinking that romantic love will complete us. This is the underlying message of every chick flick ever made. (I confess, I watched *Pretty Woman* at least a dozen times, and for years I waited for Richard Gere to come and sweep me off my feet.) But it distracts us from the greater love we have inside.

What can we do to break free of this myth? The answer is a 180-degree turn in our approach to love, which means overriding our societal conditioning and making a habit of connecting with the love inside ourselves, the foundation of the Love for No Reason program. Relationships based on this inner love are naturally more fulfilling.

One of my Love Luminaries, Amely Greeven, told me a great story about her own turnaround with romantic love:

> When I was twenty-five, I worked at *Vogue* magazine, New York City's bastion of image, luxury, and desire. Despite all the "beauty" and "romance" we sold as a magazine, there was very little beauty or romance in the environment. Instead, it was a hectic place with lots of pressure and competition.
>
> I was a stressed-out editorial assistant and I quickly befriended one of the other young assistants, a beautiful woman named Tish. She was African American, petite and sexy, with a tribal headwrap and funky Adidas sneakers. (Can you imagine how she stood out in the world of Manolo Blahniks?)
>
> Like many twentysomethings in Manhattan, what Tish and I wanted in addition to our hotshot jobs was a super-duper romance, a blow-your-mind boyfriend. Candidates for this job were few and far between, especially in the headquarters of fashion!
>
> Yet when we'd talk about our desires, I was always surprised by Tish's attitude. She wouldn't join in on my loop of "Where is he? Life's a bummer without him (boo-hoo)," about our inability to find "the one." Quite the opposite.
>
> Any time I started going there, like a little songbird Tish would start to trill, "I don't need a man to feel love. Life is my lover!"
>
> Then she'd grab an imaginary microphone and sing a Stevie Wonder song or something equally upbeat, getting me to join her.
>
> I had never heard anyone say that before. I remember thinking,

Yeah, right . . . But at the same time, my deeper self knew instinctively what she meant and it tickled me. How fun it must be to go through life like that, I felt. What adventures might I have? I started jumping on board with that attitude—or at least aiming for it. Life became a charmed game.

Tish introduced me to a new way of looking at the world—through a much bigger lens of love. Today, although Tish is happily married with two children and I haven't found my super-duper romance yet, we both still feel that "life is my lover."

To get a jump start on debunking the myth of romantic love in your own life, try using Tish's motto "Life is my lover" several times each day—especially when you're looking to someone else to fill you up with love.

Myth #2: The Myth of *I'll Love You If* . . .

Another common misunderstanding about love is that I need to agree with you, approve of you, or like you in order to love you, and vice versa. When someone doesn't match our template, we call the whole love deal off.

Some of the conditions we place on love are *I'll love you if*

- *you share my values.*
- *you give me what I need.*
- *you remember my birthday.*
- *you're not too fat or too skinny or bald or _____* (fill in the blank).
- *you love me in return.*

It takes a lot of energy to try to control others so they'll give us what we want or need. And still, no matter how hard we try, we can't get them to do it perfectly, so there are always times when we withdraw our love. In these situations, both sides lose.

Loving people doesn't mean you have to enjoy their company, want to see more of them, or even respect their values. It means you're willing to keep your heart open to them, show them compassion, and accept them for who they are.

I once heard an anecdote about how the spiritual teacher Ram Dass has worked to overcome this myth in his own life. His goal is to love all people unconditionally and to view everyone as a part of God or the Beloved. To this end, he's placed a picture of a politician he intensely disagrees with on his dresser along with pictures of Buddha, his guru, and other saints. Every morning he stops to look at the pictures for inspiration and he notices how different he feels when he comes to the photo of the politician. It serves to remind him of his intention—and how far he has to go. He says, "Mother Teresa has described this as 'seeing Christ in all his distressing disguises.'"

This is a great exercise for anyone. Find a picture of someone who really pushes your buttons; it could be a politician, a certain type of person that you judge, or someone you know personally whom you have difficulty accepting. Put the picture somewhere you'll see it every day and let it serve as a reminder of the ideal: to love more unconditionally.

Myth #3: The Myth That Love Makes You Weak

Everybody knows that nice guys finish last, right? We tell ourselves, *I can't go around being loving to everyone. I'll get hurt. People will think I'm wimpy. I need to protect myself.* This is how fear tries to talk us out of opening our hearts and going for love.

We believe that love will make us sentimental and that people who live from the heart are somehow vulnerable and weak. We've lost sight of the enormous strength of love. Because something is gentle and soft, we think it's less powerful. But the Tao Te Ching says, "The softest of all things overrides the hardest of all things." The softest thing in the world is an open heart. The hardest thing in the world is a closed, constricted heart. The open heart welcomes everything and, in doing so, grows in power.

Writing about this myth in his book *The Power of Unconditional Love*, Ken Keyes Jr. says we think "unconditional love requires going along with everything a person does." But it doesn't mean being a doormat or pushover or allowing people to mistreat you. It does mean being anchored to the state of love while you take appropriate action—which could be standing up for yourself, holding boundaries, righting wrongs, ending a relationship, or saying no.

Open-heartedness may not always mean being loving in your manner.

But when you're *being love*, you're strong and able to do whatever is right in the moment while staying connected to your heart.

Love Keeps Knocking at Your Door

The love you seek is seeking you at this moment.
—Deepak Chopra, author and physician

Once you break free of the love myths, you begin to see that love is everywhere. In fact, every experience we have is an invitation to love. Even when we hit up against our limits to love, love continues to knock at our door, and it's up to us to hear and respond.

I heard many stories from the Love Luminaries about how love's first invitation was a gentle tap, but if they didn't answer, it became louder. If they still ignored the invitation, love broke down the door, many times in the form of serious illness or personal crisis. Whatever it took to get their attention.

Why wait until love has to shout? Ask yourself: Is love knocking at *my* door? Have I put limits on love that may be blocking it? What myths do I believe that might be hindering my ability to love more fully? In the next chapter, we'll look at how you can remove those love limits and invite love to come in.

CHAPTER 3

Your Love-Body: Activating the Neurophysiology of Love

There is no mistaking love. You feel it in your heart.
It is the common fiber of life, the flame that heats our soul,
energizes our spirit, and supplies passion to our lives.
—Elisabeth Kübler-Ross, psychiatrist and author

*W*hat does it take to live in a state of pure love 24/7? Wishing
for it isn't enough. I know that from personal experience.

At the start of writing this book, my whole life revolved
around learning about Higher Love. I ate, slept, and dreamt about Love for
No Reason. Soon I began to notice pure love welling up inside at scattered
moments throughout the day—usually when I was appreciating something beautiful or feeling grateful. And while those flashes were inspiring,
I wanted to understand how I could make the experience more lasting.

I thought of the many times I'd given talks and afterwards had been
asked questions about the Law of Attraction and *The Secret*. At almost
every event, someone would stand up and say, "I've watched *The Secret* two
hundred and ninety-three times. I think about my goals every day, but it's
not working."

My answer was always the same, "Thinking about your goals and believing in them is a good start, but you still have to get up off the couch and take action." Now I gave myself the same advice. I wanted to *be* love, but what action could I take?

From my interviews with the Love Luminaries, I knew that Love for No Reason wasn't a mental attitude that they talked themselves into every morning. I've been around enough "mood-makers"—people who suppressed who they really were and pretended to be something they weren't—to see that the Love Luminaries were different. They weren't pasting a veneer of loving behavior over irritation or loneliness. The compassion and care I felt radiating from them went all the way to their core.

I knew that to make the shift myself would mean learning to access a distinct type of energy and then making it a habit. Instead of just taking an occasional trip to the state of Love for No Reason, I wanted to move there.

Everything Is Energy

Take a moment to look around you and notice what you see. Whatever you're looking at—whether animal, vegetable, or mineral—all of it is made of a single miraculous ingredient: energy.

This view that everything in the universe is energy has been scientifically verified. For over a hundred years, physicists have been examining the structure of matter, and today Einstein's revelation about the relationship between matter and energy is universally accepted.

When I interviewed Love Luminary David Morelli, the host of the *Everything Is Energy* radio program, he explained it this way: "Even what seems like solid matter is actually pure energy vibrating in particular patterns and frequencies. Our flesh-and-blood bodies are composed of energy, and we're surrounded by the same energy in a multitude of different forms. The universe is one big energy soup!

"This isn't a new idea. For thousands of years, wisdom traditions have told us that the entire world—the infinite variety of people, plants, animals, stones, stars, and so on—are just different expressions of the same universal life force."

What does this mean for us in our everyday life? The energy of our bodies and the energy of our thoughts and feelings are one and the same energy, simply vibrating at different speeds. This is why our thoughts and feelings have such a profound influence on our bodies. Vibrating at some frequencies feels good, while vibrating at others feels bad. We experience this reality every day in a thousand different ways when we simply pay attention.

For instance, after an argument, have you ever felt like a punching bag, exhausted and battered—even though no one has laid a finger on you? Or maybe you've had a "superfluid" day, the kind of day when the people and resources you need seem to magically appear, and you feel strong, clear, and invincible. This flowing and balanced energy frequency creates completely different biochemical and electrical energy signatures in our brains.

Pure, unconditional love is the highest frequency of vibration there is. The more you experience Love for No Reason, the more habituated you become to living at a high energetic vibration, and the greater your effect on the world around you. When we radiate love, we send out a powerful vibration that impacts all other life forms: humans, animals—even plants.

Author and Love Luminary David Spangler told me a remarkable example of this:

> In the early 1970s, I was one of the directors of Findhorn, a deeply spiritual community in Scotland dedicated to living and working in partnership with Nature. The residents of Findhorn made a regular practice of consciously sending love to the plants in the garden. The results were spectacular. Without the use of chemical pesticides or fertilizers, the gardens at Findhorn produced extraordinary flowers, fruits, and vegetables—that at times bordered on the miraculous.
>
> One day, Peter, a cofounder of the Findhorn community, asked me to join him in his study, where he was having tea with a local minister and his wife. We sat and chatted politely for a little while and then Peter suggested we tour the grounds to see the rosebushes that had been planted a little over a year ago. Peter explained that the minister was a rose horticulturist who had helped with the selection and planting of the roses but hadn't been back since to see their progress.
>
> As we traipsed around the gardens looking at the various rosebushes, I noticed the minister becoming more and more agitated. Suddenly, he stopped walking and cried, "Enough!"
>
> We all looked at him in alarm.
>
> "What I'm seeing is completely impossible!" he thundered.

Seeing our puzzled faces, he continued more calmly, "I have a confession to make. You see, my wife has been dragging me up here for the past three years on my vacation because she loves this community. I, on the other hand, have been firmly convinced that you're all crazy. All that rubbish about cosmic energy and plants and love. It's ridiculous! But she brings me here when I would much rather go fishing. So, to prove that what you were doing here was nonsense, I offered to help you with the planting of your rosebushes.

"I've studied roses for over thirty years, and I know what will grow in this soil and in this climate. When I drew up the list of roses for planting at Findhorn, I selected varieties that had no chance of surviving here. *No chance!* Every one of these roses is totally wrong for this location and has never been known to grow here. Some shouldn't even grow outside of a hothouse. Yet here they are, all of them, thriving!" He paused, looking at us intently. "I would never have believed this if I hadn't seen it with my own two eyes."

Seeing the roses had convinced him that people's energy could affect the world around them. From that day on, the minister became one of Findhorn's staunchest supporters.

Love Is Letting Go of Fear

It's long been acknowledged that there are just two primary energies in the universe: love and fear. Everything that's not love—anger, hatred, hurt, sadness, guilt, frustration—is a form of fear.

Love and fear have two very different effects. Love expands you, while fear contracts you. Check it out for yourself: for ten seconds, think of a situation in which you feel afraid, angry, or hurt. Notice what happens to your body, your posture, and your breathing. Now switch gears and for the next ten seconds think of a situation in which you feel love. Again, notice what happens to your body, your posture, and your breathing.

When you feel fear or any of its variations, you hunch your shoulders, at least metaphorically, and cave in on yourself to protect your heart. You tighten and stop breathing. When you feel love, your spine straightens, you breathe more deeply; you open up to life.

Love and fear truly affect every cell of your body. Researchers at the Institute of HeartMath measured the effect on the body's immune system. They found that when subjects were feeling love and compassion, there was a boost in immune functioning as measured by levels of secretory IgA, which is the body's first line of defense against illness. On the other hand, when subjects experienced fear and frustration—even for just five minutes—their immune functioning was suppressed for up to six hours, leaving them more susceptible to viruses, bacteria, and parasites.

Having judgments about ourselves or others or feeling unworthy shuts us down to love. We get lost in fear and pain and we lose touch with the essence of who we are. This drives us to look for love from the outside, which can't make us happier or healthier for long. Any temporary satisfaction, like a sugar rush, evaporates quickly, leaving an even bigger vacuum in its wake.

On the other hand, when we experience Love for No Reason, there's no space for fear and its negative cousins to enter. As it says in the Bible, "There is no fear where love exists."

Marianne Williamson writes in her classic and life-changing book *A Return to Love*, "Love is what we were born with. Fear is what we have learned here. The spiritual journey is the relinquishment—or unlearning—of fear and the acceptance of love back into our hearts. Love . . . is our ultimate reality and our purpose on earth. To be consciously aware of it, to experience love in ourselves and others, is the meaning of life."

The Love for No Reason program raises your energetic vibration to the frequency of love by giving you exercises and techniques that will help you lessen fear. Moment by moment, day by day, you'll strengthen your love body.

The Anatomy of the Love-Body

Just as we feed our physical body food and water to nourish it, the love-body flourishes on a steady diet of love. And as I heard over and over from the Love Luminaries, the heart is the portal to that love. (Love Theme #3.) Yet, as central as the heart is, it's not the whole story. Your love-body provides supporting players to bolster your heart—six of them, to be exact. Together these seven players form Team Love for No Reason.

According to many different wisdom traditions, we have seven main centers in our energy body. If you've attended a yoga class, you've probably heard them called by their Sanskrit name: the chakras. Author and physician Deepak Chopra explains that these centers "serve as junction points between the body and consciousness."

These energy centers are located in a vertical column from the base of the spine to the top of the head. Though the centers aren't yet documented by modern science, there are indications that something significant is in fact occurring in the body at the sites of the centers. Dr. Candace Pert, an internationally recognized expert in the field of psychoneuroimmunology, has done research documenting the body's "nodal points"—clusters of emotional receptor cells along the spinal cord where a high concentration of neurotransmitters and neuropeptides are released. What's remarkable is how closely the location of these nodal points corresponds to those of the energy centers.

Eastern systems of medicine, including India's Ayurveda and traditional Chinese medicine, say that the centers relate to specific aspects of our physical and psychological well-being. If the energy flow is blocked in a center, we may experience mental, physical, or emotional dis-ease in the systems governed by that energy center.

While volumes have been written about these energy centers, I've seen little about how our ability to experience love is affected by them. I became intrigued by this possibility when I noticed how characteristics that all of the Love Luminaries shared—the qualities of Love for No Reason—were correlated to the specific qualities traditionally attributed to each of the energy centers.

For example, one common trait among Love Luminaries is a sense of feeling safe in the world, which allows them to open their hearts. Knowing that the first energy center at the base of the spine is related to feeling safe and secure, I wondered, *How does that center support the experience of love?*

As I began to look at all the centers and their qualities in terms of how they supported Love for No Reason, I got excited: had I stumbled upon the anatomy of the love-body?

I saw that each of the energy centers represents certain qualities of Love for No Reason; strengthening the center and its qualities helps you open to love. Let me be clear: this is *not* a book about chakras but a book that uses the energy centers as a model to help you learn how to expand your ability to be in the state of Love for No Reason more and more of the time. Each energy center is like a doorway to love.

The energy of love flows into our lives through the following seven doorways:

1. **The Doorway of Safety:** *Being in the Here and Now.* This doorway is connected to the energy center I call the safety center, which is located at base of the spine and is related to feeling safe, secure, and grounded.
2. **The Doorway of Vitality:** *Turning Up the Juice.* This doorway is connected to the energy center I call the vitality center, which is located in the area of the sacrum or lower abdomen and is related to feeling vital and alive—both physically and emotionally.
3. **The Doorway of Unconditional Self-Love:** *Loving Yourself No Matter What.* This doorway is connected to the energy center I call the unconditional self-love center, which is located in the area of the navel or solar plexus and is related to feeling empowered and worthy of love.
4. **The Doorway of Openness:** *Living with an Open Heart.* This doorway is connected to the energy center I call the openness center, which is located in the heart and is related to being open to fully giving and receiving love.
5. **The Doorway of Communication:** *Coming from Compassion.* This doorway is connected to the energy center I call the communication center, which is located in the area of the throat and is related to being able to listen and express ourselves from a place of love.
6. **The Doorway of Vision:** *Seeing with the Eyes of Love.* This doorway is connected to the energy center I call the vision center, which is located in the middle of the forehead, also called the third eye, and is related to intuition and the ability to see inner and outer truth and beauty.
7. **The Doorway of Oneness:** *Connecting to Wholeness.* This doorway is connected to the energy center I call the oneness center, which is located at the top of the head, and relates to feeling connected to a larger whole: God, Spirit, Higher Self, Nature, the Divine, or the Universe.

When a center is healthy and strong and we experience the quality related to that center, the doorway to love is fully open. When the center is

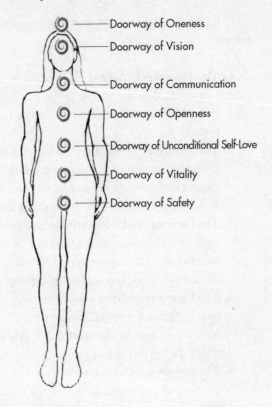

imbalanced or weak and we aren't experiencing the quality related to that center, the doorway is partially or fully blocked, and our ability to love is hindered.

It's not a sequential process; you don't have to strengthen the first center in order to work on the second center, and so on. There are many people in the world who have strong and healthy seventh energy centers but whose lower centers are weak. And if any of the energy centers are weak, we can't fully experience Love for No Reason on an ongoing basis.

Whether or not you believe that these energy centers exist, you can still use this model to develop the seven main qualities that will support the experience of Love for No Reason in your life. Following this program will allow you to open the doorways to love.

The Heart: The Master Command Center for Love

*Awake, my dear. Be kind to your sleeping heart. Take it
out into the vast field of light and let it breathe.*

—Hafiz, fourteenth-century mystic poet

Physically, the heart is the most important organ in our body. It's the first organ to develop in the fetus and the last to shut down when we die. Many would argue that the brain is more important, but the truth is that the brain and heart significantly influence each other's functioning. What most people don't know, however, is that the heart affects the brain more than the other way around.

Research shows that the heart sends more neurological information to the brain than the brain does to the heart. In addition, the Institute of HeartMath found that the magnetic field generated by the heart—what's measured on a magnetometer—is five thousand times stronger than that of the brain. Even more surprising is the discovery that the heart is a major player in the process of manufacturing and releasing hormones and neurotransmitters, some of which affect important brain processes. In fact, based on research by J. Andrew Armour, MD, PhD, one of the pioneers in the field of neurocardiology, many scientists, researchers, and neurocardiologists now understand that the heart has its own independent nervous system, a complex system of neural cells called the "brain in the heart." All these factors help explain why the heart is so crucial for our well-being.

When it comes to love, our energetic heart or heart center has a similar status. It's the CEO, the top dog, the chieftain—the master command center leading and being supported by all the other centers. To experience and live in Love for No Reason, our heart center has to be open and balanced.

In fact, unconditional love has been connected to the heart in every tradition throughout history. The Vedic literature speaks of the lotus in the heart, and the Sufis of the diamond in the heart. In Islam, the heart is considered "the Throne of the Infinitely Good and Compassionate." In Christianity, God's love for humanity is symbolized by the Sacred Heart.

Judaism's Kabbalah considers the human heart the true location of the Ark of the Covenant, the sacred container which contains the Torah or the word of God. Many scriptures call the heart "the seat of the soul."

Though modern society places more importance on the logic and analytical skills of the brain, it's actually the heart that's central to our fulfillment. Just making this paradigm shift is a significant step to experiencing more unconditional love in life.

Heaven and Earth Meet in the Heart

While it's true that the heart is the main portal where the energy of love is given and received, it needs the support of the other energy centers to remain open.

Here's an analogy that may make this clearer: Think of love as water flowing through a hose, with a sprinkler located at the heart center. If the hose is kinked anywhere along its length, the full amount of water won't get to the sprinkler. In the same way, our love energy needs to flow easily through all the energy centers for us to fully experience love at the heart center.

In addition to being the go-to spot where we access Love for No Reason, the heart center has another important function. It's where the spiritual and the physical aspects of human life merge. The Taoists believe that the human body is the link between heaven and earth—like a tree with its roots planted deep in the ground and its branches stretching up into the sky.

There are three energy centers below the heart center and three above. It's long been understood that the lower three centers deal primarily with the energy of the earth—our physical existence—while the top three centers are related to more spiritual energies.

The heart, which is both spiritual and physical, is the bridge. It transmits the combined energies of the earth and the divine into our human experience. Picture an infinity symbol standing upright. The upper three centers (the top half of the symbol) and the lower three (the bottom half) meet and "marry" at the heart center. The essence of being human is taking the divine and the earthly aspects of ourselves and integrating them through love.

Then Love for No Reason flows out into the world through us. We become a blessing to ourselves and everyone else.

The Love for No Reason Program

In Part II you'll learn to open the seven doorways to Love for No Reason—one chapter for each doorway. The chapters include two separate approaches—or Love Keys—to help you develop the quality that will open that doorway. Based on my research and interviews with the Love Luminaries, I've also included tools and techniques that help you establish the neurophysiology of Love for No Reason. These fall into one of two categories:

1. They remove the blocks to your experience of unconditional love by helping you dissolve limiting beliefs, transform negative habits, and release emotional and physical toxins.
2. They allow you to directly tap into or create a resonance with that state of unconditional love.

This unique holistic program addresses love from all angles—physical, mental, emotional, and spiritual. Each impacts and strengthens the other.

I suggest you take a week on each doorway, taking time to integrate the keys, tools, and techniques introduced in each chapter. You may need more time on some of them. Be sensitive and kind to yourself. After all, being anything but loving to yourself is counter to this program.

As you are working with the Love for No Reason program, you may experience, as I did, an interesting phenomenon: love brings up everything unlike itself to be healed. You may find that old issues, fears, and discomforts are stirred up like clouds of dust when you clean an attic.

When this happens, it means that you're getting rid of old garbage—outworn ideas, beliefs, and memories that have been sabotaging your ability to fully love. You don't need to sort through the garbage or catalogue it. That will only slow you down. Keep on doing the program and the dust will gently be cleaned away.

Well Begun Is Half-Done

*When you are truly clear about what you want, the entire
universe stands on tiptoe waiting to assist you in miraculous
and amazing ways to manifest your dream or intention.*

—Constance Arnold, radio host

As you begin the Love for No Reason program, it's important that you become crystal clear in your heart and mind about your desire to live a life of unconditional love. You will get the best results from this program when you start with an intention that resonates deeply in your heart.

When you want something to grow, you start by planting a seed. You can water the ground and put in fertilizer, but without the seed nothing will happen. If we want Love for No Reason to flower in our lives, we have to plant the seed of our intention first.

To do this, write your love intention below. Make sure to be positive in your intention. Focus *only* on what you want, not on what you don't want. For example, my Love for No Reason Intention is "I am living with an open heart and I bring unconditional love to every experience I have." You'll know you've found the right intention for you when you're uplifted by just thinking it.

My Love for No Reason Intention:

_____

Now take a few minutes to visualize your life as if you were living from the state of Love for No Reason. Imagine what it would be like.

- How would it look and feel?
- What would your relationships be like?
- How would you interact with your children?
- How would you feel at work?
- How would your daily commute be different?
- How would you be treating yourself?

There is tremendous power in visualizing your desired life. Countless studies have demonstrated the effectiveness of visualization for improving athletic and academic performance and for speeding healing. A particularly interesting study was conducted at Harvard Medical School showing the effect of mental imagery on learning to play the piano. One group imagined playing a sequence of notes, while the other group physically practiced that sequence. After five days, both groups showed the same changes in the brain's motor system and played the sequence equally accurately.

That's why it's important to regularly visualize the outcomes you want. Einstein said, "Imagination . . . is the preview of life's coming attractions." Consciously picturing and feeling a love-filled life will inspire you and get your energy rolling in the right direction.

To supercharge your intention, add the feeling of love to your visualization. Anything done with love has more power. In another study, conducted at the Institute of HeartMath, twenty-eight people were each given a sample of DNA in a test tube. They were instructed to send an intention, infused with feelings of love, to the DNA strand to wind or unwind. Those people who were able to experience more love, as measured physiologically, had a much greater ability to affect the DNA in the way they had intended.

A good way to keep your Love for No Reason intention front and center in your life is to pick a physical symbol to have as a daily reminder. It can be a heart-shaped rock that you carry in your pocket or place on your desk. Or maybe a piece of jewelry—a ring, pin, pendant, or bracelet—that sends a Love for No Reason signal to you all day long. Find a T-shirt that reminds you of Love for No Reason or choose a ringtone for your phone that has an association with Higher Love for you.

Remember, once you set your intention, habituating the state of Love for No Reason simply means practicing the love keys until they become second nature. It's just a matter of doing a little each day. Gretchen Rubin, the author of *The Happiness Project*, calls this small and steady approach one of her secrets of adulthood: "What you do every day matters more than what you do once in a while." In chapter 11 you'll find suggestions for keeping Love for No Reason growing in your life.

You're about to embark on an incredibly exciting adventure, one that will lead you into a new and wondrous world inside yourself and will allow you to be a more loving person than you ever imagined you could be.

So, let's get started on the Love for No Reason program and begin living a more open-hearted life.

PART II

The Love for No Reason Program: How to Develop Your Love-Body

Your task is not to seek for Love, but merely to seek and find all the barriers within yourself that you have built against it.

—Rumi, thirteenth-century Sufi poet

CHAPTER 4

The Doorway of Safety: Being in the Here and Now

Love is based on our capacity to trust in a reality beyond fear, to trust a timeless truth bigger than all our difficulties.

—Jack Kornfield, author and teacher

When I was a little girl, one of my favorite experiences in life was to listen to the murmur of my parents' voices in the living room as I drifted off to sleep. My cozy bedroom, dimly lit by a small night light, felt like a cocoon of comfort, and the presence of my parents just down the hall cemented my feelings of safety and peace. For years I called this my "All's right with the world" experience.

I know that I was fortunate and that not all childhoods include such idyllic moments. Yet no matter what's happened to us in our past, we all have the potential to feel the same peace inside. And when you carry that sense of security within you—wherever you are—it allows you to open up your heart and let love flow in your life.

This deep anchoring in well-being beyond worry is what you feel when the Doorway of Safety is open.

But when this doorway is blocked, you feel more shaky than solid.

You worry—sometimes for no apparent reason—about the fundamentals of life like your job, health, and home. To onlookers, you may appear distracted, indecisive, or ungrounded. Your home may get messy, your kitchen cupboards empty, your bank account overdrawn.

Or just the opposite. You may hold on tight to your money, plagued by the constant fear of not having enough. You may become obsessive about neatness and order, attempting to compensate for feelings of insecurity or powerlessness. You may try to get more done, multitasking like mad. Or you may find yourself unable to focus and act at all.

Whatever the symptoms, the bottom line is that your brain gets overwhelmed and mistakenly triggers your body into stress episodes over minor events. Molehills morph into mountains.

There's a single phenomenon at the source of all these negative states. It's the F-word. *Fear.* When fear builds up in the safety center, it does a number on love: we contract and our hearts constrict. We may seek security in other people and end up in the wrong relationships or refuse to risk getting hurt and cut ourselves off from the people around us. When fear dominates us, we lose touch with the love at our core. If we don't feel an inner sense of safety, we may find ourselves falling into the abyss of No Love. Strengthening the safety center is about lessening our fear and feeling safe no matter where we are.

Finding Our Feet

Over fifty years ago, psychologist Abraham Maslow wrote about a hierarchy of human needs. He said that the need for security is so fundamental to human development that we can't fulfill any other part of our potential until it's satisfied. To give and receive love, he said, we must first trust that we are safe in our surroundings. But the deeper truth is that when we are internally stable and centered in the here and now, we can relax enough to open our hearts—no matter how unsafe our circumstances appear.

When this doorway's open, we feel calm and present in the moment. We don't rush, we don't panic, and we're at ease even when we're busy. The mantra we hear is a low, slow pulse: *Don't worry, don't hurry; you'll be all right.*

Picture an elephant moving across the wide savannah. Her huge feet move at a steady, swift pace, and each step makes ginormous contact with the ground. This wise-eyed beast is so weighty and unflappable, it's reassuring just to be near her! When the Doorway of Safety is open, we tap into that elephantine confidence inside ourselves, enabling us to walk surefooted through an unpredictable world.

Getting Rooted in Love

The Doorway of Safety is the first of the seven energy centers or chakras we'll be looking at in Part II. Cultivating the qualities associated with each center will support your experience of unconditional love. Remember, when the energy center and its qualities are weak, that particular doorway to Love for No Reason is closed. But when the energy center and its qualities are strong, that doorway is open, and Higher Love can flow, brightening every aspect of your life.

In ancient wisdom traditions, the safety center is known as the root or base chakra. Located at the bottom of the spine, its energy circulates around and under the base of the body, around the pelvis, through the large intestine and down the legs and feet.

If you drew arrows through this center, they'd all be pointing south, pulling invisible energy downward and keeping you planted in solid ground. The more firmly a plant or tree is rooted in the earth, the larger bloom or growth it can support. To grow and flourish in love, we too need a strong root.

Sounds simple enough. But how many people do you know, including yourself, who feel absolutely rooted and secure in their lives, irrespective of their income, job, or relationship status? How many people never get lost in worry over the what-ifs? Modern life has brought us many gifts but also some serious challenges. It's given us fragmented families and competitive workplaces and taken away the safety nets we've relied upon for hundreds of years, leaving us with little to hold on to for stability.

Plus, we have a million things begging for our attention. It's been said that we get more information in *one day* than a person three hundred years ago got in his *entire lifetime*! This information avalanche feeds our scattered and overwhelmed state.

No wonder we often feel anxious and don't even know why. It's as if we're sponges soaking up the stress surrounding us.

The good news is that we *can* create that unshakable safety inside. I think of people who have it—many of whom are the Love Luminaries in this book—as human redwood trees: majestically grounded, difficult to knock over, and soothing to be around. Most didn't get that way overnight. They developed inner security with practice, by grounding themselves firmly in the present moment and finding a deep bedrock of trust in life—two keys to unlocking the Doorway of Safety that you'll learn in the coming pages.

Turning Off the Stress Response

As I mentioned in chapter 3, love and fear are mutually exclusive energies. Either we're functioning from love, or we're functioning from fear. If we're running our fear programs—worry, anxiety, nervousness—love is essentially off-line.

Fear expresses itself physically and mentally as a tightening, limiting force. It sends us into survival mode, or fight or flight, which causes our brain to shut down its normal functioning and direct more energy toward self-protection. Our whole system gets depleted from constantly defending itself.

Love Luminary Dr. John Douillard is a brilliant practitioner of Ayurveda, India's traditional, holistic system of medicine that has been practiced for more than five thousand years. In our interview, Dr. Douillard told me that because modern-day stress levels trigger the fight-or-flight response so often, we're actually building bodies of fear. Worries don't just disappear into thin air after we think them; they leave a toxic trail of neurochemicals, like cortisol and norepinephrine, that get stored in our bodies. These emotional toxins are just as harmful as the chemical toxins from our air, water, and food that are stored in the fat cells right alongside them.

This residue not only hampers the functioning of your body, it hinders the functioning of your mind. "Emotional toxins make us think and do the same dumb stuff, again and again and again," Dr. Douillard says. What's worse, we get used to this state of free-floating fear and start to think it's normal.

To take fear off-line, Dr. Douillard says we can begin by reversing this agitated physiology and creating a safe, relaxed state in our cells instead.

"We have to convince the body the war's over and life is not an emergency. When we feel safe, those toxins get released out of the fat cells and newer, better molecules of emotion—neurotransmitters of love and happiness like oxytocin and dopamine—can become available."

Recent studies on compassion, trust, empathy, and altruism support this idea: the circuitry of love—the unique brain functioning underlying these states of love—activates only when the stress response is switched off. Researcher Esther M. Sternberg, MD, of the National Institutes of Health explains that unselfish, benevolent love appears to activate "certain aspects of the relaxation response in addition to blocking aspects of the stress response."

In my interview with Love Luminary Dr. Stephen G. Post, the author of *Why Good Things Happen to Good People: How to Live a Longer, Healthier, Happier Life by the Simple Act of Giving,* he told me, "It's neurologically impossible to be engaged in outward acts of lovingkindness and also be experiencing a state of high stress or negativity inside. The higher action, loving, cancels out the lower one, fearing."

I've personally experienced how love and fear are mutually exclusive. For most of my life, I've been one of those people who go into fight or flight at the drop of a hat. My brain simply has an oversensitive alarm switch. Or as a brain scientist once told me, I have a hot amygdala. (Unfortunately, that's not the same as calling me hot.)

For years I tended to overreact, and my friends and family had become immune to my constant shrieks of panic over small upsets—"*Eeeek!* Where are my keys?" "*Oh no,* I closed the file without saving it!" As you can imagine, this wasn't good for my body, and it was especially hard on my heart. Spending so much of my day being freaked out left me little time and energy to experience love.

About ten years ago, I went to see a therapist who suggested a simple exercise for taming my hair-trigger response to life. She told me to consciously relax my perineum, which is located at the base of the body, between the rectum and the sexual organs. (The location of the safety center!) I wondered how something so simple could really help, but I tried it anyway. For the next week, every time I'd feel tense, overwhelmed, insecure, or afraid, I'd put my attention on the perineum and find it was clenched.

As soon as I relaxed it, I could breathe again. I'd immediately be able to think more clearly and things didn't seem as scary or difficult.

Today it's become a habit that helps me "roll with the punches." Instead of hyperventilating over every little thing, I'm more centered and can be more loving—to myself and everyone else in my life.

This simple process has been one of the many tools I've used to help myself tame my stress response and unlock the Doorway of Safety.

Unlocking the Doorway of Safety: The Two Love Keys

In my interviews with the Love Luminaries, I was continually struck by how these very diverse people shared so many similar qualities. For example, I noticed that when they spoke with me, they were deeply present: though they were busy people, they didn't seem rushed for time and they were fully focused on our conversation. Also, they frequently acknowledged the things in their lives that supported their well-being—daily routines, people, pets, as well as more abstract backups, like nature, Spirit or simply the universe. It was clear to me that having these supports in place helped them remain open to the flow of love and life.

The two Love Keys for this doorway will allow you to develop these Love for No Reason traits too. They're easy but potent ways to increase your experience of this redwood-tree state in yourself. One involves connecting downward and grounding, like planting your taproot deep into the soil; the other involves extending your branches outward and developing a *felt awareness* of all that supports you. Both contribute to a sense of safety, which enables you to be in the here and now—the only place you can truly experience love.

The Love Keys for the Doorway of Safety

1. Get Grounded
2. Sense Your Support

The Grounding Key unlocks your natural ability to feel secure in the physical world, assured you've got all the time and resources you need. It involves slowing down and connecting to the earth and the present moment.

The Support Key unlocks your inner trust that there's plenty in life to lean on. It involves recognizing, appreciating, and making use of the support that already exists within and around you.

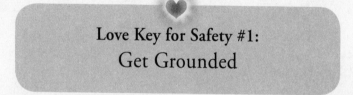

Love Key for Safety #1:
Get Grounded

Have you ever arrived at a destination, only to realize you had no idea what route you took to get there? Or finished a meal and realized you barely tasted the food? When our minds are lost in thought or worry, we go AWOL from the present and we start living on autopilot. If you're so distracted that you forget who you're calling by the time you finish dialing or you find yourself putting your car keys, rather than the milk, in the refrigerator, how can you be present enough to feel love's flow?

This ungrounded state hits me hardest on "flying days" when I've been captive thirty-six thousand feet in the air speeding at 550 miles an hour in a metal machine. As soon as I get home, I make a point to do things that let me feel the opposite of flying. I plug back in to the physical world. I start by taking off my shoes and socks and putting my bare feet on the earth. I stop moving and stare at the sunset. I cook (if steaming vegetables and plugging in my rice cooker counts as cooking).

These simple activities are universal ways of getting grounded. They help curb our anxiety by slowing us down and calming our nervous system. The mental world moves at light speed, especially when it's agitated. The physical world moves a whole lot slower. You can't rush a setting sun, and soup has to simmer until it's done.

When teacher and healer James Keeley told me how Mother Nature helped loosen the knots in his heart, I knew he was a Love Luminary. His story, which follows, is the first of the fourteen full-length stories from my Love Luminary interviews that illustrate the points throughout the book. James explained to me that getting grounded reconnected him to a place deep inside himself that he'd known as a child but had forgotten. His journey of coming home to himself began with the painful recognition of how far off course he'd wandered.

James's Story
Lost and Found

There are four questions of value in life . . . What is sacred? Of what is the spirit made? What is worth living for, and what is worth dying for? The answer to each is the same. Only love.

—Actor Johnny Depp's character in the film *Don Juan DeMarco*

I was twenty years old and lost. I was a kite without a string, a boat without an anchor—a party animal with an aching heart.

When I'd finished my stint in the military, I had no idea what to do next. I decided, *What the hell, I might as well have fun.*

So I moved to Fort Lauderdale and set about having as much fun as I possibly could. My daily routine was a hedonist's dream: hanging out at the beach by day, parking cars at a swanky restaurant in the evenings, and partying late into the night.

On the surface, I appeared fine, even happy, but underneath, I was disillusioned. I felt emptiness, sadness, and a sense of pointlessness, which I numbed out with all the drinking and fun. I felt disconnected from my heart.

Then one night my soul sent out an SOS. The answer I received set me on a new path.

The party was in full swing. The beer had been flowing for hours and I'd had a lot of it. Suddenly the room seemed too small, too hot. I needed some air—and to go to the bathroom. I made my way to the door, weaving through the crowd of people yelling to each other over the blaring CD.

Outside, the breeze felt cool and sweet. I stumbled over to the bushes and relieved my full bladder. I looked up into the night sky studded with stars, and suddenly the meaninglessness of my life felt intolerable. I had the thought, *If this is as good as life gets, then I'm in big trouble.* It was a cry for help—the first sincere prayer I'd ever prayed, though at the time, I didn't recognize it as one. I was cynical about religion and had no conception that it was possible to have a real relationship with God.

The answer to that prayer showed up a few weeks later, in the form of a book. A friend's father had sensed my plight and sent me *The Tracker*, Tom Brown Jr.'s story of his experience as a young boy being taught by a Native American elder how to live in the wilderness. I began reading and was immediately hooked. I was fascinated by the author's accounts of tracking, setting up shelters, and finding wild sources of food. But when he talked about learning the Native American beliefs of being one with the Creator and being in harmony with all living things, I found myself choking up, tears filling my eyes. It reminded me of the feelings I'd had as a young boy.

I'd grown up in a small town in Pennsylvania and spent a lot of time outdoors. There were some woods by my house where I'd built a little fort. I remembered sitting in it, listening to the birds, and just being quiet. Reading Tom Brown's words, I saw that the peace and wholeness I'd touched in those times in the woods were what was missing from my life.

I began saving every penny I could to attend Tom Brown's tracking school. I had it in my mind that I was going to become his apprentice. I fantasized about living at the school with him and absorbing all he had to teach me.

When I got to the school, it was everything I'd hoped it would be. As I worked in the woods with this amazing tracker, my awareness settled down, relaxed, and expanded. I felt a groundedness, a slowing down, a state of being one with nature—something so large and grand and beautiful that it opened me up to a deeper kind of love than I'd ever known before.

One day, our class did a Native American healing ceremony for one of our classmates, who sat in the middle of the circle. We were instructed to feel the love inside our hearts and let it flow through us to the person we were trying to heal. Opening to that love, I was overcome by it. Yet I also felt so at home. I thought, *Whatever this healing stuff is, it's what I'm meant to do.*

When the two-week class was almost over, I managed to pull Tom aside and tell him about my plan to stay and have him mentor me.

He looked at me and said, "Well, where you from?"

"Pennsylvania," I answered.

"There are a lot of woods in Pennsylvania," he said with a wry smile.

I understood what he was telling me: *If this is what you want to do, go do it.*

I took his advice and spent the next forty days living in the woods. My best friend at the time came with me. When you're living in the wild, it only takes a few hours each day to do the things necessary for your survival, so we had a lot of time to meditate, reflect, and roam the forest. Those days in the wilderness connected me to a flow of life much bigger than myself. Becoming a part of that flow put everything in perspective and gave me reasons to live. It turned my disillusionment into love of life—an excited, ecstatic, exuberant state of looking forward to what's around the next corner.

I recently found a journal I kept during that time and came across this entry: *Today I realized that love isn't something that happens between two people, it's something you're either open to or you're not.* That was my first glimpse of a state of love that's natural to all of us. I learned that it's only our unwillingness to be in the moment that keeps us from experiencing Divine love and knowing that we're connected to everything and already have everything we need.

This insight is the foundation of the work I do today helping others find that place of love and trust within themselves. After the forty days in the wilderness, I signed up for a school where I learned about herbs and energy healing. This led me to a career as a therapist and a teacher offering people and corporations a practical approach to healing and spiritual development. It's turned out to be a career that makes my heart sing.

Not long ago, I went for a hike and spent an hour sitting on top of the ridge near my home in the mountains of northern West Virginia, just feeling life flow through me. I love my wife and two beautiful children with all my heart, and the love that's expressed through being a husband and father is replenished when I step out of my house, my routine, my sessions with clients, and step back into the wilderness. It's like letting go and floating on a river, allowing the current to take me where it will. In the wilderness that deeply silent sense of peace and harmony is easier to experience.

In my healing workshops, people thank me for bringing so much love to the class. I say, "I didn't bring any love. I just kept acknowledging the love that was already there until you all caught on and also realized it was there!"

Being in nature, grounded and connected to the earth, is what first allowed me to catch on to the constant presence of love. And that has transformed me from a lost boy—out of touch with life's meaning—to a deeply fulfilled man who delights in every moment.

No Shoes, No Phone, No Problem

You don't have to spend forty days in the wilderness like James did to get the benefits of nature's grounding. Simply gazing at the sky or the trees from indoors has a soothing, healing effect. In my interview with Love Luminary Bernie Siegel, he told me about a study showing that patients who can see nature from their hospital windows get better more quickly than those who have no view.

Still, it's better to get your dose of nature up close and personal. According to a study done at the University of Essex in England, just five minutes spent outside in "green exercise," including cycling, walking, and gardening, boosts a person's mood and level of self-esteem. Another study done at the University of Rochester in New York found significant increases in vitality and resistance to physical illness from spending time in nature. Professor Richard Ryan, who led the study, said, "Nature is fuel for the soul."

In today's world we suffer from what author Richard Louv calls nature-deficit disorder. So whenever possible, go outside and stand, sit, or lie on the earth—it could be grass, sand, soil, or snow—and you'll feel more love for yourself and your life. Being outside also triggers a relaxation response in your body. This may be because the earth's electromagnetic frequency thrums at a third of the speed of the busy brain. When you're somewhere free of buildings and wires, and you take a little time to just be, nature settles you down to match its slower wavelength.

With our shoes on our feet, headphones in our ears, sunglasses on our faces, and air-conditioned cars around our bodies, we modern humans are out of touch with nature's rhythms.

Love Luminary Janet Sussman, who is a writer, musician, and intuitive counselor, told me that if we plugged into nature's heartbeat more often, we'd feel less unsettled and flighty. "Today we don't truly know what it means to be 'connected.' What it meant in ancient times was that in every single step you took, there was a pulsation of information, light, love, and consciousness coming from the earth into us. There wasn't any asphalt or anything that would be in the way, so there was never any disconnection."

She went on to explain that the urge that I have to walk barefoot on the earth after being on airplanes for hours is a way to feed this quality of groundedness in myself. "The feet are exquisitely sensitive. They take information in and feed it up to your root," she said. "The ultimate result is never feeling alone or separate, and always feeling completely held, loved, protected, and known by the earth."

Kicking off your shoes may sound far too simple as a method for creating such a powerful effect, but it's long been understood that putting your bare soles on the earth's surface lets you absorb some of its *chi*, or life force. Relationship expert and Love Luminary John Gray told me he believes that one of the reasons indigenous peoples have gotten sicker in the past fifty years is that they've picked up the Western habit of wearing rubber-soled shoes and flip-flops and have lost naked contact with the planet.

There are many exciting new studies that support the theory that being in direct contact with the earth's energy improves our health. The May 2010 *Townsend Letter*, a newsletter documenting alternative health research, discusses *Earthing*, a book by Martin Zucker, integrative cardiologist Stephen Sinatra, and Clint Ober: "The energy you feel from walking barefoot is the ground's electric energy rising up into your body. Research is now revealing that this energy creates a distinct and uplifting shift in the physiology. It promotes health, vitality, and better sleep, harmonizes and stabilizes the body's basic biological rhythms, knocks down and even knocks out chronic inflammation, and reduces and eliminates pain. This disconnect from the natural resource right under our feet may likely be a totally overlooked and major factor behind the alarming rise of chronic disease in recent decades, and inflammatory-related conditions in particular. The sun provides essential Vitamin D; the earth provides essential Vitamin G—which stands for GROUND!"

If you're one of those people who consider the whole back-to-nature, bare-feet-on-the-earth concept some hippy-dippy notion, think again; getting grounded this way is important for your health. And strengthening the safety center helps open your heart.

Slow Down, You Move Too Fast

Another powerful way to get grounded is to bring our attention to what's right in front of us. But this can be a real challenge when we're faced daily with the stress of today's insanely fast-paced world.

Over sixty years ago, pioneering researcher Dr. Hans Selye first popularized the word *stress* to describe the body's reaction to certain stimuli. Small amounts of stress are created whenever we're forced to switch the focus of our attention. Back then, it was considered stressful to switch focus more than ten times per hour. What would Dr. Selye think of our potential for stress today, when the average TV show cuts between shots every three to six seconds to keep us engaged? That's ten to twenty focus changes *a minute*—or six to twelve hundred of them an hour!

On top of this, we have an alarming epidemic of attention deficit disorder and a national obsession with multitasking—these days we keep more balls in the air than most professional jugglers. It's plain to see that the pace of life has gotten out of control. Our attention is everywhere but where we are. This isn't good for experiencing love—or for our physical health.

A study reported in the *Journal of Experimental Psychology* found that multitasking led to the release of stress hormones and adrenaline into our systems. What's worse, when we switch our attention so quickly and continuously, "the brain doesn't have the time to make the neural connections in the cortex humanitatis—the part of brain that makes us civilized creatures," according to Dr. Daniel Siegel, author of *The Mindful Brain* and a clinical professor of psychiatry at UCLA Medical School.

There's a Simon and Garfunkel song that begins, "Slow down, you move too fast," which gives you an idea how to start opening this doorway. The practice of mindfulness, which is bringing your full attention to what you're experiencing in every moment, will ground you and counter that agitated state.

As Eckhart Tolle and many others have taught, harnessing the "power of now" calms the busy mind and engages the heart, creating stability and equanimity. When your attention is 100 percent filled with the now, there's no room left for fear about the future—or regrets about the past.

Dr. Ellen Langer, a psychology professor at Harvard whom I interviewed for my *Happy for No Reason* PBS television show, has done extensive research on the effects of staying present. One fascinating study gave women who disliked football the task of watching the Super Bowl. One group was asked to find six interesting and unusual things about the players while the other group was given no instruction. The group that was guided to an activity that caused them to pay close attention to what was happening enjoyed the game significantly more than the other group.

Being fully engaged and present in your body is a great way to ground yourself, opening yourself up to more joy and love. The following exercise, which I learned from Love Luminary Judith Blackstone, a psychotherapist and the author of *The Enlightenment Process*, counteracts the prevailing MO of "doing ten things at once and being everywhere but here." Carol and I took Judith's workshop on The Realization Process. We noticed right away how present, clear, and loving Judith was. During the workshop she shared the following exercise. I was amazed at the power of this simple process and the richness it added to my experience of life.

Exercise

The Realization Process—Embodiment

By inhabiting the internal space of your body, you deepen contact with yourself and become more grounded and present in the moment. This sets the foundation for you to experience your true essence of love. Take the time to do this exercise completely, following each step carefully. Notice the profound sense of presence you feel when you finish.

1. Sitting comfortably, close your eyes, and begin by focusing on your breath. Watch how your breath comes in and out through your nostrils.

2. Feel that you are inside your body, inhabiting your body. Imagine your awareness being pulled down into your body as though weights were inside your body pulling your awareness in and down. Instead of just thinking about or being aware of your body, you can feel that you actually *are* the internal space of your body. There is no difference between your body and your self.

3. Feel as though you are inside the various parts of your body, starting with your feet. Be in the soles of your feet, feeling the skin as though you were inside your skin feeling outward. Inside each part of your body, attune to the feeling of your own aliveness, what it feels like to be you, living inside your body.

4. Feel that you are inside your lower legs and your knees. To help yourself feel that you are inside your body, place your hands on each side of one knee. Feel that you inhabit the space between your hands. Experience how it feels to be your knee being touched by your hands. Now feel that you are inside your thighs. Attune to the feeling of your aliveness inside your lower legs, knees, and thighs.

5. Bring your attention to your abdomen and feel that you are deep inside your pelvis and stomach area, attuning to the quality of your aliveness inside these parts of yourself.

6. Proceed with the same process to the area of your chest, your shoulders, arms, and hands. Attune to the feeling of your aliveness inside these areas.

7. Feel that you are inside your neck, and inside your whole head (your face and your brain). Attune to the feeling of your aliveness inside your neck and head.

8. When you have completed inhabiting each area of your body, inhabit your whole body at once. Attune to the feeling of your aliveness, inside your whole body at once. If we say that the body is the temple, you are sitting inside the temple of your body.

9. Next bring your attention to the space outside your body, in the room. Experience that the space inside your body and the space outside your body is the same, continuous space; it pervades you. You are still inside your body, but you are permeable; your body is pervaded by space.

10. Sit quietly for a few minutes before opening your eyes. Then, with your eyes open, see if you can still sit inside your body, and feel that the space inside and outside your body is the same, continuous space.

Used by permission of Judith Blackstone, www.RealizationCenter.com

Love Key for Safety #2:
Sense Your Support

The whole of my childhood was spent running. I traveled from assurance to assurance . . . I felt sure that nothing was unfriendly, that the branches I used to swing on would hold firm and that the paths, no matter how winding, would take me to a place where I would not be afraid.

—Jacques Lusseyran, twentieth-century blind French author and activist

Feeling alone, unsafe, or afraid of life's challenges freezes up your love flow faster than a cold front in winter. How can you relax into love if you're afraid of what may be lurking just round the corner? You can disarm these anxieties when you lean into a larger truth: *I am supported. I trust I'll be taken care of, even if I don't always know how or by whom.*

The Love Luminaries all project an inner confidence of "being held" by life. Their ability to love unconditionally comes from feeling supported unconditionally. To live with a wide-open heart ourselves, we need to sense the three distinct circles of support in our lives—physical, emotional, and spiritual.

The first circle relates to the physical aspect of support: the feeling that you can sustain your basic needs and that you're safe—no matter what's going on outside.

The second circle involves the emotional aspect of support, the people—and sometimes the pets—whose presences help you to feel safe and comforted. It includes your immediate tribe—your family and friends with whom you share your daily life—plus your extended tribe, like neighbors, colleagues, and members of your community. Being aware that there are people you can count on for help and encouragement makes it easier to live with an open heart.

When you consciously register the trust you have for the people in your life, it activates the brain centers and hormones associated with trusting. This strengthens the neural pathways for Love for No Reason.

The third circle of support is a spiritual one. Across the board, my Love Luminaries all reported they had a fundamental trust in what Einstein famously called the "friendly universe." Einstein said that the most important decision you can make is whether to believe you live in a friendly universe—one that is always supporting you.

People living in Higher Love have a deeply felt sense that they're part of something bigger and there's some benevolent order to events. This circle of support is what ultimately brings us the redwood-tree stability. When we feel the universe is friendly, we develop the most profound and reassuring kind of support there is: unconditional trust. Love Luminary Rosemary Trible's story, which follows, illustrates these circles of support and their effect on the heart.

I first met Rosemary at a speech I gave in Virginia. After the event, a lovely woman approached me, and what I noticed right away was the warm, accepting air she had about her. Later, during our interview, I discovered that Rosemary's serenity, which clearly comes from a place deep inside herself, had been lost for a time. As a young woman, Rosemary had to rebuild her life—and her ability to trust.

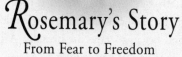

Rosemary's Story
From Fear to Freedom

*Three things last forever—faith, hope, and love—
and the greatest of them all is love.*

—1 Corinthians 13:13

A dream can turn into a nightmare in an instant. One minute you're walking in a beautiful sunlit garden and the next, you're being chased, panting and afraid, by your own personal brand of monster. My life was like that garden until a monstrous event filled it with fear.

In 1975 I was twenty-five years old and had been married for four years. It was a happy, exciting time for me. My husband, Paul, was a lawyer with his eyes on a future in politics, and I was the host and producer of a daily talk show called *Rosemary's Guestbook* on a regional television station in Richmond, Virginia. My audience was primarily female, so I often dealt with subjects that were relevant to women's lives.

Two weeks before Christmas that year, I aired a show on sexual assault—an issue that wasn't usually discussed on television in those days. Afterwards, the station was flooded with phone calls and letters as hundreds of women shared their painful experiences and the fear they had been hiding. I wept hearing their stories and reading their letters. So many victims . . . so much pain.

A week later I decided to tape a few programs in one day so I could be free the week of Christmas. Rather than make the hour-long commute home, I opted to check in to the hotel across the street from the studio and spend the evening preparing for the morning's tapings.

By eleven o'clock I was having trouble staying alert, so I went down-stairs to the hotel restaurant and got a cup of coffee. I got back to the room and was sitting down at the desk when I heard the window curtains rustle in back of me. Suddenly a man grabbed my neck from behind. Pressing the cold steel muzzle of a gun to my temple, he hissed in my ear, "Okay, Miss Cute Talk Show Host. What do you do with a gun to your head?"

I was terrified. Struggling to free myself as much as I dared, I pleaded for him to let me go, but he held me in a stranglehold. Then he threw me down on the bed and began to rape me brutally. A ski mask covered his face; all I knew was that he was very strong.

The pain was excruciating, but the terror was worse. Trying to keep from going into shock, I repeated the Lord's Prayer over and over to myself. I had always been a person of strong faith, but now, as I struggled to feel God's presence, my heart cried out, *How can I live through this?*

Finally, still holding the gun to my head, he whispered in my ear, "I will kill you if you tell." And then the terrifying words, "I know where you live." Then he backed away, climbed out the window onto the roof of the parking garage, and slipped away into the night.

I shut the window and, despite his threat, immediately called the front desk and reported what had happened. Then, shaking from head to toe, I called Paul. "I've been raped," I sobbed on the phone. "I need you. Please come and hold me." Then I huddled in a chair, weeping, my arms wrapped around my knees. I felt filthy, alone, and overwhelmed by fear.

Hotel security responded at once, as did the police, but there was no trace of the rapist, nor any useful evidence. When Paul arrived, he cradled me like a child, repeating over and over, "I love you, sweetheart. It's going to be all right." Finally, exhausted, I fell asleep in his arms.

Though I managed to go on air the next morning—I was afraid my attacker would know I hadn't kept the rape a secret if I didn't—I did the show like a robot. Afterwards, the station manager told me he would host the rest of the Christmas week shows to give me some time to heal.

When I got home, I went straight to bed but slept fitfully; my body was bruised and my heart felt completely broken.

Christmas came and went, but nothing was the same. The rape itself had been horrible beyond imagining, but even more devastating was the dagger of fear that had struck deep in my heart. My safe, happy world, and the trusting person I had been, were shattered. I was afraid of being touched and got nervous when a stranger even looked at me.

After the holidays, I continued the daily show on autopilot. Thankfully, after two months my period came; I was not pregnant. It was a great relief, yet fear still consumed me. Every day as I commuted to work or ate a meal, I could hear my attacker's chilling words, "I know where you live." I knew I needed help but couldn't seem to find it. I tried counseling but worried I'd never truly feel like myself again; I kept telling myself, "Rosemary, why can't you just get over this?" Though I tried to hide my emotions and push down the pain, a storm still raged inside me. After three months of constant distress, I resigned from the television show I loved.

What could I do to return to the Rosemary I'd been before the rape? This was the question that commanded all my attention. I knew I couldn't heal this wound alone, so I called my best friend, who was living in Texas at the time. In college, René and I been closer than sisters and our theme song had always been James Taylor's "You've Got a Friend." Now I "called out her name" and asked her to come to Virginia to help me heal. Like the true friend she is, she came.

I'd once heard that if an elephant in Africa is injured and falls down, he will likely die because of the weight of his heavy body on the wound. In this situation, two elephants will often come alongside the wounded one and literally hold him up, for days if necessary, until the elephant is strong enough to stand alone.

René and Paul became my supporting elephants. They pressed in close and I leaned on their courage. Whenever I felt fearful, they reminded me that I was a woman loved by her husband, adored by friends, with a life worth living—worth fighting for. If I gave in to the fear, it would rob me of all the good that was right there in front of me. They held me up with their love until I was able to stand alone.

I also did a lot of praying during this time. My trust in God had always been a source of comfort for me, but since the rape, I had felt confused. Despite that trust, I hadn't been protected. Now my faith was shaken. I asked God to help me understand and to heal.

Gradually I began to feel better, though I did still experience moments of heart-pounding panic. Then in May, seven months after the rape, I found out that Paul and I were going to have a baby. *Oh, joy!* I thought, *I can finally put this all behind me.* Meanwhile Paul had decided to run for Congress. He was elected in November 1976, and we moved to Washington DC, where our daughter Mary Katherine was born.

Those were happy, healing days, taking care of Mary Katherine. One day, however, after a stroll around the neighborhood with my now three-month-old baby, I walked up our front walk and was suddenly stopped cold by the sight of our front door. It had been smashed in! Someone had broken into our home.

In a flash, all the old fear came flooding back—heightened tenfold because of the baby in my arms. It was clear that the intruder was gone, so after calling Paul to notify the police, I put Mary Katherine in her bed. I was shaking with fear and didn't want it to affect her. I went to my own bedroom and fell on my knees. I cried out to God, "I can't go back to being a victim every moment of my life. You have got to be with me and save me from being destroyed by this fear again."

As soon as I said those words, I felt the presence of a beautiful Spirit envelop me. It was like being wrapped in a soft, warm blanket. My fear left me and I was filled with peace.

In that moment of clarity, I thought of all I'd gone through since the rape. I saw that although it had broken my heart, it had also given me much deeper compassion for others. I wondered, *What if I stopped thinking of myself as a victim and instead saw that I was a survivor who had maybe even gained something from my ordeal?* This revolutionary thought gave me a strength I had never felt before. As I waited for Paul to come home, I felt a thrill of hope. What would life be like, knowing that I was truly safe because even bad things that happened to me could be used for good in my life?

From that day forward, my feelings of well-being and security grew steadily. I understood that trusting in God didn't mean that scary things wouldn't happen in my life. It meant that anything, however scary, could be okay if I trusted that it had a purpose in my life and could serve me and others in some way.

Thirty-five years later, I continue to see how much I learned from that terrible night. I have a kind of love I don't think I would have gained without that trauma. I was always a caring and compassionate woman, but I wouldn't have had the same sensitivity and depth of love that I do now. It's as if I'm a clay pot that's been cracked and God's light shines out most brightly through my broken places. That light is a kind of love that allows me to enter into the suffering of others. For a lot of people, that's very uncomfortable. For me, it is a great joy. If I can hold the container of someone else's pain, I can help them see their own light coming through the cracks, heralding a new beginning and new freedom.

Today I spend a lot of time working with women who've been raped or sexually abused. It's gotten to the point that I can sense if a woman has been through that kind of trauma just by looking at her. And at my best, I can become like a candle, able to lean toward another and light her wick from my flame.

I would never have chosen to be raped, of course. And yet I am deeply grateful for my healing journey from fear to freedom. My heart is more full of love than it ever was before, and I have a more mature relationship with God. I look to Him, not for safety and protection, but for support in opening my heart and becoming of greater service to others. I pray that God continues to use me as the elephants use each other in times of distress. Let me be one whom others can lean on until their hearts are healed and they can love again.

❤ ❤ ❤

Enjoyment, Growth, or Both: The Key to Spiritual Support

Whenever anything in nature seems to us ridiculous, absurd, or evil, it is because we have but a partial knowledge of things.

—Baruch Spinoza, seventeenth-century philosopher

Rosemary's journey to a more expanded state of love was aided by the presence of her two "elephants," Paul and René, but tremendously accelerated by her understanding the events in her life in a new and larger context. Suddenly a previously invisible support became visible. When we sense our spiritual support, nothing new is created; we simply wake up to what's been there all along.

In sports, they call the sense of being surrounded by fans and supporters the "home court advantage." It gives you a boost in energy and confidence when you know that the majority of people in the stands are on your side. What if everywhere you went, that same network of support was already in place? What if the whole world really were your home court?

The truth is that at the deepest level of life, we *are* supported unconditionally—even when we don't realize it. Fear and pain color our perception of the world, blinding us to the love and care that are there for us. A favorite expression that reminds me of this is "Life doesn't happen *to* you, it happens *for* you."

A similar friendly-universe saying comes from Love Luminaries Jim and Jori Manske, mediators and certified trainers of Nonviolent Communication, a system of speaking and listening from the heart that we'll explore further in chapter 8. In our interview, the Manskes told me, "Everything that happens to you is either for your enjoyment, for your growth, or for both."

When I heard that, I loved it! Now when things seem frightening or unpleasant and I start to tense up, I do a quick inner check, asking, "Is this for my enjoyment, growth, or both?" The next time you face a challenge, ask yourself the same question.

I also love the way Love Luminary Janet Sussman explains this sense of support: "We usually think of trust as 'trusting we'll get what we want.' A higher level of trust is unconditional trust. This means 'trusting that everything I get will be for my higher good.'" When you recognize that everything that happens—enjoyable or not—ultimately helps you become wiser, kinder, or richer in experience, you're able to relax.

Or, to paraphrase the Rolling Stones, you can't always get what you want, but you always get what you need. Realizing this truth often takes the passage of time. With reflection and distance, you can see more clearly how an event has served you. With practice, you can learn to trust this larger-picture benefit even while the events are unfolding.

Your rational mind may find this concept a stretch. In his book *The Heart's Code,* physician Paul Pearsall writes that trusting in a friendly universe can be challenging because the brain has an "inborn negativity bias" against the idea. Our brain is used mainly to solve problems of survival, he writes, so it's convinced that the universe is threatening.

Our heart, on the other hand, sees the beauty, connection, and love all around us. Pearsall says you'll only agree that you live in a friendly universe when you can press the pause button for the brain and let your heart answer instead.

When you "sense your support," you feel that someone's got your back—whether it's you being there for yourself, your sister at the end of the phone, or the forces of nature collaborating, even if mysteriously, for your higher good.

There's no denying that terrible and tragic things do happen sometimes. It can be a scary world out there. But ultimately the safety and security we crave is inside us: knowing that we can handle whatever comes our way. The next exercise will help you become aware of the support around you, opening the Doorway of Safety—and your heart.

♥   ♥   ♥

My dear colleague Rick Hanson is a Love Luminary extraordinaire and one of the people I most respect for his brilliant work combining psychology, brain science, and contemplative traditions. In addition to all his impressive credentials—neuropsychologist, meditation teacher, and the author of the best-selling *Buddha's Brain: The Practical Neuroscience of Happiness, Love, and Wisdom*—Rick is a wise, deep, and open-hearted man. He developed the following exercise, based on the principle of the brain's neuroplasticity, to help you create the habit of sensing your support.

Exercise

Circles of Support Process

This exercise helps you to sense how you are supported in life and then to consciously register that sense of support to rewire your brain's neural network. This rewiring allows you to experience greater inner calm and safety and to open more fully to love.

1. Find a protected setting—perhaps in your favorite spot at home, in a church or temple, or under a tree—somewhere you feel safe. Close your eyes and notice how you're feeling. Are you feeling more watchful, more nervous deep down than you truly need to be?

2. Bring to mind the sense of being with someone who cares about you; recall a time you felt relaxed and safe; remind yourself that right this minute you're safe.

3. Take a few deep breaths with *long* exhalations and relax. Keep helping yourself feel more sheltered, supported, and safe—and less vigilant, tense, or fearful.

4. Let these feelings of safety sink into you so you can remember them in your body and find your way back to them in the future.

5. Mentally take stock of your circles of support—physical, emotional, and spiritual. Review the resources inside and around you that you can draw on to deal with whatever life throws at you. Again, let your mind and body register the feeling of being supported and safe. Spend at least one full minute savoring each circle of support. The longer, the better. When you feel complete, open your eyes.

6. To reinforce this neural pathway, each day notice the ways in which you are being supported in your life. Pay attention to them and mentally register them. Take them in. Whenever you feel anxious, breathe and find that bodily sense of safety and support you've been practicing. Recognizing the support you have and remembering that feeling of inner safety will help you relax in the current moment.

Used by permission of Rick Hanson, www.rickhanson.net

Summary and Love for No Reason Action Steps

Getting grounded and sensing your support are the keys that open the Doorway of Safety. You support the opening of your heart by slowing down and connecting to the calm core of security within you. Use the following action steps to increase the flow of love through this energy center:

1. Periodically pull the plug and reconnect with nature. Walk outside, kick off your shoes, and feel the earth beneath your feet. Allow the grounding quality of nature to draw you back to your center.

2. To quickly switch out of fight-or-flight mode, take a few deep breaths and consciously relax your perineum, located at the base of your body.

3. Practice mindfulness by bringing your full attention to what you're experiencing in the present moment.

4. Use the Realization Process to "inhabit your body" and become more grounded.

5. When you're facing a challenge, sense the support of a friendly universe by looking for the ways that the situation is ultimately serving you. Ask yourself, *Is this for my enjoyment, growth, or both?*

6. Using the Circles of Support Process, take stock of the support—physical, emotional, and spiritual—that is all around you. Consciously registering feelings of safety and support creates neural pathways that allow you to relax.

CHAPTER 5

The Doorway of Vitality:
Turning Up the Juice

Love is that splendid triggering of human vitality.

—José Ortega y Gasset, twentieth-century Spanish philosopher

Learning to live with unconditional love while writing this book has stretched me in so many ways. For example, love and deadlines have *not* gone hand in hand in my life. In the past I always managed to get things done, but the price was usually a stressed-out body and a constricted heart. But this time, with my manuscript due date breathing down my neck, my tried-and-true methods for getting words on the page simply stopped working. For years I'd been used to running myself ragged, pulling all-nighters at my computer, and pushing beyond my limits. Now I just couldn't do that to myself anymore!

Instead of forcing a brainstorming session at the end of the day, I found myself switching off everything work-related and curling up to watch a movie.

Instead of rewriting pages until my eyes glazed over, I'd luxuriate in a bath and let my frustrations seep out of me, allowing the hot water to nourish my body and spirit.

I'd inevitably wake up revitalized the next morning. Life would feel good again, and my heart would reopen to the task at hand, which in my case was investigating love's mystery. Clearly, some higher part of me was staging an intervention for the sake of spreading love's true message!

I realized that love can't be studied—or experienced—as effectively from a state of exhaustion. Its energy can't be channeled by pushing the envelope, ignoring my feelings, or forcing a result. Love was telling me gently but firmly, *I'd be delighted to come hang out with you, but not when you're in that crazed, overworked place. It's no fun for me, and you won't even notice I'm there.*

This experience taught me some surprising lessons about energy and vitality—and their connection to love. It forced me to look closely at ways I supported Higher Love in my life—and ways I blocked it. I learned that cultivating a sense of physical and emotional aliveness, finding delight in daily life, and welcoming all my feelings open the Doorway of Vitality, which is essential to increasing the flow of Love for No Reason.

The Wake-up Call

Fresh, invigorating, sparkly, juicy—these words describe how you feel when love's living large in your cells. What all these words point to is a sense of vitality. At your core, love and the feeling of aliveness are intimately related. You naturally experience more love when you're more awake and vital.

If we're asleep in any way—be it tapped out, maxed out, bummed out, or zoned out—our hearts close up shop. When that deadened feeling hits, whether it's after a long, sedentary day or an adrenaline-driven one—or it's from stifling our true emotions—love's flow slows to a trickle. Our bodies may feel sluggish or exhausted, numbing our minds to the point that we even forget we *have* a body that needs a little TLC. Our senses can become so dulled that we may not be sure what we're feeling. Think zombie.

To find our vitality and love again requires paying attention to what's really going on inside us, even when it's easier to stay numb. Opening the Doorway to Vitality makes us feel genuinely alive.

The vitality center, the second of our seven energy centers, is located in the area of the lower abdomen, sex organs, and sacrum. Related to our physical and emotional well-being, it's where we connect to the energy and feelings continually coursing through us. The ancient Vedic texts sometimes call it the "sweetness" chakra, because of its connection to the senses and pleasure, as well as sexuality and reproduction. It governs not only the actual birth process but also every act of creative expression, whether it's completing an assignment at work, planning a meal, doing a crafts project, or playing with your kids.

When this center is healthy and balanced, you have more zip and life has more zest. You're more awake to colors, tastes, textures, and scents. You feel emotions more deeply and authentically as they move through you like the variations of the weather. Your senses are more enlivened and you're more in touch with your heart.

Unlocking the Doorway of Vitality

Strengthening the vitality center doesn't mean getting amped up on Red Bull. It means waking up your body, senses, and emotions, breaking up any stagnancy or staleness, healing your workaholic tendencies, and nourishing and recharging your life.

There are two keys for opening this doorway, one related to your body and the other to your emotions. Both of these help to balance your energy flow by creating strong habits of self-care and awareness.

The Love Keys for the Doorway of Vitality

1. Give Your Body True Nourishment
2. Feel Your Feelings

The Nourishing Key helps you nurture your physical body by paying attention to what you truly need and by drawing on the subtle energy that's available all around you. In the words of reggae singer Bob Marley, you "lively up yourself!"

The Feelings Key invites you to ride the waves of your emotions with the grace of a surfer, so their powerful energy moves freely through you instead of shutting you down or throwing you off balance.

Love Key for Vitality #1:
Give Your Body True Nourishment

One of the ways we block our ability to love is by neglecting the needs of our bodies. Love Luminary and author Geneen Roth, whose story is included in this chapter, wrote a line that's always stuck with me: "Passion, strength, and joy cannot take root in exhausted, burdened, half-dead bodies." In other words, we can't ignore our bodies and expect to experience Love for No Reason in its fullness.

Yeah, yeah, we all know that exercise, eating right, and getting enough rest enhance our experience of life and love. But we still seem to have a hard time making those a priority; more urgent tasks bump them off the top of our to-do list. We get caught in a vicious cycle: the more overwhelmed and stressed we are, the less we're able to take care of ourselves, which creates more stress . . . and down the tube we go.

The tendency to make poor decisions under stress is actually rooted in your brain. In a study conducted at Stanford University, scientists randomly divided the participants into two groups. One group was asked to memorize a two-digit number; the other, a seven-digit number. Then they offered both groups a choice of snack, either a fruit salad or a slice of chocolate cake. Those who memorized the two-digit number were twice as likely as the other group to choose the fruit salad, while those who memorized the seven-digit number were twice as likely as the other group to choose the chocolate cake. The stress of trying to remember the long number overloaded the part of the brain involved in self-control and willpower and made it harder for the participants to do what they knew was better for their health.

Memorizing a seven-digit number is child's play compared to the demands most of us face. Is it any wonder that when it comes to making healthy choices in our lives, we reach for the chocolate cake or its equivalent?

A lot of people compensate for their less-than-ideal lifestyle choices by using sugar or caffeine to get through the day. In fact, *Time* magazine recently reported that 170 million Americans (more than half the population) are hooked on caffeine. This addiction is a clue to just how tired we are.

Unfortunately, using caffeine to perk us up actually stresses the body over time. Studies show caffeine has a similar effect to the stress hormone cortisol, so that surge you feel with your espresso is akin to your fight-or-flight response. Over time this weakens the adrenals, fatigues the thyroid, and throws off the hormones that help sustain your energy levels throughout the day. Because women are more prone to thyroid imbalances and adrenal burnout, caffeine appears to be more profoundly damaging to women than men. Love Luminary and relationship expert Alison Armstrong said it best when she told me, "Relying on caffeine is like using a credit card. You're borrowing energy you don't have, and you have to pay it back with interest later." As time goes by, we get deeper and deeper in energy debt.

The solution lies in starting small. I'm sure you've heard the saying about a long journey beginning with a single step. Begin the journey to vitality by doing just one thing that truly nourishes you. Then do it again. When you keep on doing that one small action, it starts a larger chain reaction, flipping your feedback loop from negative to positive—in the same way that a small change to a ship's rudder can cause a huge change to the ship's course.

Love Luminary Dr. Sue Morter discovered how one act of true self-nourishment shifted her energy permanently. Sue, a chiropractor and an internationally recognized authority on science, spirit, and human possibility, has a deep understanding of the mechanics of energy and the body. I've known Sue for years and she radiates clarity, vitality, and an unmistakable aura of love. In our interview, Sue shared the story of what happened when she let go of her voracious do-more drive, which had been blocking her ability to open her heart fully.

Sue's Story
The Choice

*I*t was early in the morning. As I surfaced from sleep—before I even opened my eyes—I felt the pain like a hammer pounding on the left side of my head. I moaned softly, thinking, *Oh, man. Is it going to be one of those days?*

For the past year, at least once a week I'd been having migraine headaches that were so debilitating I couldn't get out of bed, much less go to work. I had also been having chronic and severe pain in my neck and across the top of my shoulders. Just getting dressed every morning was an ordeal; each movement of my arms made me wince and grit my teeth in agony.

The whole situation was ridiculous. In my chiropractic office I could rid other people of those exact same pain patterns every day of the week. Why couldn't I help myself?

Tests had ruled out anything life-threatening. It was obvious to me that my physical problems stemmed from deeper issues in my life. For as long as I could remember, what I wanted and needed—and especially what my body needed—had taken a back seat to my compulsion to accomplish whatever I thought the perfect daughter, then student, then professional woman should accomplish.

I saw how I was exhausting myself, constantly trying to live up to the demands of my internal slave driver, who insisted I always do the "right thing." And while this style of functioning had paid off in my achievements and professional and social standing, my body had paid the price.

I couldn't seem to escape my perfectionism. I'd grown up that way, and it was the only thing I'd ever known. I didn't know what to do—other than to try very hard to ignore the problem and keep powering through. And that approach was getting really, *really* old.

Fortunately, something had been stirring below the surface. For quite a while, I had felt drawn to the study of spirituality. I went to many lectures and attended workshops and retreats on meditation, yoga, and Eastern philosophy. But instead of changing my old ways of being, I simply carried them right into these new realms. As I tried to be the picture of the ideal spiritual aspirant, I continued to ignore what was best for my own body, as well as my mind and spirit.

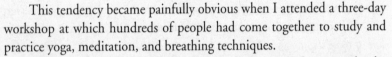

This tendency became painfully obvious when I attended a three-day workshop at which hundreds of people had come together to study and practice yoga, meditation, and breathing techniques.

When I arrived, one of the organizers asked me to volunteer to be the workshop leader's personal assistant during the workshop. I hesitated for a moment—I needed this weekend of spiritual practices to recharge my batteries—but as usual I put my needs aside for a "greater cause." I figured if I helped the workshop leader, the attendees would get more attention. Stuck in my pattern of trying to do the right and perfect thing, no matter the personal cost, I agreed.

By the third afternoon of the event, I was exhausted. I had gotten little sleep the last two nights and had been on the go nonstop since early that morning. Though I'd plowed through my assignments as fast as I could, the sheer number of them, plus my need to make sure they were done to my exacting standards, had kept me from attending many of the meetings.

I was on the phone, arranging for a private meeting for the workshop leader. The event was almost over and after this call there were just two tasks left to do. I could hear the question-and-answer session going on in the room down the hall, punctuated by bursts of laughter. It sounded like everyone was having a wonderful time. I wanted so much to join them, but I felt strongly that my list of tasks should be done first. I was trying to perform, to rise to the occasion, to do the right thing. In other words, I was doing what I always did.

The meeting arrangements taken care of, I hung up the phone and put my head in my hands. I thought I was getting one of my migraines. I felt the energy start to buzz in my head the way it did right before the pain began. But then, instead of my usual response of tensing up and trying to hold the energy in my head, something inside me gave way. I felt the energy drop into my chest and heart, where it expanded and then melted, dropping deep into my belly, landing in my lower abdomen. For a few seconds, my whole body vibrated with the energy, and then the energy burst from my mouth. To my surprise, I heard myself say, "I'm *not* going to finish this list now. I'm going to the hall to join the group!"

Something in me had finally snapped. For once, I was going to do what *my* body wanted!

I entered the large meeting room quietly. The group was just beginning a breathing exercise. I sat down quickly, hoping no one would notice what I considered my dereliction of duty. I knew the exercise they were doing and joined in, taking long, slow abdominal breaths, in and out. In and out. I felt my mind settle down as I focused completely on my breathing. In and out. In . . . and out . . .

The next thing I knew, I was completely expanded. I felt much bigger than my body.

I was still me, still totally present, but I was extremely large. I could see 360 degrees around me all at once, and all there was to see was bright light—ten times brighter than the brightest day I'd ever experienced. Yet it wasn't the kind of brightness that I wanted to shade my eyes against.

I was *part of* the brightness.

The space around me was larger than any area I'd ever witnessed, even when flying in an airplane and looking out on the endless blue sky above the clouds. It was immense.

And I was *part of* the immensity.

Far below me, I could see what looked like a marble, but I knew it was the earth. Part of me was still embedded in the earth, and with each breath I took, I felt a wave of love and well-being flow through me. I was breathing love to the planet.

In fact, I was nothing *but* love.

I had no sense of time passing but I was still in this huge, brilliant, loving space forty-five minutes later when the exercise ended and it was time to rest. I lay down and experienced the grand finale of a Fourth of July fireworks display inside my brain. Tremendous light burst again and again: it was as if I could see synapses firing and neurons activating. I was in a state of bliss and wanted to stay there forever.

It took me a few days of rest and nurturing myself to fully integrate this experience. At the course, someone else had done the last two items on my list of things to do, and amazingly the sky hadn't fallen!

When I returned to my normal routine, I noticed that the pain in my neck and shoulders had disappeared. I felt as though I were a completely different person, and at the same time, more myself than ever before. I felt relaxed, happy, and full of love for the people around me.

These feelings continued in the weeks and months that followed. I experienced a new state of equilibrium: my body was supporting my activities, and my activities were supporting my body.

Today I'm so grateful for my life. My neck and shoulders remain pain-free and my headaches have completely disappeared. And the energy! I have far more than I ever dreamed possible back when I was driven to nurture everyone besides myself. This enables me to travel and teach and speak—all the things I most love to do.

Best of all, I've stopped spending every waking minute trying to analyze what has to be done for everything to be perfect. It's not that I don't care; I simply have a deep sense of knowing that everything will be fine. That everything *is* fine.

That one choice, to listen to myself and nourish myself in a way I'd never dared to before, has led to a life of continually choosing nourishment. Taking care of my own body, mind, and spirit has made me better able to help others *and* opened up a world of love inside me. What could be more perfect than that?

What Is True Nourishment?

I was there that day in 2001 when Sue made this life-altering choice. Her transformation has been a real inspiration to me, as I can sure relate to her perfectionist/pleaser tendencies and the way that they zap your vitality. If you're also one of those people who are forever putting their own needs on the back burner, your true nourishment begins with daring to consider that you'll be of more use to yourself—and the people around you—if you keep yourself in top form.

Making the choice to nourish yourself may not lead to a transformation as swift and dramatic as Sue's, but it will get you going in the right direction immediately. The commitment to taking care of your body is the first step. The second step is to make the right nourishment choices; the quality of what you nourish yourself with really matters.

Most people get enough nourishment each day to keep their blood flowing, their heart pumping, and their brain working to a more or less adequate degree. But to light up your love-body, you need a higher vibration nourishment than you need to simply stay alive: high-quality exercise, high-quality food, and high-quality breathing!

What follows is the lowdown from some of the top experts in the field on giving your body the high-quality, true nourishment it needs.

Truly Nourishing Exercise

All exercise is nourishing, but when you really enjoy the exercise you're doing, you take it to the level of true nourishment. I learned this firsthand after a year of promoting *Happy for No Reason*.

I was burned out. I'd traveled 250,000 miles that year for speaking engagements and had done almost two hundred interviews. With that relentless schedule, I'd all but given up exercise, and the exercise I did force myself to do was a drag. While trekking on a treadmill did make me feel better whenever I got around to doing it, it didn't put me in touch with the juicy state of unconditional love inside that I knew was possible. Luckily, my assistant, Suzanna, came to the rescue when one day she sent me off to an exercise/dance class called Zumba.

I said, "What the heck is Zumba?"

She laughed and said, "Don't ask. Just go."

I put aside my worry about the time I was taking from my other responsibilities and jumped in the car. I'd always loved to dance, and when the music started, my inner Tina Turner woke up. My body was so busy keeping up with the instructor's high-octane movements that my laundry list of to-dos faded into the background. Five minutes in, I was smiling. Ten minutes in, I was laughing out loud. By the end of the class, I was electrified!

I felt more alive in that sweaty studio than I'd felt in over a year. I quickly developed a Zumba habit, going several times a week. Boogying and salsa-ing to the music cleaned out the residue of stress and left me sparkling on the inside. It also triggered a powerful resuscitation of my whole body and spirit. The more I fell in love with dancing, the more I fell back in love with life.

We think that the value of exercise lies in raising our heart rate or building strength or flexibility. And of course it does, but that's only part of the picture. Along with all the benefits we normally associate with working out, exercise that you like doing not only nourishes the physical body but opens your heart. For me, Zumba provides true nourishment because I adore doing it. For others, yoga, tennis, cycling, or lifting weights might be the ticket that sends them soaring. To give *your* body true nourishment, find the exercise or movement that takes your energy to the highest level by bringing you the added bonus of an open heart. You're more likely to keep doing it, and in addition to staying healthy, you'll be working out your love-body as well.

Truly Nourishing Breathing

Breathing is breathing, right? Not really. The yogic tradition of India has long known how certain techniques of breathing—the most fundamental movement in our body—can actually make more energy available to us. With a well-executed inhalation, we grab more of the *prana*, or life force, that surrounds us.

You'll remember from chapter 3 that according to quantum physics, everything in the universe is energy vibrating at varying speeds. This universal life force that manifests in all the different forms around us is called *prana* in some Eastern traditions, *chi* in others. In the West, we don't have a special name for that subtle, all-pervasive energy, but we know it when we feel it.

Think of being in a lush garden, or in the woods, or beside an ocean or waterfall. Now compare that with being in line at the Department of Motor Vehicles, or in the aisles of a giant superstore, or in any windowless office space with recycled air and artificial lighting. There's enough oxygen in each of these places to keep us alive, but in the natural places, the level of *prana* is higher and more nourishing. It's one of the reasons our hearts automatically open when we're in nature.

Western science has isolated at least one component of *prana*: negative ions. These invisible molecules are found in high concentration in certain places, such as in the mountains, and near crashing water, like the ocean, waterfalls, and in the shower. Research shows that negative ions have profoundly positive effects on the brain and body, reducing depression, anxiety, and irritability and increasing mood-elevating alpha waves, serotonin, and the flow of oxygen to the brain. This is why you feel so clear and alive when you're walking on the beach or even sitting near a fountain.

Truly nourishing breathing allows you to inhale more *prana* anywhere you are and exhale toxins more completely. It improves all your body's processes, from digestion to elimination to thinking to healing, and it supplies your love-body with what it needs to be strong and vital.

Studies done on certain yoga-based breathing techniques show that they improve mental clarity, promote relaxation, reduce cortisol and anxiety levels, and strengthen the entire cardiovascular system. The exercise for this key (at the end of this section) is a simple breathing and movement exercise you can do anytime you feel dull or anxious; it both revitalizes and calms you, setting the stage for Love for No Reason to enter.

As Love Luminary Sweet Medicine Nation, a spiritual teacher of Choctaw descent, told me, "The word for love and breath is the same in many languages." Improve one and the other follows.

Truly Nourishing Food

You'd think we'd all know how to eat right by now. Most weeks, eight out of the top ten books on the *New York Times* best seller list are either diet books or cookbooks. But we're as confused as ever: one day chocolate is terrible for you and the next day it's the miracle antioxidant. Yet what none of these books address is the connection between food and unconditional love: what you eat can help open your heart!

The simple formula for a diet of true nourishment is to eat food that gives you more energy than it takes. In my interview with Love Luminary and nutritional consultant Sherry Strong, she told me, "After eating, we should experience the same energy we feel when we're in nature—serene, expanded, and inspired.

"When you eat food that's closest to how it's found in nature, it remains full of life force. It's fully charged, like a cell phone that you've just taken off the charger. Even though it's not plugged in anymore, there's plenty of energy left in the batteries for a while. When I eat food that's still got a good amount of life force in it, I have a smile on my face and experience a deep sense of love in my heart."

This idea was a revelation. The thought that what I put in my mouth could make me feel as good as I feel when I'm walking on the beach inspired me to eat that way more often. To ensure your diet has the same heart-opening effect as being out in nature, choose food that's high in *prana*. This means avoiding what Sherry calls the "lethal recipe": refined grains, refined sugars, refined oils, refined salts, and chemical additives, which are so taxing to break down and digest that they drain your body of energy. Fresh fruits and vegetables that burst with enzymes and nutrients, and ingredients that are closest to their original state from field, ocean, or farm will fund your body's energy account instead of depleting it.

Eating high-*prana* foods (intelligent foods filled with life force) will definitely boost Love for No Reason, but only if your body is able to digest it fully. When your body is full of toxins, it can't digest well and absorb the nourishment. Love Luminary and expert Ayurvedic physician Dr. Suhas Kshirsagar shared how important it is to detox our systems from unhealthy foods and emotions. "People keep their cars clean, inside and out, but do they take the same care of their bodies? It's important to do regular cleanses to get rid of toxins. This will declog your channels and correct the imbalances in your body." I've taken Dr. Kshirsagar's advice. At least twice a year, I go to his clinic to do a special Ayurvedic cleansing/purifying program called *panchakarma* that's designed to purify the entire system, on both the physical and emotional levels. It not only keeps my vitality level high but also deeply nourishes my heart. I leave feeling clean as a whistle, balanced, and at peace.

High-*prana* food and a toxin-free body are important for giving yourself true nourishment, but there's one more ingredient in this recipe for vitality: loving what you eat. If you're scarfing down high-*prana* food but don't like how it tastes, you're not going to get the full Higher Love–inducing benefits. You may need to wean yourself off the intensely flavored substances that pass for food these days, and cultivate a taste for "real" food. Be patient; with time your taste buds will learn to appreciate the fresh, clean flavors of a Love for No Reason diet. And if you get tempted to eat junk food, remember: nothing tastes as good as an open heart feels.

Delight, Pleasure, and Joy

The final way that you give your body true nourishment is through increasing your daily dose of delight, pleasure, and joy! These have the power to turn up your juice as much as any superfood or supplement.

You increase delight by feeding your senses—not in a self-indulgent way, but by paying attention to the pleasures available to you in every moment. Savoring life's beauty and pleasure have positive physical and emotional effects, as research by Loyola University's Dr. Fred Bryant and others shows. Delight activates the parasympathetic system, which calms and soothes your body, creating a whole host of benefits, including strengthening the immune system, balancing your hormones, and uplifting your mood.

Unfortunately, with our busy lifestyles, we can go for days barely registering the scents, sounds, and sensations that are in our environment. To feed your senses, free yourself from your time-clock mentality, and be open to experience the world around you.

A story I read in the *Washington Post* offers a great example of the limits our busy lifestyles place on our joy. The journalist Gene Weingarten, who won a Pulitzer for his piece, set up a fascinating social experiment to measure how our perception of beauty is influenced by its setting. He asked famous violinist Joshua Bell to play one of the world's most difficult and exquisite violin pieces on one of the world's most expensive violins at a Washington, D.C., metro station at rush hour. With a collection box at his feet, Joshua looked just like any other street musician, but his talent—and his music—were absolutely spine-tingling.

Thousands of commuters raced past the virtuoso, talking on cell phones and checking BlackBerries. Only seven people stopped to listen. The passerby with the strongest reaction was a three-year-old boy. He stood entranced, only moving when his mother picked him up and carried him off.

This story shows how we often overlook the moments of beauty, pleasure, and delight that surround us each day. How many virtuosos are we missing because we don't let ourselves hear their music? How many fantastic flavors are we missing because we're watching television or reading the paper while we eat?

Living with our senses wide open is a skill we can practice. It's how we embody love in our lives.

The following exercise combines breathing and movement to truly nourish your body and strengthen your vitality center. It was taught to me by Love Luminary Anat Baniel, founder of the Anat Baniel Method, a process that helps the brain form new connections so that you can overcome limitations and experience optimum vitality. While the simplicity of the movements can be deceiving, I've worked with Anat's method, and I've found it to be a very powerful way to feel more freedom, energy, and ease in my body, and more openness in my heart.

Exercise

Free Your Hara—*Awaken Your Vitality*

This exercise will help you free the energy in the area of your vitality center (also known in the martial arts as the *hara*, the center of being) through specific movements and breath. You'll be moving and breathing in ways that will wake up your brain and expand your breathing capacity, your energy, and your aliveness.

1. Sit at the edge of a chair with your feet flat on the floor. Place your hands behind you on the seat of the chair and lean on your hands throughout the exercise. It's important to move gently and slowly through these steps.

2. Leaning on your hands, round your back, and pull in your belly as if you were slouching forward (see photo 1). Exhale as you do this. Then reverse the movement: roll your pelvis forward, arch your back, and push your belly out, making a big round belly

(see photo 2). Inhale as you do this. Do this entire movement four times and pay close attention to the sensations in your belly, lower back, hip joints, and spine.

3. Repeat step 2, except this time, reverse your breathing: Inhale as you round your back and pull your belly in. Then exhale as you roll your pelvis forward, arch your back, and push your belly out. Do this four times.

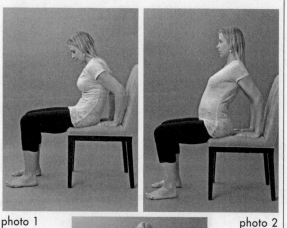

photo 1   photo 2

photo 3

4. Lift your right hip off the chair and roll it toward your left side, pushing your belly out. Your weight will have shifted to the left hip (see photo 3). Inhale as you do

this. Return to your starting position as you exhale. Do this movement four times. Repeat the same movement to the other side four times.

5. Combine all four movements. Still leaning back on your hands, make a full circle with your pelvis: round your back, roll your pelvis over to the right, and continue all the way around to complete the circle. Notice the movement in your rib cage and spine and allow your whole back to move freely with your pelvis. Breathe at your own pace. Do this circle four times in one direction. Then reverse the direction and do it four more times. Feel the vitality and life force within you.

Do this exercise any time you want to experience greater energy and aliveness.

Used by permission of Anat Baniel Method,
www.anatbanielmethod.com

Love Key for Vitality #2
Feel Your Feelings

The Guest House

This being human is a guest house.
Every morning a new arrival.

A joy, a depression, a meanness,
some momentary awareness comes
as an unexpected visitor.

Welcome and entertain them all!
Even if they're a crowd of sorrows,
who violently sweep your house
empty of its furniture,
still, treat each guest honorably.
He may be clearing you out
for some new delight.

The dark thought, the shame, the malice,
meet them at the door laughing,
and invite them in.

Be grateful for whoever comes,
because each has been sent
as a guide from beyond.

—Rumi, thirteenth-century Sufi poet

What happens when those unpleasant, no-fun feelings arrive on your heart's doorstep? If you're like most people, you slam the door in their faces or turn off the lights and hope they'll go away. You try to avoid them at all costs. Unless you're a drama queen, in which case, you invite them in and chain them to a chair, holding on to them long beyond their natural course.

There's a lot of scientific evidence linking the mishandling of our uncomfortable emotions to disease. Repressed emotions in particular have been linked to immune-system-related diseases, asthma, high blood pressure, cancer, and depression.

You might think that the antidote to repressing emotions is expressing them. However there are also studies showing that this isn't the case: venting emotions after trauma is a predictor of worse psychological outcomes, and expressing anger and hostility lead to increased risk of heart disease. A study done at the Institute of HeartMath showed that just one five-minute episode of anger depressed the immune system for up to six hours.

What I discovered from my research is that stifling your emotions— or expressing them excessively—are equally damaging for your love body.

Luckily, there's a third option: *feeling* your feelings.

Ideally, our feelings are supposed to flow through us, but for a variety of reasons, we often stuff them down or amp them up. Here are some of the reasons you may try to suppress your emotions.

- **Feelings are often uncomfortable, even painful.** When we experience emotional or physical pain—or are even just afraid we might—our primitive brain activates our "approach or avoid" response. We're afraid the feelings will overwhelm us. Our natural instinct for self-preservation kicks in and we run the other way.

  In my interview with Love Luminary Raphael Cushnir, who's an expert in the dynamics of feelings, love, and the human heart, he described what's going on in the brain. He said, "I believe there's a glitch in our brain. One part of it—the limbic brain—generates an emotion. For optimal functioning, we need to feel that emotion completely. When we do, the feeling dissipates. That's the way it's supposed to work.

  "But then there's another part of our brain—the primitive brain— that protects us from danger. The problem is that the primitive brain can't distinguish between an external threat, like footsteps in a dark alley, and an internal threat, like loneliness or jealousy or rage. So quite literally, the primitive brain thinks that painful emotions are going to kill us and doesn't want to feel them. This creates a conflict. The limbic system is saying, *Feel this,* and the primitive brain is saying, *No way.* Until we rewire the brain to realize the painful feelings won't really kill us, we'll get caught in this glitch and avoid feeling our feelings."

- **Feelings aren't always acceptable.** When we don't want to feel the way we do about something—or think we *shouldn't* feel that way—we resist our emotions, trying to wrestle them into submission.

- **Feelings are seldom logical or reasonable.** When we can't explain or understand our feelings, we may discount them or simply try to ignore them. The intellect tries to override the heart.

For a lot of us, stuffing our feelings comes from our training as children: how many toddlers' squeals of delight and howls of protest are met with shushes, frowns, or worse? Rather than risk acting on our emotions, we often decide it's better to steer clear of feeling them altogether.

But when you avoid, deny, or pull back from your emotions—positive or negative—instead of truly feeling them, they get bottled up inside. This stops the flow of your energy and squashes your vitality as effectively as holding your breath, starving yourself, or going without water. When you deaden yourself to your feelings, you deaden yourself, period. You shut down your life force and, by extension, your capacity to experience love.

On the other end of the spectrum from repression, excessive or prolonged expression of your emotions is equally damaging. Being a drama queen, throwing tantrums, holding grudges, or wallowing in self-pity also stop the flow of energy and love in your life.

Feeling your feelings, simply and naturally, triggers their release, like melting ice into water. Heavy emotions lose their rocklike density and can move again. Then love too is able to stream in and out of us freely.

One of my feel-your-feelings heroes is Love Luminary Geneen Roth, the author of the number one *New York Times* best seller *Women, Food, and God*. Geneen has been conducting workshops and writing about compulsive eating, food, and love for over thirty years. After struggling with her weight for much of her life, Geneen finally stopped dieting when she realized that it was her heart that was hungry, not her body. In the following story, Geneen shares how making peace with herself began with being willing to face her feelings head-on.

Geneen's Story
The Deeper Song

When I was in high school, a girl I'll call Randi Williams had big hair, a stomach as flat as a board, and legs that—I swear—were at least 12 feet long. Me? I had hair that was the only thin part of my body, a face as round as the moon, and legs that looked like tree trunks. Randi ate French toast for breakfast, quenched her thirst with

chocolate milkshakes, and snacked on tiny, white, powdered-sugar dough-
nuts, a dozen at a time. I tortured myself with diet pills, skinless chicken,
and breakfast cereal that tasted like sawdust.

When I looked at Randi, all I could see was what she had that I didn't.
It wasn't long before I came to the conclusion that I was definitely living
the wrong life, and that if only I could live in Randi's body instead of mine,
I would be happy—blissfully, eternally happy.

Since adolescence, I've gained and lost over a thousand pounds. I've
been anorexic, sixty pounds overweight, and every point in between. But
mostly overweight. My closet was stuffed with eight different sizes of pants,
dresses, and blouses. For years, I was addicted to amphetamines and laxa-
tives. I threw up, fasted on water, and tried every diet possible: the Atkins
Diet; the Prunes and Meatball Diet; the Thousand-Calorie-a-Day Sugar
Diet; the Coffee, Diet Shasta Creme Soda, and Cigarette Diet; and Weight
Watchers. All of them worked for a week, a month, even a year.

And then I wouldn't be able to tolerate the deprivation one more
minute. Not one. At the breaking point, I'd become the reverse of myself.
Order would flip to chaos, restriction become abandon. Like a werewolf
at the full moon, I'd become a creature of the night, a wild thing with
little resemblance to the daylight human. I'd rip and tear and crash my
way through the boxes and cans and bags of food with a voraciousness so
intense it was as if I hadn't eaten in years. After eighteen months of living
on raw foods and juices, I spent two months inhaling whole pizzas and
chunks of salami. Then just as suddenly as it started, dawn would break
through the trance and I'd flip into being civilized again.

Compulsive eating was a way to distance myself from the way things
were when they weren't how I wanted them to be. I didn't want to sit in
the center of my own life. To ask myself what was actually going on when
I wanted to eat even when I wasn't hungry. Crazed with self-loathing and
shame, I vacillated between wanting to destroy myself and wanting to fix
myself with the next best promise of losing thirty pounds in thirty days.
At one point, a few hours from committing suicide after gaining eighty
pounds in two months, I made the radical decision to stop dieting.

At first, it was easier to imagine people coming back from the dead or
Brad Pitt asking me to marry him than to imagine dropping the war with
my body. But as I began to look at myself with openness and understand-

ing, I saw that eating was *not* the problem. And that by treating it as if it were—by dieting, depriving myself, hating my body—I was treating the symptoms without working on their cause.

I used to think (well, okay, sometimes I still do) that the less I showed up, the less it would hurt when I lost anything. Accepting the unpredictable fragility of life was just too much. The minute that I began to feel or sense or think something that was uncomfortable, I wanted to get out of Dodge. And food was the straightest route.

My obsession with food ended when I stopped leaving myself and began staying in the present moment. I learned a version of inquiry— a philosophical/scientific/psychological/spiritual process that has been around for thousands of years. The version I learned was a body-based approach that started with observing my direct experience. My teacher said, "Instead of trying to change it all, start noticing what's already there. Pay attention to what you already feel. Sad. Bored. Happy. Hungry. Miserable. Ecstatic." She said that if I was curious about the feelings and beliefs that were taking up my attention, they would change, open, dissolve.

I didn't believe her at first. This kind of inquiry requires inhabiting a feeling completely. I thought that I would drown in sadness, be consumed with anger. I thought that keeping the feelings away was what was allowing me to function and that in practicing inquiry I'd be unable to cope.

But it turns out that being with feelings is not the same as drowning in them. With awareness and presence, it's possible to be with what you believe will destroy you without being destroyed. It's the way into love.

The truth is, it's not about food. It's never about food. And it's not even about feelings. It's about what's below them. What's in between them. What's beyond them. Disengaging from the roar of can'ts and won'ts and let-me-outta-heres, I paid attention to the deeper song, the deeper truth: me without my story of me. I fell in love with the life force, what Eckhart Tolle calls the "animating presence," that blazes through my body.

In the first few weeks of eating what I wanted, I confused what I wanted with what I hadn't allowed my body to eat without guilt. Since I'd been dieting for seventeen years, my list of forbidden foods was long. I was so elated with my resolve to never diet again that I didn't notice that I was bumping around in a sugar haze from eating only raw and cooked chocolate-chip cookies. What I didn't understand was that I didn't want the cookies; I wanted the way being allowed to have them made me feel: welcomed, deserving, adored.

What I soon noticed was that any food or way of eating (in the car, standing up, sneaking) that spaced me out, drained my energy, made me feel terrible about myself lost its appeal. In this new galaxy without gravity, it became apparent that eating was only about one thing: nourishing my body. And this body wanted to live. This body loved being alive. Loved moving with some measure of ease. Loved being able to see, hear, touch, smell, taste—and food was a big part of how I could do that. The way I ate was another way to soar.

When I stopped dieting, it was because I glimpsed the possibility that my crazy eating was the sanest thing I'd ever done. If I didn't reject it, try to be good or measure up to an external standard of right eating or right body size, if I was curious and open about each part of it—what I was eating, how I felt while I was eating, what happened in the moments before I suddenly found myself hacking away at frozen cake in an attempt to get the whole thing into my mouth ten minutes ago—the eating itself would lead me back to the feelings, beliefs, fears that created the addiction. Once I understood what I was using food to do, I could ask myself if there was a more direct way to have what I wanted without hurting myself in the process.

The students in my workshops often say to me, "But if I don't eat to push down my sadness, then I have to feel it—and then what?" I point out that the sadness is already present and that the only thing that eating does is add another source of sadness: after the food is gone, the original source of sadness is still there except that now they have topped it with the sadness or frustration or hopelessness about their conflicted relationship with food. Contrary to their fantasies, eating has not taken away their sadness, it's doubled it.

There are many ways to deprive yourself: You can deprive yourself of cookies or you can deprive yourself of feeling well after you eat them. You can deprive yourself of feeling your sadness or you can deprive yourself of the confidence and well-being that come from knowing you won't be destroyed by feeling it.

Not long ago, a good friend called to tell me she was dying of cancer. The same day, another friend called to tell me her mother just died. Yet another friend's father fell down the steps and broke his neck. Then, there was the rain, which never stopped once all day. The rain that split a few trees in our backyard, broke my favorite outdoor planter with the sunflowers, and then decided to come pouring through our living room. Oh, and there was the small matter of the fifteen stitches on my face (from having a cancerous mole removed) and the fact that I looked like a rainbow-colored Scarface. My eyes were black and blue, my cheeks were yellow, and the wound was bright red.

So all in all, it was an eventful 24 hours. And yet, life was calm. There was a sense that everything was as it should be; there was no resistance to any particular event. Not that I wasn't sad. I was. I didn't want my friend to die. I felt deeply for my other friends. And I wished I would have known to move that sunflower pot out of the way of the wind. (My face? Well, I had a really cool cobalt-blue bandage with stars and galaxies covering the wound. It wasn't exactly my color—I like yellow and golds—but still.)

When I don't argue with what is already happening or has happened, when I don't want anything to be different than it is, there is calm. There is sadness, grief, disappointment—yes, even hunger—but it is all happening on the surface. Underneath, there is a sense of stillness. Of rightness. Of no problem.

Underneath, there is love.

Like Geneen, many people use food to avoid feeling their feelings, but there are many other ways to dodge emotional discomfort: sex, drugs, rock and roll—or whatever's the current distraction of choice. What they all have in common is that they shrink your ability to feel. Whichever method you choose, you can be sure of one thing: it's not going to get you where you really want to go. Becoming unconscious to avoid pain is only a useful strategy when you're on an operating table. In life, the only way out—the only way to truly be free—is through.

Avoidance: Variations on a Theme

In today's world, we're rarely taught the healthy way to handle strong feelings: head-on and fearlessly. Instead we've devised a million different avoidance tactics, which all fall into three main categories. Which of the following do you rely on most?

1. **The Watercooler Approach:** You endlessly rehash the story of what happened, whose fault it was, and why you're suffering. Many people mistake this for feeling their feelings, but it's actually a way of remaining separate from them, buffered from the real discomfort that aches underneath. It doesn't help, and in fact, it hurts you. HeartMath researchers found that reviewing and rehashing the things that make you angry, frustrated, irritated, or worried can throw off your autonomic nervous system balance, create incoherent heart rhythms, and negatively affect your hormonal and immune system balance.

2. **The Spiritual Bypass:** You jump straight to the moral or higher lesson in the situation, without acknowledging there's some raw emotion alive and kicking underneath. Symptoms of spiritual bypass include using expressions like "What doesn't kill you makes you stronger" or "This is God's will," long before you've arrived at that wisdom inside. It's pretending you feel fine when you don't.

3. **The Numb-out:** You contract away from the pain, physically putting up armor around it by stiffening your body, breathing more shallowly, or going to sleep. Or you engage in behaviors that distract you from your pain, like eating, drinking, gambling, shopping, or sex. As Geneen's story shows, this reaction often creates a secondary problem for you to fix—obesity, alcoholism, addiction, debt, and so on—further misdirecting your attention from the initial pain that caused it.

When faced with difficult emotions, we look in every direction but the one that will take us back to ourselves and the love that's at our core. Using this key is the antidote to avoidance.

What "Feeling Your Feelings" Feels Like

It's important to understand that *feeling* your feelings "is not the same as expressing, exaggerating or acting out," as Love Luminary Raphael Cushnir writes in his book *Setting Your Heart on Fire*. "All it requires is a gentle focus, a turning toward what's actually present." You do this not in your mind, but in your body.

As soon as you catch yourself beginning to practice any of the avoidance techniques—getting caught in the "story," trying to talk yourself out of your feelings, or reaching for that chocolate cake, glass of wine, or your keys and credit card for some retail therapy—take a deep breath or two and pay attention to what's going on in your body instead.

Part of what makes negative emotions so painful is our tightening against them. Try this simple practice to help maintain openness that I adapted from Raphael's work. I've recommended it to lots of people and they love it.

To begin, think of a negative feeling that you resist (such as anger, jealousy, sadness, or fear). Next recall how you feel standing in a hot shower—the stream of hot water cascading over your body. Use your felt memory to actually re-create the expansion, relaxation, and openness of that experience in your body.

Now bring this same sense of bodily relaxation to feeling that negative feeling you resist. Notice how your body relaxes and expands, and in that bigger space, the stuck feeling can now start to move. It wiggles around and starts to flow through you—and out. When you remove the interference to the flow of emotions, like leaves on a river, they stay with you briefly and soon move round the bend.

It takes courage to open to discomfort. But the amazing thing about this technique is that once you're willing to feel your feelings, no matter how painful they start out, they actually hurt less as you open to them. In fact, with practice, this opening even becomes pleasurable.

In my interview with Love Luminary Arjuna Ardagh, author, speaker, and founder of the Living Essence Foundation, he told me, "Anything fully felt turns to love." This is because the feeling, having completed its mission, dissolves, revealing the presence of Love for No Reason underneath, which, like the sun, has been there all along.

The Power of How

A few weeks before this book was due, I woke up early one morning with the thought *I have to interview Tom Stone.* Tom had been a friend and colleague for thirty years, but I hadn't seen him in over a decade. I knew he was doing cutting-edge research on human potential and had written a book called *Vaporize Your Anxiety without Drugs or Therapy.* I had the strong feeling that he held an important piece of the Love for No Reason puzzle that I had to hear.

Two hours later, I had just given a telephone interview and on an impulse asked the host if there was anyone he knew who really represented the Love for No Reason message. He said, "You may not have heard of this person, but I've just been introduced to his work and I'm blown away. His name is Tom Stone."

Thank you, universe! I got the message loud and clear. I called Tom and it turned out that his office was five minutes away from the house Carol and I were staying in to work together on the book. My memo from the universe had been delivered just in time: Carol and I had just two days left of our writing retreat.

Within just a few moments of walking into his office the next morning, Carol and I could both feel that Tom radiated love. When we asked him to describe his experience of Love for No Reason, the first words out of his mouth were, "Love is not an action, not a giving or receiving; it's a state of being. There's only one true form of it and that is unconditional. Love that isn't unconditional is just need. Everyone is intrinsically unconditional love: it's our nature." Carol and I looked at each other and grinned. It was our first two love themes, almost verbatim.

Tom continued, "One habit that keeps you from experiencing love is avoiding emotional pain and negative feelings. We have a deep-seated fear of being overwhelmed by them and do our best not to feel them."

Tom told us that the purpose of feeling your feelings is not to get rid of them but to let them fulfill their purpose—which is bringing our awareness to the things in our lives that need our attention. When we feel our feelings, they complete this mission, which allows them to dissolve naturally.

In 1997 Tom developed the technique below that he calls the CORE—Center of Remaining Energy—technique for resolving emotional pain quickly and thoroughly. After practicing the CORE technique a few times, you may find that within seconds you're able to resolve even very powerful emotions.

Exercise

The CORE (Center of Remaining Energy) Technique

This technique allows you to feel your feelings fully. It guides your awareness into the center of the energy field of your incomplete feelings and completes the experience of the energy that's been held in your body.

1. Sit comfortably and close your eyes.

2. Notice any anxiety or uncomfortable emotion you're feeling in your body. That anxiety or emotion has an energy field. If it didn't, you wouldn't be able to feel it. Notice where in your body you feel that energy.

3. Locate the area of greatest intensity in the emotion or anxiety's energy field.

4. Let your awareness go right into the center of the most intense part of the energy field. If you look for it, you will very likely find a little vortex or "eye of the hurricane" at the very center of the intensity. Feel right down into the center of that for a few minutes.

5. One of three things will happen:

    a) The sensation will become more intense.

    b) The sensation will seem to stay the same.

    c) The sensation will start to fade away or soften.

Notice which one of those you are experiencing.

6. Continue to allow your awareness to feel right into the center of the most intense part of the energy of the sensation.

7. Bring your awareness in closer, like a laser beam, to whatever is left of the sensation, again finding the center of intensity in the remaining energy. Feel down into it, experiencing the essence of the energy. The goal is to feel down into the energy of the sensation so thoroughly that there's nothing left to feel.

8. If there's any sensation of the energy left, continue to place your awareness in the center of the most intense part of whatever is left of that energy. You're not looking for insights, just to experience the energy.

9. You may need to do this a few times for the energy to feel complete.

10. When you feel complete, spend a few more minutes just sitting easily with your eyes closed before getting up.

Used by permission of Tom Stone and Great Life Technologies,
www.greatlifetechnologies.com

Summary and Love for No Reason Action Steps

Giving your body true nourishment and feeling your feelings are the keys that open the Doorway of Vitality. Don't underestimate the power of making one new, energy-enhancing choice. Use the following action steps to increase the flow of love through this energy center.

1. Pump up the *prana* in your body by choosing foods that give more energy than they take.

2. To stop racking up energy debt, break the caffeine habit. Look for more sustainable forms of energy—like enough sleep and proper nourishment.

3. Experiment with some new types of exercise—such as dance, aerobics, or yoga—until you find one that not only gets your blood flowing but also makes you smile.

4. Make time each day to breathe deeply and when possible spend time where you'll breathe in a good dose of negative ions.

5. Practice the Free Your *Hara*—Awaken Your Vitality exercise anytime you want more energy and ease in your day.

6. Make a practice of noticing and savoring the beauty, joy, and delight in your environment.

7. To welcome your feelings, imagine you're in a hot shower or bath. Feel your body expand and relax. Now bring the same state of physical relaxation and openness in your body to the practice of feeling your feelings.

8. Use the CORE technique to complete your feelings and free yourself to open your heart.

CHAPTER 6

The Doorway of Unconditional Self-Love: Loving Yourself No Matter What

Find the love you seek, by first finding the love within yourself.
Learn to rest in that place within you that is your true home.

—Sri Sri Ravi Shankar, spiritual leader and humanitarian

The family story I heard most often growing up was told by my mother. At almost every family gathering, she'd describe how in the years before I was born, she was so overwhelmed taking care of my older sister and brother that she'd often say, "If I ever get pregnant again, I'm going to drive the car into the ocean! I can't handle any more kids!" At the time, our family lived in San Francisco, just blocks from the Pacific. She always ended this story looking at me with a loving smile and saying, "Oh honey, I'm so glad I didn't drive into the ocean."

I knew both my mother and my father loved me dearly, but because I'd started out as an unplanned and clearly unwanted pregnancy, I had absorbed a very different message on a cellular level. At each step of my fetal development I took in another layer of my mother's unconscious communication that I wasn't welcome. So somewhere deep inside, I always felt that there was something wrong with me; I was unwanted and I wasn't good enough. "I'm not okay" became my mantra.

From an early age, life became a constant struggle to overcome the negative effects of this core belief. I would try anything to make myself feel "good enough"—anything that would prove I was wanted and worthy of being here. But no matter what I did, nothing could plug the hole inside.

As an adult, when I started speaking professionally, it made sense that the topic I wanted to specialize in was self-esteem for women. I studied with Jack Canfield, the world's number one expert on self-esteem, and began teaching self-esteem programs. They say we teach what we most need to learn, and over time I did start to feel better about myself—at least on the outside. I felt dynamic, vital, attractive, and successful. And I was happy that I was able to manifest many of my goals and dreams.

Yet no matter how many standing ovations I got, no matter how many millions of books I sold, no matter how many times a man said, "I love you," and no matter how good my body looked, I still felt like the girl with cooties. Any rejection, whether real or imagined, sent me into a tailspin, triggering the same feelings of humiliation and hurt I used to feel in school when I was the last one chosen for the team.

My inner "cootie girl" was one of the major blocks to experiencing unconditional love in my life. I didn't believe I was worthy of love. I was hard on myself and, consequently, I was equally hard on the people around me.

Then a couple of years ago I had a wake-up call. One day I noticed myself using a very sharp tone with Sergio, and I suddenly recognized it as the same harpy-like voice inside my own head. I realized how my judgments of other people reflected how harshly I judged myself. As I thought about this over the next few days, I saw that if I continued to relate to people this way, I would never get what I wanted or be the person I wanted to be. Harshness and punishment never lead to love; love blossoms with kindness and care.

It was then that I started to feel true compassion for myself—for both the harpy *and* the cootie girl. As a reminder to bring compassion to these parts of me, I taped the Angel Card for compassion (one in a deck of seventy-two inspirational cards, each depicting an angelic quality with a word and a drawing of an angel) on my computer monitor.

It's still there today. If I start to beat myself up or become impatient with others, the compassion card helps me remember to ask myself what I can do to be gentler and kinder to myself *right now*, so I can start to feel love for myself—not because of anything I've done, but by aligning with a love that doesn't depend on success or approval.

Almost all of us carry around this same underlying belief of "I'm not good enough"—or some variation of how we are flawed or inadequate. Yours might be "I'm not smart enough," "I'm not worthy," or "I'm not lovable." It doesn't really matter which edition of the "I'm Not Okay" manual you have, when you don't love yourself, you hold yourself back from receiving life's richest experience: Love for No Reason. It's like having a winning lottery ticket and not showing up to claim the millions.

To make matters worse, you look outside yourself to try to fill yourself up—with food, drugs and alcohol, achievements, relationships, you name it. It's the ultimate bottomless pit. This explains why so many people are overweight, addicted, frustrated with their jobs or their relationships, and passing unhappiness and lack of love on to their kids. The truth is that until we fill the inner void, nothing from the outside can ever make us feel "enough"—at least for very long.

You may be thinking, *I've heard this before, but how do I do it?* The good news is you've already begun. Reading this book has most likely caused you to reexamine your paradigm about love. And it's set you on the path of learning to access Love for No Reason and clearing away the blocks to living it every day.

When you love yourself unconditionally, you're kind to yourself, have compassion for yourself, and accept yourself as you are. You don't love yourself just for "good reasons," such as your talents and good qualities, which are the basis of your self-esteem. While self-esteem is healthy and important in moderation, it has its limitations. Loving yourself for good reasons keeps you focused on external factors, like your accomplishments and successes.

And what happens if you can't maintain those positive qualities? Your self-esteem disappears. Or worse, it turns into harshness and self-disparagement. You beat yourself up for letting yourself down.

When you strengthen the self-love center, you stop condemning and abandoning yourself and start being there for yourself, no matter what— even in the midst of pain, in the midst of the things about yourself that you think are unlovable.

You're also able to be fully empowered. That means you create appropriate boundaries and take responsibility for your own experience of love. This then becomes the basis for loving others unconditionally.

Love Luminary and psychologist Dr. Art Aron says that a lack of self-love is a terrible handicap in relationships. In our interview, he cited a study conducted by Dr. Sandra Murray and Dr. John Holmes that showed that people who didn't love themselves overreacted to problems in relationships, perceived signs of rejection where none existed, and put down their partners as a defense mechanism, reducing the closeness between them. The high self-love subjects in the study, on the other hand, were less sensitive to rejection, appreciated their partners more, and felt closer to them, even when they were told their partner thought there was a problem in the relationship.

Opening the Doorway of Unconditional Self-Love removes one of the most devastating blocks to the giving and receiving of love. It clears the way for an open heart.

Tending Your Inner Fire

The self-love center, traditionally called the third or solar plexus chakra, is located in the center of the body, in the area of the stomach and navel. It physically affects the organs of digestion, the pancreas, and the liver, and its psychological and emotional influences are felt on the level of our core beliefs: *Am I adequate? Am I lovable? Do I have the power to create the life I want?*

The solar plexus chakra is associated with the element of fire; like the sun, it powers your own personal solar system of body, mind, and spirit. When this energy center is healthy, you not only efficiently digest the food you eat, transforming it into energy and the basic building blocks for wellness, but you're also able to effectively digest your life experiences.

The result is a clear and balanced sense of self: self-acceptance and self-compassion combined with a quiet invincibility and a connection to your individual will.

Unlocking the Doorway of Unconditional Self-Love

The Love Luminaries all agreed that it's possible to cultivate unconditional self-love, even if you've spent a lot of time beating yourself up, as I had. With practice, you can learn to bring the higher vibration of Love for No Reason to yourself, just as you are, and feel compassion for yourself even when things go wrong.

Opening the Doorway of Unconditional Self-Love doesn't mean simply using positive affirmations or telling yourself, "I love you" a hundred times a day, as you probably won't believe that anyway. It means replacing old habits with new beliefs, attitudes, and behaviors. When you make self-love a practice, you actually develop new neural pathways in your brain that support the experience of unconditional self-love, making it easier and easier over time to spontaneously be a kinder, gentler, more powerful you.

Strengthening the self-love center is essential for building your love-body. If you want to be unconditionally loving to others, first you have to be unconditionally loving—consistently and generously—to yourself. Here are the two Love Keys that will release the flow of this transformational current of self-love. They work together to raise your love set point and dissolve the upper limits that block the flow of Love for No Reason in your life:

> ### Love Keys for the Doorway of Unconditional Self-Love
>
> 1. Love The Unlovable in Yourself
> 2. Honor Your Power

The Self-Love Key expands your capacity to love yourself the way you are—not the way you think you "should" be—by practicing loving-kindness, compassion, and acceptance for yourself no matter what.

The Empowerment Key strengthens self-love by helping you connect to the source of true power within yourself.

Love Key for Unconditional Self-Love #1:
Love the Unlovable in Yourself

The "not good enough" voice in our heads is one of Higher Love's sneakiest enemies. The voice (which almost everyone hears, just at different volumes) usually originates from an outside source—parents, teachers, siblings, or classmates—but once it's internalized, we become so used to it, it does its damage without our even being aware that it's there. Although my inner critic was already a familiar presence by the time the following incident occurred, she really found her voice that day.

The year was 1971 and hot pants were all the rage. In case you weren't around for that particular fashion flurry, hot pants were three-inch-long shorts that barely covered your butt, usually in wild psychedelic colors and patterns.

I was thirteen years old at the time and the fact that my nickname was Chubs didn't stop me from squeezing into my very own pair of bright pink hot pants. All the girls in my school were wearing them and—no surprise—I wanted to be one of the crowd.

The day of my hot pants debut, I walked home from school with my best friend, Chris. At my house, we decided to call another girl I'll call "Susan" for a good old "who likes who/he said, she said" teenage gossip session. Chris dialed the number on the kitchen phone, and I went to my bedroom to use the extension there. As I picked up the receiver, I heard Susan say, "Can you *believe* Marci wore *hot pants* today—with *those* thighs?"

My face burning with shame, I silently put down the receiver. I took off the tiny pink shorts and stuck them in the very back of my closet, where I would never have to see them again.

But I couldn't get rid of Susan's voice as easily. Every time I looked in the mirror, I heard, "Can you *believe* how fat you are?" Later, when I was nineteen and didn't have a boyfriend, that same voice asked, "Can you *believe* what a loser you are?" And years after that, when I gave a talk and thought someone in the audience looked bored, the voice was still there: "Can you *believe* what a lousy speaker you are?"

It took years for me to hang up the phone on my "inner mean girl," a term that Love Luminary and self-love advocate Christine Arylo uses to describe the inner critic that lives inside our heads. My "mean girl" had a steady job and she didn't want to lose it! She was successfully employed full-time, pointing out every "unlovable" part of myself and every reason I wasn't "getting" love from outside.

To circumvent her, I had to outsmart her same old "Can you believe . . . ?" refrain.

Transforming the Inner Critic

*Pay no attention to what the critics say; no statue
has ever been erected to a critic.*

—Jean Sibelius, twentieth-century Finnish composer

Inner critics like "mean girl" are pros at what I call the three Cs: comparing, competing, and criticizing. They're always on the lookout for people to measure you against—someone smarter, more attractive, more successful, and so on—a surefire recipe for misery and a closed heart.

Then, once they've identified an ideal image to compare you against, they egg you on to compete—knowing you can't possibly live up to such high standards. You're then left trying to compensate for your inadequacies by finding fault or tearing down the other person: "So-and-so's not so great," or "That guy had a lucky break. He doesn't really deserve his fame/ power/money," and so on. This creates insecurity and bitterness—certainly not the hallmarks of Love for No Reason.

But the inner critic's specialty is, of course, criticism. It specializes in offering a constant stream of criticisms and judgments, such as "You should have known better," or "You ought to be different." Basically, it picks on you because it knows all your weak spots.

Your inner critic's invective acts like poison on your system. Thankfully, the Love Luminaries offered some effective antidotes to this toxic condition:

Give Your Inner Critic a Name: In my interview with Christine, she told me about Inner Mean Girl Reform School, the program she's codeveloped with Amy Ahlers to free women from the damaging effects of harsh, self-critical thoughts and behaviors. (It works for men too.) The first lesson on the syllabus is to name your inner mean girl or guy (IMG for short) who mutters defeating or hateful things inside. Mean Patty, Loveless Lulu, and Eeyore are just a few of the names that Inner Mean Girl Reform School students have come up with.

Naming the voice, with a dose of humor, is a way of becoming separate from it. It's one aspect of you—an unruly one at that—but it's not your deeper self that's speaking.

When you step away from that voice enough to name it, you soon observe that its stream of unsupportive comments is more white noise than hot newsflash. You can notice the comments, but keep going without engaging with them.

Learning to defuse the IMG is vital for your emotional well-being. Numerous studies show that self-criticism and a preoccupation with personal mistakes and failures are strongly correlated with negative emotional states and behaviors such as depression, eating disorders, and anxiety.

Find the Critic's Deeper Message: Refusing to engage the IMG is an important first step toward reducing its power over you. But to send it packing, you have to find out why it is there. This involves going inward to ask, with kindness and openness, *What are you trying to do for me?* What you find may surprise you.

My friend, speaker and Love Luminary Terri Tate, told me her experience:

> My mother was a very unhappy woman. Her unhappiness, which would be called depression today, and her colorful ways of expressing it

served as a model for the voice in my head that harried and harassed me for most of my life. I later came to call this voice the Witch Upstairs.

The Witch lay in wait for me every morning. Before I had even fully opened my eyes, she'd begun listing my inadequacies and the calamities that the day might hold for me, causing my gastrointestinal tract to seize up in anticipation. The disapproval and many sharp criticisms I received as a child gave the Witch Upstairs plenty of good material to work with.

After I grew up, the Witch let me know in no uncertain terms that my marital status as a two-time divorcée was evidence of my defective character and, worse, likely to have a terrible effect on my two sons. Then, at forty-five, I was diagnosed with oral cancer from which I had a 2 percent chance of survival. This sent the Witch into overdrive; she was making dire prognostications and second-guessing every health decision I made. Her reverse cheerleading was driving me crazy.

Then, one morning, I woke before the Witch Upstairs did. As I lay there in the unfamiliar silence, I had a sudden flash of understanding. The Witch was only trying to help. She wanted what was best for me but didn't know any other way to communicate. In her own twisted way, she was showing me how much she cared.

When the Witch woke up and started to make her usual dark predictions, I quickly interrupted her, first thanking her for caring so deeply about my welfare, then telling her firmly that unless she had any constructive ideas to share, she could just butt out.

She sputtered angrily, but she could tell I meant business. Every time she started to harangue me, I simply repeated my willingness to listen to anything helpful she might like to contribute. After a few false starts, she surprised me by saying, "Oh what the heck, it's your body, do what you want. Doctors don't know everything."

After that, I began standing up to the Witch rather than simply taking—and believing—her abuse, and this weakened her. As time passed, I found myself less and less affected by the Witch's worldview.

Finally, I knew it was time to send her packing. At an imaginary retirement party, I gave her a gold watch for more than fifty years of faithful service and bought her a condo in Boca. She kicked and screamed, but her ravings just didn't touch me anymore.

Today, life is so much easier without her. Still, even now, whenever I get tired or stressed out or blue, she's on the first red-eye back from Florida, ready to relive the glory days of her reign. When she returns and tries to assert her old control, I remind her that I am under new, nicer management now. I thank her again for her efforts at keeping me safe and then kindly but firmly suggest that she do some shopping or enjoy a round of golf—or whatever it is retired witches do. She glares but toddles off, a pathetic figure really. We both know she's lost whatever power she had—whatever power I gave her—and that I am doing fine without her. Better than fine really, great!

And although she'd never admit it, we also both know that beneath her venom and bluster, that's what she's wanted for me all along.

What Terri discovered was the main ingredient for loving the unlovable in yourself: self-compassion. When you stop listening to the inner critic, the voice inside you becomes softer and more loving. The pain-body is reduced as the love-body expands.

Mean Girl or Guy, Meet Self-Compassion

Unconditional self-love means treating yourself the way you'd treat a beloved friend. Pema Chödrön, the wonderful American-born Buddhist teacher, calls this *maitri*, the Sanskrit word for unconditional friendship with yourself. She says that *maitri* is a practice, something you actively cultivate through lovingkindness and self-compassion.

Self-compassion is one of the hottest new areas of study in the field of positive psychology. According to research conducted by Dr. Kristin Neff, of the University of Texas in Austin, "higher self-compassion is associated with greater psychological well-being: less depression, anxiety, rumination, and thought suppression, and with greater life satisfaction and social relatedness." In Britain, Paul Gilbert, professor of clinical psychology at the University of Derby, has done initial studies showing that self-compassion reduces self-criticism and shame. He conjectures that self-compassion may be connected to the release of endorphins and the bonding hormone oxytocin.

Having compassion for yourself doesn't mean behaving irresponsibly or giving yourself license to do whatever you want. In fact, research by Duke University psychology professor Dr. Mark Leary shows that people who practice self-compassion take full responsibility for their actions, but they don't tip into self-abuse or add an extra layer of catastrophe to a situation. In one study, for example, Dr. Leary found that self-compassionate dieters who went off their diets were less likely to continue to overeat than those who beat themselves up for their lapse.

When you're feeling judgmental toward yourself, try using this easy-to-remember process that Carol and I came up with—the ABC of self-love:

> *Awareness:* Become aware of any negative feelings you're having toward yourself.
>
> *Be with the feeling:* Allow the experience to be there without expressing it or trying to make it go away. Let it be there without trying to change it.
>
> *Compassion:* Bring the same kindness and compassion to yourself for having this feeling as you would bring to a dear friend.

Mastering self-compassion requires coming into a new relationship with yourself—especially being kind toward the inner you when you've usually been harsh. The next story shows what this journey looked like for one woman as she moved from self-rejection to self-love.

I heard about Love Luminaries Sally Sals and her husband, Robb, from a mutual friend who said that Sally and Robb absolutely radiated love. When I interviewed them, I had to agree. Sally and Robb are truly living lives of Love for No Reason. Sally told me that Robb has always been an unconditionally loving person—he was just born that way—but that it took a life crisis to spur her to dissolve her blocks to unconditional love, both for herself and others.

Sally's Story
Healed by Love

You can't survive long without a functioning liver. In my case, my family and I had been told I had just three days. I was well into my third day, and if a liver donor couldn't be found in the next few hours, I was going to die.

It was right before my fiftieth birthday. I had been rushed to the hospital, delirious and vomiting bile, only to be informed that my liver was failing. I was shocked. How could this be? I didn't drink and, as far as I knew, I didn't have a liver disease. The doctors were stumped too. After a day of extensive testing, they ruled out cancer and hepatitis. Clearly something was very, very wrong, but what?

In the end they called what I had "liver failure for no medical reason." The direness of my situation catapulted me to the top of the national waiting list for a liver transplant. There were only three people ahead of me.

Barely conscious, I lay in my hospital bed, being kept alive through transfusions. With each passing hour, my chances of surviving dwindled. As the third day wore on with no call to say a donor had been located, my family and friends came to say their good-byes.

Then, hallelujah! With only hours to spare, a liver was found for me and I was whisked into the operating room.

The doctor who performed my surgery told me that my liver was the worst he'd ever seen. It looked, he said, "as though it had been chewed by a cat." It was literally eaten away. And the cause remained a total mystery.

After the surgery I was put into the only room on the floor with a beautiful view of the Golden Gate Bridge. I remember looking out the window and feeling incredibly grateful. I was amazed that God had allowed circumstances to work out so that I could live. I had never felt loved in such a profound way before.

The area of love and relationships had never been easy for me. Three years earlier I had divorced my husband of over twenty-five years. Two of our four kids were on their own, and we shared custody of the two youngest, ages twelve and sixteen. Though I loved my family, I was fearful and mistrustful of most other people, scared of being rejected or hurt.

Rejection had been a central theme of my life, especially as a child. I felt as though my brother and sister, who were much older than I was, didn't want me around, and my parents, who were both alcoholics, basically ignored me. To compensate, I became a people pleaser, always going along with what others wanted, hoping to be loved, or at least liked.

Now I thought, *God, if you can get me a liver at the last hour and put me in this beautiful room, I'm going to trust you. I don't know who or what I am. I certainly don't know how to love myself, or anyone, really. So please send me whatever and whomever to teach me what love is. I want to live it, be it, and model it.*

This intention was the start of a long journey, one that would teach me how powerfully love—or the absence of it—could affect my life.

After a few weeks, I was released from the hospital and sent home to recover. In those days, after an organ transplant, the doctors gave you loads of immunosuppressants to prevent your body from rejecting the new organ, which left you terribly vulnerable to infections. In my case, though, the liver I'd received appeared to be a good match, and I wasn't in and out of the hospital like so many people who receive transplants. Slowly but surely, I began to pick up the threads of normal life.

But it couldn't be the same "normal" I had known. I wanted my second chance at life to be different from the safe but emotionally numb prison I'd created for myself before the transplant. I spent the next year trying many different healing modalities—including acupuncture, homeopathy, and chiropractic—and practiced trusting my intuition about what was good for me. I also made a concerted effort to take greater care of myself and do nice things for myself. I scheduled massages. I took baths. I bought myself flowers. I did all the things I thought were self-love. The changes I felt were gradual, but it seemed as though I was making progress.

Then, about a year after the transplant, I got sick as my body started to reject the new liver. There was nothing the doctors could do. Unless I got another liver, I would soon go into liver failure again. They sent me home with a pager and told me they'd call if a new liver became available for a transplant.

I carried the pager around, in shock that this was happening again. As the days passed and my liver grew less and less functional, I turned yellow and felt increasingly ill. I also got scared. The doctors had told me that it no longer mattered whether I took my immunosuppressant meds or not. Worse, they'd said that even if I did get another liver, there was no guarantee I'd survive. In other words, I was probably going to die!

I waited three weeks for a call, but none came. At the end of that period, on one of my visits to the hospital, I met a woman who had just had her third liver transplant in as many years. She was the most miserable, resentful person I'd ever met, complaining nonstop about her husband, her health, *everything*. Observing her, I suddenly remembered something I'd once heard about Chinese medicine. According to that system, each organ is related to a specific emotion, and problems of the liver are related to too much anger, both expressed and repressed.

It was clear to me that this woman's anger was more destructive than anything modern medicine could do to help her. I didn't want to be like her —constantly wearing out my liver and having to get a new one. It was time to take matters into my own hands. The doctors had given up on me; I would have to do my own "inner surgery." I had to see if there was something inside *my* mind and heart that was causing my liver to fail!

At home, I settled onto the couch with a pad of paper and a pen. I sat still and went deep within. (I had never done anything like this before.) I asked myself, *What do I believe?* As the answers came to me, I wrote them down. I didn't judge or censor them. When I was finished, I read over what I had written. I was shocked by many of the beliefs I'd been carrying around without knowing it, but one stood out in bold relief. There in black and white was the sentence *I believe there's a punishing God and I'm being punished because I'm a terrible person.*

No wonder my attempts at self-love hadn't been successful! Trying to love yourself when you don't believe you deserve love is like pouring water into a sieve. The love isn't around long enough to make a difference.

Determined to root out this attitude, I went within again, mental scalpel in hand, to find out *why* I believed I was so bad. The answer was surprisingly simple: as a child, being "me" meant being punished.

In our household, my parents had zero tolerance for voicing dissatisfaction, crying, or expressing anger. Actually, almost all expressions of emotion were big no-nos that led to harsh reprimands and physical punishment. I realized I was a living example of something I'd once heard: when your parents reject and punish you for expressing your emotions, you usually end up doing the same thing to yourself. Any strong feeling I had, especially anger, was completely repressed, usually before I was even aware I had the feeling. The sad truth was that for most of my life I'd had no idea what I felt or who I was—and I hadn't wanted to know. I was mired in guilt and shame and felt somehow responsible for everything that had gone wrong in my family.

I had to learn to forgive, love, and accept myself right here and now, or the inwardly directed self-rejection would continue to destroy my liver.

Something in me welled up for that child who still lived at the center of my inner self and who felt so unloved and so unworthy. In my mind and heart, I put my arms around the little girl who was me and said, *Honey, you didn't do anything wrong. I forgive you and I love you.* The affection and understanding I felt were real and sincere, and a surge of warmth and light filled me.

That inner embrace was the turning point. From that moment on, I began to be kind to the little girl inside me. I treated her as if she were my own beloved child. I began tucking her in at night and waking her up in the morning with love and kisses. At restaurants, I'd check inside, asking my little girl what she wanted. When I went out for a walk, I'd ask her, *Where do you want to go, honey?*

I was gentle with myself, which included letting myself feel all my feelings, including anger. Instead of saying, *You shouldn't feel that way* or *Stop crying! Don't be a baby,* I was patient and understanding. I told myself, *It's okay, honey. You can have those feelings.*

To my surprise, doing this actually helped my feelings dissipate and resolve themselves. I was able to come back to an inner place of peace and acceptance more quickly and stay there more of the time.

This process of being loving with myself had powerful physical effects as well. Since the transplant, my level of bilirubin (a component of red blood cells associated with liver function) had been tested twice a week. Too much bilirubin meant something was wrong. The day I'd sat down on the couch for my "inner surgery," my bilirubin level had been sky-high. Over the next nine months it went all the way down to normal. The doctors couldn't explain it. They called it a miracle; I called it Grace.

That was eighteen years ago, and I never had to have the second transplant. As the months and years have gone by, I've continued to be a loving parent to the little girl inside. This has allowed me to be a better parent to my flesh-and-blood children as well.

My whole life, I'd been looking for love and acceptance, affection and attention outside but couldn't find it. Only when my heart became fully capable of opening to true love, first for myself and then for others, could I draw love into my life in the form of wonderful friends and the most loving partner imaginable!

Ten years ago I met an incredible man and fell deeply in love. We're now married. My husband, Robb, is a model for living with an open heart, and our relationship has been one of the most beautiful experiences of my life, allowing me to experience unconditional love—love for no reason—given freely and joyfully.

Though I wouldn't wish my brushes with death on anyone, I am grateful for the wake-up calls. They taught me something I probably wouldn't have learned in any other way: not only do we deserve to love ourselves, we literally can't live without it.

💜   💜   💜

Self-Forgiveness

As you can see from Sally's story, what often blocks self-love are feelings of guilt and shame. Like many of us, Sally had somehow come to believe that she didn't *deserve* love after what she had done (or not done) as a child. So, how can we get beyond guilt and self-punishment to self-love?

Love Luminary Dr. Frederic Luskin, the director of the Stanford Forgiveness Project, shed some light on this question by making a clear distinction between regret and guilt. He says, "Regret is our conscience's way of telling us that we've behaved in a way that's violated our sense of right and wrong. This feeling of remorse drives us to make amends: we may apologize or try to repair the damage we've caused. With regret, *even though we feel bad about how we've behaved, we don't feel bad about ourselves as people.* Regret serves a positive function in that it helps us safeguard our value system, but it doesn't include self-attacks.

"Guilt, on the other hand, is a negative force. Like regret, it also includes feeling unhappy with ourselves about a particular action. However, instead of trying to make amends, we turn on ourselves and the guilt becomes destructive. It's no longer our actions in question but our basic selves. This self-attack contributes to low self-love, self-destructive behavior, and depression. In such a weakened state it's difficult to make amends. The path out of the self-attack that characterizes guilt is learning to forgive oneself."

When you forgive yourself, you make peace with something you did or didn't do that you feel bad about. Though you can't change what happened in the past, you can lovingly take responsibility for your mistakes, make amends if possible, and make a sincere effort not to repeat the behavior in the future.

To keep the Doorway of Unconditional Self-Love open, it's important to separate *what you do* from *who you are.* (This is something you'll learn to do as part of the Disidentification Process in chapter 10.) You can love yourself as a person even if you make a mistake. When you forgive yourself, you stop attacking and punishing yourself and let yourself feel the sadness that is a natural part of regret. Self-forgiveness, which builds on self-compassion, requires feeling your feelings, and then being kind and encouraging to yourself, instead of punitive and demoralizing.

Bringing the Vibration of Love to Anything and Everything

Whatever you are doing, love yourself for doing it.
Whatever you are feeling, love yourself for feeling it.
—Thaddeus Golas, twentieth-century philosopher

The most direct way that you can love the unlovable in yourself is to bring the vibration of love to whatever it is you're feeling or experiencing—even if what you're experiencing is challenging or unpleasant. If you're one of those people who has a hard time loving yourself, you can begin by simply loving the fact that you *are unable* to love yourself.

Try it: think of something that you really don't like about yourself—you're too fat or too thin, or you can't balance your checkbook, for example—and instead of trying to love your excess flab or your boniness or your lameness in the bean-counting department, just love that you don't like that quality about yourself and are struggling with it. Beam love, compassion, and understanding to the person who's experiencing the challenge: you! Love Luminary Gay Hendricks, who wrote *Learning to Love Yourself*, put it this way: "Love whatever you can from wherever you are."

When you can love yourself in every situation—whether you've succeeded or failed, whether you feel good or bad, whether you're enjoying life or hating it—you've taken self-love to the unconditional level. Loving self-acceptance is the ability to simply bring love to your feelings and thoughts, without rejecting any of them—even the "unlovable" stuff. It means being able to say, *I love myself even though I'm flawed. I love myself no matter what. I love myself for* no reason! You'll feel a physical shift in your body when you do this; your heart center will feel softer and more open. You may even find yourself smiling.

The positive effects of this approach are measurable. A team of British researchers led by Dr. Paul Gilbert showed how training people to be loving and compassionate toward every aspect of themselves—even toward their tendency to be self-critical—significantly reduced mental suffering, depression, anxiety, self-criticism, shame, inferiority, and submissive behavior, while upping their ability to soothe and reassure themselves.

Isha, Love Luminary and the Australian-born author of *Why Walk When You Can Fly? Soar Beyond Your Fears and Love Yourself and Others Unconditionally*, says true self-love comes from embracing the perfection of your human experience—just as it is. "You're having a human experience, not an idealistic, saintly experience. You get angry, you feel sad, you love, you're selfish, you're generous. You accept that there is nothing wrong with you. Unconditional love like this is such a high vibration that it starts to expand very rapidly. It soon brings you to the point where you say: 'I don't want to be someone else; I love myself as I am.' Ironically, when this happens, we become the person we always wanted to be: as we embrace the things we judge, we naturally rise above fear-based behaviors and let go of our limitations."

Carol and I were so inspired by our interview with Isha that we took a weekend seminar with her. We found ourselves nodding enthusiastically in agreement the entire time she was talking. Isha has developed a system of "facets"—simple statements of profound truth that create the transformational energy of love within you. When you use the facet for self-love, it helps you to "embrace yourself in your perfection." (To find out more about Isha's program, look in the Resources section in the back of the book.)

If you're like most people, you beat yourself up thinking that it's the only way you're going to change, but actually it's only when you truly accept and love yourself that you can change. Love Luminary Hale Dwoskin, the best selling author of *The Sedona Method*, told me, "What most people call self-love—positive affirmations and putting smiley-face Post-its on the mirror—is just a manipulation. It's like pasting a thin layer of positive emotion on top of problems. If you love all your qualities as they are, good and so-called bad ones, you actually have power to change them. If you try to change them from a place of simply manipulating them, they only grow."

I've used and recommended the Sedona Method for years and found it so helpful that I included a whole section about it in *Happy for No Reason*. The Sedona Method helps you experience unconditional self-love by allowing you to let go of the harsh judgments you have about yourself.

When you connect to the Love for No Reason at your core, real self-love starts to flow. Every day, I do a very simple self-love practice that brings me into my heart and reminds me to treat myself with care. It comes in especially handy whenever I'm having a rough time or being critical toward myself or others. Throughout the day, I ask myself, *What's the most loving thing I can do for myself right now?* or *What's the most loving way I can be with myself right now?* And then I actually pay attention to the answer.

Sometimes it's having compassion for the part of me that's hurting;

other times it's forgiving myself for my mistakes or simply lightening up on myself. Often it's "loving what is"—just as it is. (I first heard the phrase "loving what is" from a model of unconditional love, Byron Katie, who wrote a great book of the same title.) There are also occasions when the most loving thing I can do for myself is taking a walk or a hot bath or calling a good friend for a chat. Whatever it is, when I love and take care of myself, I find doing so invariably serves everyone.

Tapping Your Way to Self-Love

No, you don't need to get out your tap shoes, because this next self-love solution has nothing to do with dancing. I'm referring to EFT (Emotional Freedom Techniques). This is a wonderful process in which you use your fingertips to gently tap a sequence of specific acupuncture points on the body to release blocked negative energy.

EFT was developed by Gary Craig, a Stanford University engineering graduate and ordained minister. It stimulates the body's energy meridians—subtle energy channels that have been recognized by Chinese medicine for thousands of years.

EFT releases painful emotions and creates an open, receptive state in the subconscious mind that allows new, more empowering thoughts to enter. It increases the flow of love and well-being in your body, heart, and mind. EFT has been used to clear everything from fears, anger, and anxiety to PTSD (post–traumatic stress disorder), as well as scores of other issues. Hundreds of thousands of people around the world have used this technique with often life-changing results.

When I first heard about EFT, I thought it seemed way too simple to really have an effect. How could a negative feeling I'd had about myself for forty years go away in a few minutes of tapping on some points on my face and body? It sounded too good to be true.

But I tried it and oh boy, it really works! I had chosen an issue to tap about that had been a problem for me for years: being too hard on myself, expecting perfection. After one tapping session, guided by Love Luminary Pamela Bruner, a master EFT practitioner, I noticed a lot more ease and acceptance of myself—imperfections and all. I felt freer.

Pamela shared the following exercise that you can use to release whatever's stopping you from loving the unlovable in yourself.

Exercise

An EFT Tapping Exercise for Loving the Unlovable in Yourself

In this exercise, you will be clearing the belief that you're unlovable.

1. Identify something specific about yourself that makes you feel unlovable. (For example: "I'm overweight" or "I've failed at _____" or "My partner broke up with me.")

2. Using the diagram below, find the eight points that you'll be tapping lightly, using your index and middle fingers.

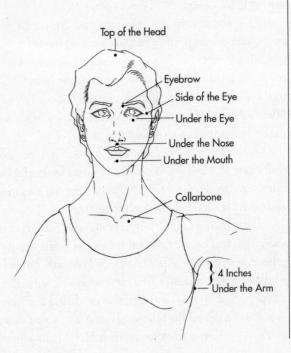

Top of the Head

Eyebrow

Side of the Eye

Under the Eye

Under the Nose

Under the Mouth

Collarbone

4 Inches Under the Arm

3. Starting at the head, tap each point long enough to say the following statement at each point:

   "Even though I feel unlovable because _____ (state why you feel unlovable—your answer from step 1). *I wonder if I could accept myself anyway."*

4. Starting at the head again, tap each one of the points long enough to say the following statement at each point:

   "Even though I still feel unlovable because _____. *I'm open to accepting myself anyway."*

5. Starting at the head, tap each point long enough to say the following statement at each point:

   "Even though I might still feel unlovable because _____, *I choose to love and accept myself anyway."*

6. Starting at the head, tap each point long enough to say the following statement at each point:

   "I deeply and completely love and accept myself anyway."

7. Take several deep, relaxing breaths. Focus on the problem again, and notice how much more ease and acceptance you feel toward yourself.

Experiment with doing this exercise regularly, choosing different issues to focus on as they arise. Over time, you will feel a much greater level of love and self-acceptance.

Used by permission of Pamela Bruner. For a video of this process, visit www.MakeYourSuccessEasy.com.

"Emotional Freedom Techniques EFT" is a registered trademark of Gary H. Craig.

Love Key for Unconditional Self-Love #2:
Honor Your Power

Your sense of personal empowerment is another aspect of the self-love center. When this energy center is healthy and balanced, you understand that the authority to create change in your life rests within you. You stand up for yourself when necessary and realize that you're the person responsible for your life—including your experience of love.

When the Doorway of Self-Love is closed, you live life as a victim—of your circumstances, of your relationships, even of your own mind. It's a contracted way of being and doesn't support an open heart.

Honoring your power increases self-love. When you stand up for yourself and are clear about what's acceptable for you and what's not, you're flexing your love-body's self-love muscles and building up their strength.

When I posted the Love for No Reason survey on my website asking what people did to experience unconditional love in their lives, I received an email from a woman in New Jersey named Janet Pfeiffer. Janet wrote that as a result of going through certain events, she had learned to be not only a loving friend to herself but also a strong advocate for her own well-being. Intrigued, we contacted her. Janet turned out to be a lovely person—and a Love Luminary. Her story, which follows, is a beautiful illustration of how self-love and honoring your power go hand in hand.

Janet's Story
R-E-S-P-E-C-T

I'm one of those women who married her high school sweetheart. Can I help it that I met Prince Charming when I was fifteen? Then, thirteen years of marriage and four kids later, my prince left me for another woman. To say I was hurt only scratches the surface. Pain, rejection, feelings of betrayal, and anger swirled together into a bitter cloud that engulfed my life.

On top of that, money was a constant worry. As a stay-at-home mom with four kids, one of whom was in and out of the hospital, I couldn't get a job, so I ran a one-woman home improvement company from my house. Somehow, between child support from my ex and my wallpapering, painting, and other handyman-type work, I managed to scrape by. But money and love, especially for myself, were both in short supply.

About eight years after my divorce, I met a man I'll call Joe. We fell in love, and within five months, we were engaged. But as soon as that engagement ring went on my finger, something changed. Joe became very possessive and didn't like it when I spent time with anyone else. When I complained, he apologized, explaining that he loved me so much he wanted me all to himself. Part of me knew this was a red flag; the other part of me loved how romantic and sensitive he was. I thought, *Well, it's early in the relationship. It's natural that he wants us to spend all our free time together.*

But a few weeks later, things got ugly. Joe and I were walking on the boardwalk at Point Pleasant on the Jersey shore when we passed a vendor selling Belgian waffles and ice cream. The aroma was heavenly. I said, "Oh, that smells so delicious!"

Joe lit up. "Do you want one?"

"Nah," I said. "I don't care for soft ice cream."

To my surprise, Joe turned to me and yelled, "What the *#@% is wrong with you?" Then he grabbed my arm, flung me away from him, and stormed off. When he returned, we drove the two hours home in stony silence. He didn't explain what had set him off, and honestly, I was afraid to ask. But as soon as we reached home, he became extremely apologetic. He cried and begged for my forgiveness, telling me how much he loved me and that he hadn't meant to hurt me. Moved by his pleading, I accepted his apology.

But as the months went by, his physical abuse escalated. After each episode, he was filled with guilt and regret, saying over and over how much he loved me and how terrible he felt about his behavior. He was seeing a counselor and begged me to be patient. Seeing his sincere efforts to change, I decided that I would stick with him.

Joe wasn't always a monster. Most of the time, he was a very loving man who made me laugh and treated me well. I knew from the start that Joe had gone through a lot. He was a Vietnam War veteran and had been through a painful divorce. I always thought of him as a "tortured soul" and felt sorry for the hand life had dealt him.

There were spells where he was making progress and I was encouraged and happy. But then he'd backslide. Eventually I resorted to hiding knives in every room of my house and wearing a hammer tucked into the waistband of my pants, in case I had to protect myself from him. I didn't want to hurt him or, God forbid, kill him, but I wanted to be able to stop him if his anger became too fierce.

I never told my family or friends about our problem: I made excuses for my bruises and cuts. Joe was never violent around my children; he probably knew that would have been the last straw. I was ashamed of my situation and at the same time protective of my fiancé.

I had started seeing a therapist a few years earlier. When I first told her about Joe's abuse, she became concerned for my safety and tried hard to convince me to leave him. When she saw I wouldn't, she took another tack and recommended I take a three-month anger management course.

I signed up, thinking I was going to learn how to manage Joe's anger. To my amazement I discovered a huge reservoir of anger simmering inside myself! I realized I was furious with myself for the way I had allowed people to treat me my whole life. I had let them take advantage of me, exclude me, say cruel things to me—not to mention how I'd let Joe physically abuse me—and I'd never stood up to them. I'd kept all that pain hidden inside, and it had turned to anger and resentment.

One night our course leader, Eleanor, introduced our group to the concept of "personal boundaries" and our right as human beings to be treated the way *we* want to be treated. It was a thrilling concept: I didn't have to just accept what anybody threw at me. I could ask myself, *What's acceptable for me? What isn't?* I could ask to be treated with respect!

But I also wondered, *Can I do it?* I'd never had the confidence to stand up for myself to anyone.

At the end of the meeting, Eleanor gave us a homework assignment. "This isn't just a concept," she said. "I want you to go home and set boundaries with someone in your life who is mistreating you."

On the drive home, I mustered all my courage and formulated exactly what I would say to Joe. When I arrived home, I sat down on the couch and told him, "I don't like it when you hit me or put your hands on me in a rough way. That has to stop." Joe was agreeable. I thought, *Wow. That was easy. I aced that assignment!*

Back at class next week, we reported on the homework. I told the class how Joe had agreed not to hit me again. "Great! And then what happened?" Eleanor asked.

"Well, he was good for a couple of days but then got mad and hit me. But he apologized more quickly than usual, so that's okay."

Eleanor looked me straight in the eyes and said, "*No.* It's not okay. You failed to set consequences with him. You told him what you wanted, but what reason does he have for changing?"

So I went back home and this time I said, "If you lay your hands on me and hurt me again, I will call the police and have you arrested." His response? "I don't know what happened to you. You used to be nice."

I said, "No, I used to be a wimp. I'm not afraid of you anymore."

A few days later, when he got rough with me, I dialed 911. Joe got so furious, he ripped the phone off the wall, but not before I'd screamed "domestic violence" into the receiver and given the dispatcher my address. The cops appeared quickly and arrested him.

I felt elated. I'd done it. I'd stood up to him. Two weeks later, when the restraining order I'd requested had expired, Joe came over and thanked me profusely. He said it was great I'd been so strong. He thought my new approach would really help him get over his problem.

One more time, I let him back into my life.

But a few weeks later when Joe lost it and shoved me against a wall, I narrowed my eyes and told him firmly, "Get out of my house, Joe. And never come back!" He left, taking all his belongings with him. I changed the locks. It was truly and finally over. I never saw Joe again.

In the following days, weeks, and months, I paid close attention to all the choices I was making in my life. I became a lot more selective about what I chose to do and who I allowed into my life. In each situation I asked myself, *Is this going to be good for me in the short term* and *the long run? Or does it have the potential at any point to cause me harm?* If it was harmful, I didn't allow it into my life. It sounds so obvious now, but it was a huge breakthrough for me.

I knew many other women were still caught in the terrible trap I had finally escaped, so a few years after Joe left, I became a motivational speaker, specializing in anger management. I also started teaching the same material, along with self-esteem classes at a battered women's shelter near my home. Violence is a way of life for many of these women, usually because horrific abuse as children made them lose their regard for themselves. I teach them about self-love.

I tell them, "When you love yourself, you don't engage in violent behaviors or abusive relationships. You don't associate with drug addicts or alcoholics. You remove yourself from those situations. You give yourself only those things that are nurturing and supportive of a healthy lifestyle." And because I've been through what they're experiencing and come out the other side, they listen to me.

When I first started working at the shelter, one of the women said to me, "You know I could be your best friend, or I could be your worst enemy." She was trying to let me know how tough she was—a way of saying, "Don't mess with me." But I replied, "No, you couldn't." She looked at me in surprise. I continued, "If you have the potential to be my worst enemy, I would never permit you to be my best friend."

Because I love myself now, I give myself only what is best for me. The people in my circle these days are kind, supportive, and trustworthy. They have integrity. And my children are doing great. There are some family members with whom I have a difficult relationship but I limit the amount of time I spend with them. The amazing thing is that I'm able to be so much more loving to those people too. I don't allow myself to be bitter or resentful or jealous or hateful, because those feelings are bad for me. I've learned to be much more loving and sensitive to the imperfections of others, and to the personal struggles they're going through. My compassion for myself has given me compassion for others as well.

About thirteen years ago, I met a kind and good-hearted man and we got married. It's a happy, healthy relationship. I love it when he expresses his love for me, but I don't *need* it. I've built up my own inner reservoir of love, all by myself. I've learned that when there's plenty for me, there's always lots more to share.

Doormats and Dominators

Though Janet's story is dramatic, most of us can relate to at least some part of it; we unconsciously give away our power in subtle and not-so-subtle ways every day. The two most common methods of jettisoning your power are by becoming either a doormat or a dominator.

Doormats are passive; lacking the strength to create and hold appropriate boundaries, they're often mistreated or disrespected. Doormats blame other people for their discomfort and hurt, feel resentful, and spend a lot of energy telling and retelling their tales of woe to themselves and anyone who'll listen. They don't fully respect or love themselves.

You know you're a doormat if you have trouble saying no or shy away from saying what you truly want or need. Other signs are that you give in to what others want to do, even though you know it won't support you. Or you stay quiet for fear of rocking the boat.

Dominators, on the other hand, appear powerful but are actually needy. They try to control others to get the love they lack inside. They don't respect others' boundaries and can often be self-absorbed and clueless about how their actions affect other people. They so desperately want to feel love that they end up grasping, causing people to run away, only compounding their sense of being unloved.

You know you're a dominator if you compensate for your feelings of powerlessness by manipulating others, being dismissive or impatient, or not allowing others to have space for their own needs. You believe that your only chance of having the experience you want—connection, care, and love—comes from keeping a controlling hold on relationships or situations.

For doormats, honoring your power means setting healthy boundaries. When I interviewed Love Luminary Katherine Woodward Thomas, who wrote *Calling in "The One,"* she told me, "When we try to love others without loving ourselves, we have a tendency to abandon ourselves, putting other people's happiness before our own. We will often give at our own expense, which could then lead to resentment—quite the opposite of what we were hoping to offer another."

If you're a doormat, you may find the concept of boundaries a novel idea, as Janet did. Doormats get so used to being walked on that they may not realize they have the power to create boundaries. It's up to you to train others how to treat you. In chapter 8 you'll learn a communication technique that will help you to ask honestly for what you need, whether in romance, at work, or with family and friends.

When you feel you're being asked to concede too much, speak up before lots of emotional charge accumulates around a situation. If you don't set a necessary boundary, you may suddenly explode over it, causing conflicts—a doormat's nightmare—and unnecessary collateral damage. With early, clear action, it's possible to remove yourself gracefully from disempowering situations, without resentment or hostility.

Creating clear boundaries also inoculates you against responding in kind to other peoples' aggressiveness. Stanford University professor and author Bob Sutton recommends avoiding, if possible, demeaning, criticizing, and bullying people. He says, "Not only are you at great emotional risk, you're also at risk of emulating the behavior of the jerks around you, catching it like a disease." If you can't get away from the toxic offenders— you may be related to them or work with them and need your job—limit your exposure and stand your ground to get the respect you deserve.

Dominators abuse their power by trying to control others. If you're a dominator, honoring your true power requires going within and recognizing that the only power you truly have is to change yourself. You can't make *anyone* do *anything*—especially make them love you.

One strategy that works for me—yes, I admit I sometimes fall into the dominator category—is to recognize that when I start to go into control and manipulate mode," I'm actually feeling scared or needy. I've turned into Cootie Girl's evil twin.

My antidote is to go inside and with gentleness and compassion find a way to give myself what I really want and need. I share my feelings with the other person if it's appropriate, and then release my attachment to their response and behavior. I take responsibility for filling my own cup.

For doormats *and* dominators, honoring your power comes when you look inside and recognize that you're in charge of your own experience of love.

Man in the Mirror

Whether you're a doormat or a dominator, paying too much attention to what other people are doing is a codependent behavior that will inevitably rob you of power. Wrestling with another person's faults or obsessing over how your problems stem from someone else's actions only puts off doing the real work of owning your part of the problem.

Carol's spiritual teacher calls this getting distracted by the "scenery"— the nitty-gritty details of what happened and who did what to whom. Keeping your sights on the scenery is classic victim behavior. You forget that the power to change lies with you, the seer—the person watching and experiencing the scenery.

To change any behavior, the first step is awareness of the problem. Next time you start to get hooked into the drama, instead of whipping out your binoculars to get an even better view of the flora and fauna, ask yourself, *Am I focusing on the scenery or the seer?* Repeatedly switching your attention back to yourself and your own ability to choose a response will soon create a strong neural pathway for that behavior.

One of the most powerful techniques I use to stay out of the scenery is what I call my "Man in the Mirror" moment (à la Michael Jackson). Whenever I start to feel hurt or unhappy with how I'm being treated by someone, I hold up an imaginary mirror to myself and consider how I might be doing the same thing to others or to myself. For example, if I feel rejected by someone, I look to see how *I'm* rejecting *myself* or how I'm rejecting others. This immediately snaps me out of victim mode and softens my heart. Instead of stewing and griping, I'm able to feel love and compassion for myself and the people I may have been unconsciously rejecting.

Leaving Triggerland

Another widespread form of giving away your power is "getting your buttons pushed." You know how that goes: someone says or does something, and before you know what's happening, you're reacting, usually in a way that doesn't foster love one bit.

When I interviewed Love Luminary Dr. Kekuni Minton, a psychotherapist and coauthor of *Trauma and the Body*, he said that this knee-jerk emotional reactivity is triggered in the limbic brain, or what he likes to call our "horse brain," because horses are extremely reactive to what's going on around them. Your horse brain remembers all the little triggers that led to stress and suffering in the past. It constantly scans for similar signs in the present and causes your body to express unwarranted fear, anger, or stress at the drop of a hat. Not a recipe for Love for No Reason, but fortunately you can learn to defuse this tendency.

Dr. Minton says you can notice when your horse brain has started to take over. "Your body language gets defensive, your muscles get tense, and your thoughts get contracted, meaning they're fearful or judgmental." If you don't do something to rein in your horse brain, the next stop is "Triggerland"—where you react rather than simply respond.

When you realize your buttons are being pushed, pause instead and ask yourself if you're reacting from a past trigger. This stops the momentum of a runaway reaction. Then you can look from a calmer place at what's really there. Your boss's folded-arm stance doesn't necessarily mean that she's upset the way it did with your previous boss. She may just be listening to you. Or when your partner doesn't ask you how your day went—again—it may be because he or she is exhausted, not self-absorbed. It's not that things won't ever bother you again; it's that you won't react to them with the same drama, fear, and harshness.

Love Luminary and author Russell Bishop, the creator of Insight Seminars, one of the largest and most successful personal transformation programs in the world, tells the following anecdote about Buckminster Fuller, a visionary I've always admired for his genius at thinking outside the box.

As you'll see, in addition to his many other talents, Bucky had mastered the skill of responding rather than reacting:

> Back in the late seventies, I had the great privilege of seeing the legendary innovator Buckminster Fuller lecture in San Francisco. When he finished speaking, the audience was invited to engage in dialogue via open microphones around the auditorium.
>
> One gentleman took the mic and proceeded to tell Bucky that he was full of beans, didn't know what he was talking about, and had no basis for his point of view. Bucky paused for a moment, looked toward the speaker, and replied, "Thank you."
>
> As Bucky turned toward another person, the gentleman raised his voice and repeated his denunciation of Bucky and his thoughts, a bit more firmly. Again Bucky paused, looked squarely at the speaker, and replied, "Thank you."
>
> Once again, Bucky turned to another, and once again the gentleman raised his voice, repeated his diatribe, and offered quite a bit of angry energy to his comments, asking why he was being dismissed so summarily.
>
> This time Bucky responded something like this: "Did you not notice that I paused to consider what you had to say? I looked inside myself to see if some part of me was reacting to what you had said about me, particularly if some part of me were upset, prone to counterattack, or otherwise affected. I have found that when I am in that kind of reaction, there is typically something there for me to learn about myself, something for which I need to improve. In this instance, I found no reaction. Thus, you were simply sharing your opinion, to which you are fully entitled and with which I have no argument. Therefore, 'Thank you' seemed most appropriate."

Since then, Russell has tried to follow Bucky's example. He said that learning to see the reaction inside himself as feedback about himself, not feedback about the other person, has been a tremendously challenging yet uplifting experience in his life. "When I find myself irritated or offended, it can be of great value to simply ask myself, *How am I like that? What about the other person's behavior do I see in myself?*"

The more responsibility you learn to take for your own triggers, the more you'll experience that *you* are the one who determines whether your life is love-filled or love-deficient. You can decide whether to live in Triggerland or to respond thoughtfully and compassionately.

As you've seen, taking responsibility for your experiences of life and love starts with awareness. When you have a problem or difficulty, especially one that keeps coming up, it's important to ask yourself, *What I am doing here that isn't serving me, and why?*

When I was looking for an exercise for this key, I naturally turned to Love Luminary Jack Canfield, my mentor, who's been teaching people—including me—about self-empowerment for over three decades. Jack shared the following set of questions that will help you to get clear on how you're contributing to any lack of love you're experiencing in life and to come up with steps you can take to create something better.

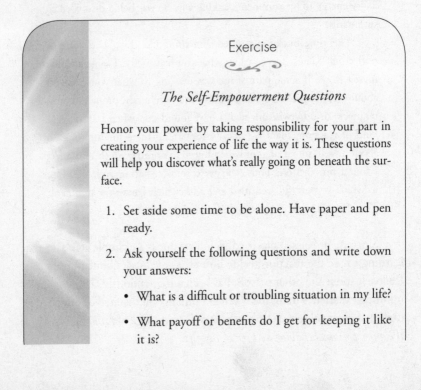

Exercise

The Self-Empowerment Questions

Honor your power by taking responsibility for your part in creating your experience of life the way it is. These questions will help you discover what's really going on beneath the surface.

1. Set aside some time to be alone. Have paper and pen ready.

2. Ask yourself the following questions and write down your answers:

   • What is a difficult or troubling situation in my life?

   • What payoff or benefits do I get for keeping it like it is?

- What costs do I pay for keeping it like it is?

- How am I creating or allowing it to be like it is?

- What am I pretending not to know?

- What do I want?

- What actions could I take and what requests could I make to get it?

- When will I do that?

3. Put the actions you came up with on your calendar and follow through. Or tell a trusted friend what you've committed to do and ask for their support in doing it.

Used by permission of Jack Canfield, www.JackCanfield.com

Summary and Love for No Reason Action Steps

Loving the unlovable in yourself and honoring your power are the keys that open the Doorway of Unconditional Self-Love. Use the following action steps to increase the flow of love through this energy center.

1. When you catch yourself being sharp and critical—or feeling overly clingy or needy—take a moment to ask yourself, *What is the most loving thing I can do for myself right now?* or *What is the most loving way I can be with myself right now?* Listen to and act on the answer. Notice how your inner critic softens when you give yourself a dose of compassion and self-care.

2. Give your "inner mean girl or guy" a name. The next time you feel picked on by your inner critic, address it by name,

ask it what positive purpose it's trying to serve, and incorporate any of its suggestions that feel useful.

3. Use the ABCs of self-love (Awareness, Being with, Compassion) to dissolve self-judgment.

4. Whenever you're having a hard time loving yourself, use the EFT technique and tap your way to greater self-acceptance.

5. Become aware of when you slip into doormat or dominator mode. If you're a doormat, start by writing down clear and concrete requests for what you want. Then move up to expressing them. If you're a dominator, go inside and find a way to give yourself what you really want and need. Share your feelings with the other person if appropriate, and let go of your attachment to their response.

6. The next time you get hooked into a drama, ask yourself, *Am I focusing on the scenery or the seer?* Use the "Man in the Mirror" moment to focus your attention back on yourself.

7. To honor your power and take responsibility for your experience of love, use the Self-Empowerment Questions exercise.

CHAPTER 7

The Doorway of Openness:
Living with an Open Heart

There is a light which shines beyond the world,
beyond everything, beyond all, beyond the highest heaven.
This is the light which shines within your heart.
—The Chandogya Upanishad

*A*hhhh. At last, we get to talk about the heart. Especially the warm, full, delicious experience of an open heart.

When Love Luminary Debra Poneman, my friend and first mentor (over thirty years ago), told me this story about her son Daniel, I was moved to tears:

When Daniel was thirteen, his entire eighth-grade class was scheduled to go on their big end-of-the-year trip to Washington, D.C. Daniel and his friends were really looking forward to it. The plane ride, the cool hotel with a swimming pool, and taking pictures with the girls on the Capitol Mall was all they talked about for weeks.

Two nights before the trip, I attended a parents' meeting where the travel itineraries were distributed and the hotel roommate assignments were announced. I listened to hear which of his friends Daniel would be rooming with and was confused when all the names had been announced except for his. As I was about to point out that he'd been left off the list, the teacher added, "Oh, and Daniel Poneman will be with Ricky (not his real name) and Ricky's aide."

My heart sank. Daniel's assigned roommates were an autistic boy and his aide, a man in his early thirties. My first thought was *Daniel's going to get left out of all the cool things that he and his buddies were planning. How am I going to break this news to him?*

I consider myself to be a loving and compassionate person, but this was a tough one for me. I was so afraid that Daniel would be disappointed. I was in mother-bear mode; I decided that if necessary I would call the school and see if we could work this out a different way.

When I got home after the meeting, I told Daniel about every other detail from the evening before I mustered the courage to share the roommate news. "Daniel," I said, "the roommates were also announced at the meeting. I want you to know that if you're really upset, I'll go to school tomorrow and try to get this changed: they put you in a room with Ricky and his aide."

He looked at me quizzically for a moment, not sure if I was kidding him, and then said simply, "Mom, they didn't *put* me with Ricky; I *asked* to be with Ricky. I knew if I wasn't with him, he'd get left out, and you know, Mom, it's *his* eighth-grade class trip too."

I looked at Daniel, my heart swelling to the bursting point. I had been proud of my son for many things in his life, but this was my proudest moment.

What makes one person, like Daniel, loving and giving—and another not? According to the world's spiritual traditions and the Love Luminaries, it's the openness of a person's heart.

The heart they're referring to can't be seen on an X-ray or MRI, but we feel its power. Our energetic heart is where we experience the energy of pure love.

When you live with an open heart, you effortlessly radiate love because the channel connecting you to the love at your core is unobstructed. You're able to give and receive love as freely and naturally as you breathe in and out. Kindness, compassion, forgiveness, and gratitude become second nature, and hostility, hurt, indifference, and loneliness dissolve.

The openness center is where the rubber meets the road for Love for No Reason. While the other six energy centers have to be healthy to keep your heart open, they're the supporting actors in this particular play. The heart, the star of the show, is where love is actually felt, received, and expressed. If the heart center isn't open, love simply can't flow.

Strengthening this center of the love-body paves the way for you to experience love in connection to others and the world. It's the path to true benevolence, heartfelt service, and healthy relationships.

To make sure the Doorway of Openness is flung wide, you have to clear away the blocks that shut down your heart.

Love Central

The openness center is traditionally called the fourth or heart chakra. Physically, this center influences your chest area, including the heart, lungs, ribs, and breasts, and radiates out to the shoulders, arms, and hands.

According to the yogic science of chakras, the heart center is also connected to the functioning of the thymus gland, the part of the immune system in the area of your sternum that makes pathogen-fighting T cells. When the heart chakra is closed or stressed, it can throw the thymus off, which makes you more vulnerable to infections, cancer, and chronic illness. If there were such a thing as an owner's manual for the heart, it would come with the warning: a closed heart can be hazardous to your health.

When I first heard about the heart center's connection to the arms and hands, I was surprised. But it actually makes perfect sense: we use the arms and hands to receive and express love—through hugging, touching, applauding, and by extending a helping hand to others. Love also flows out from our hearts into the world through our hands when we make something with them—be it a painting, a meal, a handwritten letter, or even a typed email.

My dad was a master of handmade expressions of love. As a dentist, he brought his whole heart to his work. Whether filling a cavity or fitting a crown, he always treated his patients with kindness and love. During World War II, he was stationed in the South Pacific. When he wasn't working as an Army dentist, he would pour his love into handcrafting gifts for my mother. One piece that he created was a beautiful heart-shaped neck-lace made of mother-of-pearl, set in gold with my mother's initials carved on the back. My mom adored that necklace and wore it throughout all their sixty-three years together. Now I wear that necklace and it continually reminds me to live with an open heart and to bring love to whatever I do.

As the fourth of the seven chakras, the heart center sits in the middle of the chakra system. It's seen as a meeting point or bridge: the place where the integration of mind and body, or spirit and matter, happens. It's where the earthly (the lower three chakras) and the divine (the upper three chakras) marry. When your heart chakra is open, life "comes together" for you. You can handle both the physical side of life (money, job, health) and the spiritual side (your life's purpose, wisdom, and connection to the divine), while still staying firmly anchored in the energy of love.

Achy-Breaky Hearts

At twenty-nine, when I had the worst case of an achy-breaky heart I've ever had, I was lucky to find my way to the office of Love Luminary Ali Najafi, a remarkable psychotherapist and holistic health practitioner. With Ali's masterful guidance I was able to heal my broken heart. So, of course, he was one of the first people I turned to when I began my study of unconditional love and the heart. In our interview, Ali told me that in his more than thirty years of doing healing work, he's found that the heart is the main place we register hurt and trauma—providing the pain-body with most of its food.

This is why intimate relationships can be so painful: when we open our hearts to each other, we also get in touch with our stored emotional pain, which surfaces in order to be healed. But sadly, most of the time we don't heal it. Instead we put up walls or throw on armor to avoid feeling our pain. We think this will also protect us from getting hurt in the future, but it only makes things worse. The result is this energy center gets blocked or locked up tight.

According to Love Luminary and renowned Ayurvedic doctor R. K. Mishra, this blockage in the heart center is the main source of our physical and emotional problems. When we spoke, Dr. Mishra explained that the heart center, which he calls the heart lotus, is a very sensitive energy junction point that opens and closes to varying degrees in response to our experiences, just as the lotus flower opens and closes with the passage of the sun.

The ancient Ayurvedic texts say that the soul comes into the body through the heart lotus. If it's open, Dr. Mishra says, "the light of the soul— you could say consciousness—is transmitted to the brain uninterrupted. Then the brain can receive the light of love, bliss, and wisdom." When this happens, you're healthy, vital, and able to experience pure unconditional love—Dr. Mishra's definition of true health. If the heart lotus is closed, your mind and body suffer and you can only experience conditional love.

Instead of using a stethoscope to listen to the physical heartbeat, Dr. Mishra "listens" to the subtler vibrations of the heart through the time-honored technique of pulse diagnosis. He said that when he first came to the United States almost twenty years ago and started treating American patients, he was shocked by how many of them had a closed heart lotus. He believes that the main culprits are relentless stress, dysfunctional families, widespread materialism, and the pervasive media violence in our society. He also blames too much time spent in front of computers, on cell phones, and around other sources of potentially damaging electromagnetic field (EMF) radiation.

Hearing this, I thought of the statistics about heart disease I'd read recently (now *these* are scary): 2,600 Americans die of cardiovascular disease every day—that's one every thirty-three seconds—and heart disease now surpasses breast cancer as the number one killer of women. It seems to me there's a connection between the closed state of our heart centers and this epidemic of heart disease: perhaps we're literally dying of broken hearts! Using the steps in this chapter to heal your heart is a powerful prescription for a healthy body and Higher Love.

Who's the Love Boss?

Carol and I were thrilled to interview Love Luminary James Doty, a neurosurgeon and the director of the newly formed Center for Compassion and Altruism Research and Education (CCARE) at Stanford University. We discussed the relationship between the brain and the heart and which is more important in our experience of love and compassion. For millennia, love and compassion have been ascribed to the heart, yet modern science has pooh-poohed this idea as more poetry than fact, contending that the brain alone dictates our experience of love. Many scientists view the heart as a physical and electrical pump with one essential job, to drive the circulation of blood and oxygen throughout the body.

But Dr. Doty told us a story that paints a different picture about the heart's role. He said that in one of the early compassion studies, famous brain researchers Dr. Francisco Varela and Dr. Richard Davidson worked with Tibetan monks who'd spent their lives cultivating compassion. When the scientists first administered the electroencephalograph (EEG) test to the monks, they wired them up in the normal way—placing electrodes on their scalps to measure the brain's electrical activity—and told them they were interested in studying compassion.

Hearing this, the monks started laughing. The researchers thought they were amused by the funny-looking wires protruding from their heads in every direction, like space-age fright wigs. But when the researchers asked what was so funny, the monks answered that they didn't understand why the scientists were putting the electrodes on their heads, when compassion is generated by the heart!

Yet modern science may be changing its view on this brain/heart conundrum. Dr. Doty told us, "I've had discussions with top scientists in my field who believe that the vagus nerve, a cranial nerve that connects the brain and the heart and controls a lot of the parasympathetic system's calming responses, may significantly affect love and compassion. It's interesting that stimulation of the vagus nerve can have an impact on depression. Why would that be? Maybe it *is* all about your heart."

We ended our conversation agreeing that the brain and the heart are *both* involved in our experience of love and compassion. But as new research shows, the role of the heart in emotional well-being, as well as mental and physical well-being, has been vastly underrecognized.

The Physiology of Love

The Institute of HeartMath in Boulder Creek, California, is one of the leaders in the field of heart intelligence. Since 1991 it has investigated how the heart and the brain communicate with each other and how this connection affects consciousness and our perceptions. As soon as I began writing this book, I knew I wanted to interview HeartMath's director of research, Love Luminary Dr. Rollin McCraty. Since the inception of the institute, Dr. McCraty has worked with founder Doc Childre (another

Love Luminary) to add the "math," or hard quantitative research, to the study of love and positive emotion, often thought of as a "soft science."

Dr. McCraty, along with the rest of the HeartMath research team, regularly collaborates with scientific, medical, and educational institutions such as Stanford University and Florida Heart Research Institute to advance the understanding that love is a measurable physiological state—not just a mood—that has positive physical and biological repercussions.

In our interview, Dr. McCraty told me about the research that's going on at HeartMath and how we can use their findings to improve the quality of our everyday lives. Here are some of the highlights I came away with from our discussion:

Heart Rhythm Coherence: Everyone knows it's important that the heart beats, but did you know it's important *how* it beats? When we're in a positive emotional state, our hearts beat in a coherent rhythm that causes all the other systems in the body—including the brain, the immune system, and our hormones—to work more efficiently and harmoniously.

This is called heart rhythm coherence, and it's our heart's optimal state of being. HeartMath research shows that regularly experiencing heart rhythm coherence leads to greater health and slower aging.

In contrast, negative emotional states like anger, fear, and sadness create chaotic heart rhythms (heart rhythm incoherence) that tax the body, causing it to work inefficiently and with unnecessary strain. This can lead to poor health, reduced resistance to disease, compromised brain function, and shorter lifespan.

But there's a caveat: you can't generate heart rhythm coherence by simply thinking about love or appreciation; you actually have to *feel* the love *in your heart* for your heart rhythms to sync up. More evidence that the monks may have a point and that feelings are more heart-based than brain-based.

Dr. Karl Pribram, considered by many to be the founder of modern cognitive neuroscience, was one of the first to suggest that the brain is primarily a pattern storage and recognition system—not the source of our feelings. The brain interprets the signals coming from the heart and the body and labels our emotions, but the actual feelings aren't generated there. It's like getting email: your computer receives the signals and then displays the message on your screen, but the computer doesn't generate the email; it was written and sent by someone else. Research suggests a similar relationship between the heart and the brain: the brain is simply relaying the messages of the heart.

The Heart's Effect on the Brain and Body: It's only been in the last two decades that research in the field of neurocardiology has established that the heart is a sensory organ and that a large portion of the heart is made up of information-carrying nerve cells sophisticated enough to qualify as a "heart brain." Dr. J. Andrew Armour first introduced the concept of a functional heart brain in 1991. Dr. Armour and his colleagues found that the heart's brain is a network of several types of neurons, neurotransmitters, proteins, and support cells like those found in the cranial brain. The heart brain's complex of circuitry gives it the ability to act independently from the larger brain—to learn, remember, and even feel and sense. And today, there's preliminary research showing that the heart independently secretes important neurotransmitters like catecholamines—hormones involved in the fight-or-flight response—and the love hormone oxytocin, a function long attributed only to the brain. This is significant because it means that we can use techniques that help create heart rhythm coherence to increase oxytocin in our system. (See the first exercise in this chapter.)

Messages flow back and forth between the heart and the brain all day long. Although we're accustomed to thinking of the brain as the CEO of our whole body-mind experience, this may not be the case. New research shows that, surprisingly, more information seems to flow from the heart to the brain than from the brain to the heart.

It turns out that the heart communicates to the brain in four major ways: neurologically (through the transmission of nerve impulses), biochemically (via hormones and neurotransmitters), biophysically (through pressure waves measured as our pulse), and energetically (through electromagnetic field interactions).

When the heart is beating in a coherent manner, it leads to better mental performance and more mental and emotional stability. It also activates the neocortex, the higher center of the brain that drives innovation, problem solving, and discernment.

However, when we experience stressful and negative emotions and our heart rhythms are incoherent, erratic, and uneven, we actually become less intelligent. When I interviewed Love Luminary Sheva Carr, a licensed HeartMath trainer and doctor of Oriental medicine, whose story you'll read later in this chapter, she explained it this way: "When people are experiencing worry or fear, they demonstrate a scientific phenomenon called *cortical inhibition*. It's what keeps Botox doctors in business. 'The furrowed brow syndrome'—part of your face's reaction to worry or anger—is more than just a crinkle in your forehead; the frontal lobes of the brain actually seize up and lose communication and blood flow." The opposite phenomenon, *cortical facilitation*—one of the perks of living in a state of Love for No Reason—is caused by positive emotional states and heart rhythm coherence.

The Heart's Effect on Others: The beating heart radiates an electromagnetic field outward from the body that can be detected at least three feet away, much farther than the brain's electromagnetic field. That heart field carries emotional information that others can feel and sense. It can even affect the heartbeats of those around you. In one study, Dr. McCraty looked at what happened to six longtime couples' hearts while they slept. Heart-rate monitors showed that during the night the couples' heart rhythms synchronized—rising and falling exactly in step.

In another case, this "two hearts beating as one" effect actually served as life support. When twin girls in Massachusetts were born three months prematurely, they were immediately put into separate incubators. One twin seemed to be stable, but the other wasn't expected to survive.

One day, the weaker twin was in distress—her heart rate was erratic and her breathing labored—but nothing the nurse on duty tried to do helped her. As a last resort, though it was against hospital policy, the nurse put the stronger twin in the same incubator with her sister.

The healthier twin immediately snuggled up to her sister and put her arm around her tiny body. Within seconds, the weaker twin's heart rate stabilized, her temperature normalized, and she began to breathe more easily. After that, the twins were kept together. The weaker twin's condition steadily improved until both girls, healthy and thriving, were able to go home with their parents.

As the twins' story demonstrates, electromagnetic communication between hearts means that when you're in a state of love and have more coherent heart rhythms, you're automatically helping the people around you have more coherent heart rhythms too. This is why you feel drawn to open-hearted people: you feel uplifted just by being near them. You'll find more on this entrainment effect—the phenomenon of people functioning in sync with each other—and its potential implications for the world in chapter 12.

This cutting-edge heart research shows that living in a state of love is not just a sentimental idea. It's a physiological state with tremendous ramifications for health and harmony, both inside and outside. Cultivating an open heart may be the greatest cardiovascular fitness program of all.

Unlocking the Doorway of Openness: The Two Love Keys

Open the window in the center of your chest, and let spirit fly in and out.

—Rumi, thirteenth-century Sufi poet

By its very design, the physical heart is made to give and to receive. It takes blood in from the body through one side and then pumps it out from the other, circulating it throughout the body. A healthy and open heart center does the same thing with love. It sends love out into the world and receives it in equal measure; it keeps love in circulation.

That's why to develop your openness center it's important to boost your capacity to both give and receive love. The two keys in this chapter will show you powerful methods for doing so.

The Love Keys for the Doorway of Openness

1. Give From Fullness
2. Let Love In

The Giving Key helps you remove the blocks to giving so that you can love others freely and fearlessly, without burning out and with no expectation of anything in return.

The Receiving Key invites you to practice opening the doorway of the heart to receive love without resistance whenever and however it comes your way.

> ## Love Key for Openness #1:
> # Give from Fullness

For true love is inexhaustible; the more you give, the more you have. And if you go to draw at the true fountainhead, the more water you draw, the more abundant is its flow.

—Antoine de Saint-Exupéry, twentieth-century French writer and aviator

In the last chapter you read about the importance of developing love for yourself through self-compassion, self-forgiveness, and self-acceptance. Now it's time to take your self-love out on the road and share it. When you give care and love freely to others, you enliven your own heart. In fact, whether it's through compassion, loving attention, or acts of kindness, giving is one of the most effective kick starts for opening the heart.

When you give in a healthy way, you tap into the ocean of love at your core. The more you practice giving from fullness—with your own love tank topped off—the quicker unconditional love becomes your default state.

Lean into Compassion

If we could read the secret history of our enemies, we should find in each life sorrow and suffering enough to disarm all hostility.

—Henry Wadsworth Longfellow, nineteenth-century American poet

I think of compassion as Love for No Reason brimming over: extending your heart's warmth and care to wherever it's needed in the moment, whether to another person or the world at large.

Compassion doesn't mean pity or feeling sorry for people. It doesn't mean becoming overwhelmed by others' pain or having to fix all their problems. Instead, compassion is both empathy—putting yourself in someone else's shoes—*and* the desire to alleviate another person's suffering.

Having lovingkindness and compassion toward others is the central pillar of every spiritual tradition in the world. You can see it expressed in the Judeo-Christian command to "Love thy neighbor as thyself," the Koran's emphasis on kindness and mercy, and the Hindu concern for the welfare of all creatures. Buddhists have practiced meditations that foster compassion for thousands of years.

Compassion meditation involves a repeated intention to feel boundless unconditional love for others. It not only cultivates a caring attitude and kind actions, it also creates lasting physical effects in the meditator's brain.

Dr. Richard Davidson, one of the scientists Dr. Doty mentioned earlier who wired up the Tibetan monks, is one of the foremost researchers in this field and has been studying the effects of meditation for many years. Working with the monks, he was one of the first to observe the distinct neural signature of compassion: increased activity in the left prefrontal cortex, the insula, and the temporal parietal juncture—which are all related to love, empathy, and other positive emotions—and a spike in the production of gamma waves. But even more exciting was the discovery that the monks, who had spent countless hours in compassionate brain states, had the same high level of brain functioning even when they weren't meditating. Dr. Davidson said, "The cultivation of compassion actually leads to measurable changes in the brain. This positive state is a skill that can be trained."

When I interviewed Love Luminary Dr. Rick Hanson, the neuropsychologist you met in chapter 4, he pointed out another interesting finding from the compassion meditation studies. When the monks were in a state of compassion, researchers noticed that the motor circuits of their brains—the parts of the brain that enable them to get up and go—were also activated, even though the monks were lying down inside an MRI with their eyes closed. This indicates that the impulse to act, serve, and help is embedded in the experience of compassion. Rick said, "That's why when you feel this unconditional love, you want to help. You're already leaning forward, leaning into love." There's strong evidence that feeling compassion in our hearts leads to compassionate action.

Altruism and Acts of Kindness

Three things in human life are important: the first is to be kind, the second is to be kind, and the third is to be kind.

—Henry James, twentieth-century writer

Leaning into compassion through altruism and acts of kindness is a powerful way to turbocharge the love engine of your heart.

Love Luminary Bob Votruba has taken the concept of acts of kindness and run with it. In 2009 he sold everything he owned—car, business, and house—and bought a school bus that he travels around the country in with his dog, Bogart, on a special mission. Everywhere he goes, he asks people to commit to doing a million acts of kindness in their lifetime. Bob's inspiration is a simple mathematical formula: if each person does fifty acts of kindness a day, in fifty-five years they'll have done over a million acts of kindness.

Bob defines acts of kindness as the small things we do for one another: holding the door for someone, saying "good morning," smiling, letting the other car go before you in traffic. But it also means simply feeling kindness toward others from your heart: wishing all the best for every person you come in contact with or think of during the day. Bob told me, "If you combine feeling kindness from the heart with the physical deeds of kindness that you do, a million kind acts over the course of a lifetime is a totally reachable goal."

While Bob's campaign has been especially well received on college campuses, he's also finding that people of all ages—even baby boomers, who will have to work double-time to make the million mark—are enthusiastic about committing to kindness. Turning our kind intentions into a concrete goal helps us act on them more regularly.

And being kind and giving is a healthy habit to develop. According to research, giving is really good for our bodies: it increases our immune function, reduces physical pain, provides relief from asthma and insomnia— and even helps us lose weight.

You can't start too soon. When I interviewed Love Luminary and entrepreneur Brian Hilliard, he told me that his desire to help the homeless began when he was a child back in Portland, Oregon. Brian and his mother often drove across town to visit his grandmother, and their route took them right through Skid Row, where all the homeless people lived. Brian said that when he was about six years old, whenever his mother stopped at a stop sign, he began opening the rear car door and inviting the homeless men into the car with him. More than once, one of them got in and Brian's mother gave him a ride to wherever he wanted to go. This freaked Brian's mother out, but Brian couldn't resist doing it. Even at that age, he felt a deep compassion and empathy for people living on the streets. Today Brian spends many hours each week being a friend and support to the homeless people in his local area. His boundless energy, clear eyes, and shining face are all indications that his giving has been good for him as well.

It's been shown that when people give as a teenager, they reap positive physical and emotional health benefits even as much as *fifty years later.* And giving helps you live longer: researchers at the University of California at Berkeley tracked two thousand individuals over age fifty-five for five years. Those who volunteered for two or more organizations had a 44 percent lower likelihood of dying during that period. Volunteering has also been shown to lower rates of depression and prevent heart disease.

Another well-documented side benefit of being a giver is the "helper's high," which comes from the release of endorphins and other feel-good neurotransmitters in our bodies. Love Luminary Dr. Stephen G. Post told me, "There's a neurology, immunology, and endocrinology of generous emotion that's tremendously important—and profoundly healing. So while it's good for those to whom we contribute, giving is also a wonderful way for us to live our lives."

Dr. Post would know. He established the Institute for Research on

Unlimited Love in 2001, with support from the philanthropist Sir John Templeton's foundation, to fund research on the science of altruistic love. To date, the institute has underwritten studies at more than eighty universities. The bottom line of all the findings: it's good to be good! There's a strong connection between being a giving person and living a happy, healthy life.

Loving Attention

You don't need a special occasion to give. You can give any time, any place. The person you're giving to doesn't even have to know that you're giving to them. Simply directing your caring attention to others is an act of love.

While writing this chapter with me, Carol did a fun experiment to ramp up her loving attention:

> My morning bike ride always takes me past a stream of walkers, runners, and other bicyclists. I'm a naturally friendly person, and I like to smile and say good morning to everyone I pass. But sometimes I feel quiet or don't want to interrupt someone else's reverie, so I also make a point to "beam love" at the people I meet, whether I greet them physically or not. Some people smile and others don't respond at all. (Though it's interesting that 99 percent of the dogs I encounter seem to be able to feel my love beam. They always turn to look at me with interest.)
>
> One day, after having just read the research about the health benefits of hugging, I decided to turn it up a notch. Instead of just beaming love, I gave each person I passed a "mental hug." I imagined taking each person, old, young, man or woman, in my arms and giving them a warm, sincere embrace. The experience was amazing. I could feel the energy in my body become stronger, brighter, and more loving each time I did it.

The heart-opening power of mental hugs is based on two simple facts:

1. **The act of hugging is good for you.** Studies show that if you hug someone for six seconds or more, your body produces mood-

lifting chemicals that promote bonding with others, like oxytocin and serotonin. Hugging also lowers your blood pressure, gives your immune system a boost, and can diminish your experience of physical pain.

2. **Visualizing a physical action can give you many of the same benefits as the real thing.** When we *imagine* doing something, the same centers in the brain are activated as when we physically *do* the action. In imagined hugs, the reward centers are busy distributing feel-good chemistry to your cells, and the insula—a part of the brain that relates to embodied experience—is also activated. You can enjoy the same juicy feeling in your cells that you'd get from actually hugging the person.

Based on the HeartMath research about the power of the heart's electromagnetic field, we know that sending mental hugs is good for the huggees too: they're walking (or bicycling) right through your positively charged heart field. When you give mental hugs, love does the happy dance! So you can understand why Carol is as high as a kite by the time she finishes her morning rides.

Fill 'Er Up!

How heavy the empty heart; how light the heart that's full.
—Singer/songwriter Beth Nielsen Chapman

Have you ever tried to give when you were "running on empty"? If so, you probably found yourself slipping into the martyr/codependent zone. Though your intentions may be good, when you try to give more than you have, you end up burning out, and ultimately, no one wins.

Giving from fullness is like living within your means; it keeps you from getting strung out and overcommitted. As you experience Love for No Reason more of the time, your ability to give expands.

Love Luminary Sheva Carr has walked the path from running on empty to giving from fullness. Twenty years ago she traveled to war-torn Nicaragua to help, carrying what she calls "the flaming torch of idealism." Though she was just a teenager, she already knew that giving to others was a goal dear to her heart.

The following story from my interview with Sheva touched me very deeply. It shows the powerful influence we have on each other when we care. Hearing it reminded me of something my first spiritual teacher, Maharishi Mahesh Yogi, once said that has stayed with me for over thirty years, "No drop of precious love is ever wasted."

Sheva's Story
Every Drop of Love Is Precious

*W*hen I stepped off the plane in Nicaragua, I might as well have been wearing a superhero's cape, I had such an all-consuming desire to "make a difference in the world." A nineteen-year-old exchange student from Nova Scotia, I had come to work with a Nicaraguan theater company to promote literacy in the capital city of Managua.

But my plans changed when I fell madly in love with the street children. I ended up giving all my time and energy—and the prized American dollars I'd brought with me—to many of the amazing kids who were living and dying on Nicaragua's streets.

It was 1989. Nicaragua was, and still is, one of the poorest countries in the Western Hemisphere, second only to Haiti. At first I'd been shocked and appalled by the poverty, the rough shacks, the lack of sanitation, and the sheer volume of children who lived in the streets—some with their families, and others on their own. By that time, the Nicaraguan civil war had been raging for over nine years and had left more than 600,000 children homeless or orphaned. The squalor the children lived in was heartbreaking, but once I started meeting them, my heart was captured by the bright, unquenchable spirit that shone in them.

This joy seemed so at odds with their poverty, but as I got to know the children I saw that although they had nothing, they loved everything. When I sat to eat with them, they'd take my plate, which in my mind had been licked clean, and make another meal of the bones. Life itself seemed luscious to them.

Though I was enchanted by many of the children I met during my stay, there were three who stood out: Ana Raquel, Julio, and Jorge. I met Ana Raquel first.

One afternoon soon after I'd arrived, I was eating in a restaurant when a nine-year-old girl came to my table and asked me if I had a pen I could give her. Having heard that Nicaraguan kids must provide their own supplies to get into school, I had brought a big bag of pens with me. When I pulled the bag out, her face lit up. But the pens, which had worked fine back in Canada, wouldn't write!

This didn't deter Ana Raquel one bit. Within seconds, she had an assembly line of five-year-olds pulling the pens apart, sucking on the ink tubes, and putting them back together. A short while later, I had a bag of perfectly functioning pens, and I handed one to Ana Raquel and each of her young assistants, to their great delight.

Ana Raquel and her older brother, Julio, who was twelve, lived with their mother and stepfather, and five half brothers and sisters. As the oldest children, she and Julio had the responsibility of helping to feed their half siblings by selling candy and cigarettes on the street. Like many Nicaraguans at that time, this family of nine lived in a shantytown of corrugated tin shacks.

I met Jorge not long after, when a young boy of twelve approached me shyly, asking if I would buy his peanuts. I began to chat with him and learned that he had no family at all. His mother had been a prostitute and had abandoned him as a baby to be raised in the street by other, older children. Later he'd been fed by restaurateurs in exchange for hard work. Jorge had taught himself to read and write on his own, getting textbooks out of garbage cans and pencil nibs from the street. Now he was trying to make enough money to go to school (which included paying for a uniform, books, and supplies as well as tuition) by selling peanuts. What could I do? I bought his whole inventory of peanuts on the spot.

And so began my crusade to help these three children and many more. I bought them school supplies, necessities, and medicine, spending my limited store of money, a small inheritance from my grandfather I'd used to fund my trip. My work wasn't sustainable, I knew, but I was passionate, on purpose, and I felt nothing would stop me.

I gave my new friends all the love and support I could. Day after day, I bounced through the dusty streets with the dozens of little ones who flocked to my side, a gregarious red-haired *gringa* helping them to sell their wares and put food in their bellies while they put joy in my heart. I was like the pied piper of Managua, being joined by more and more children along the way.

My love for the children overrode my fear for my own safety and well-being. With the sound of machine-gun fire nearby, I tolerated the increasing threats to my safety longer than I should have. The situation in Nicaragua was deteriorating quickly, making it risky for foreigners to stay. With my pale complexion and red hair, there was no way for me to keep a low profile. I was like an unripe fruit in a land of warm, sun-sizzled skin.

Then, one afternoon, I was kidnapped at gunpoint for twelve hours and almost raped by a man who claimed he was a government official. Although I eventually convinced him to let me go, I could no longer deny the very real danger I was in. The country was a full-fledged war zone, and I was a neon-lit target.

And so, six weeks after I'd arrived, I was forced to leave the country—and with it, my children.

The day I had to go was devastating. I was filled with despair, knowing that I would probably never see these children who meant so much to me again. Corrugated tin shacks and gutters don't have mailing addresses or telephone numbers. Good-bye was good-bye. Forever.

I gave the children slips of paper with my Canadian contact information written in clear block letters, but I had little hope that they would be able to hold on to them for long. What was worse, I knew I was leaving them to a future of economic embargo, infections, crime, prostitution, and war in a country also repeatedly devastated by hurricanes and earthquakes.

How do you say good-bye under such conditions? As I was leaving, I handed the children packets of unmarked sunflower seeds, and told them to plant the seeds where there was plenty of sunlight, and bring them water every day. I said, "Each time you water your seeds, I want you to remember that I am caring for you from far away, even though we may never see each other again. Remember, you have to take care of the seeds if you want to see what they grow into, and you have to take care of yourself the same way."

Back in Canada, I felt like a total failure. It seemed to me that I hadn't been able to do anything that had made a real and lasting difference in the lives of the children I'd left behind. My love for them turned into agony as I alternated between feeling "survivors' guilt" and beating myself up for leaving.

Sick at heart, I collapsed onto my parents' couch for months. I was rushed to the hospital on more than one occasion with seizures and pain. The doctors tried to find the root of my tropical mystery illness but failed. I became severely arthritic and went into menopause at age twenty.

Time passed as I strived to heal my failing body and broken heart, learning to function within my painful limitations. I began studying medicine, both Western and alternative modalities, including acupuncture, herbal medicine, and polarity therapy. I wanted to learn all there was to know about healing in the hope that I could one day restore myself to full health and then share that knowledge with others.

During this time, by some miracle, I was able to stay in touch with Jorge through a church group doing charity work in Managua. Through them, we exchanged letters and I sent him money and gifts, including a Swiss Army knife engraved with his initials for his thirteenth birthday—his first birthday gift ever. In the letters, I told Jorge I loved him and wanted him to be happy and well. We corresponded this way for six years but then lost touch.

In 1995 my medical studies led me to a class at a stress-management research institute in northern California called the Institute of HeartMath. The teacher, a man named Robert, radiated palpable peace. *Whatever this dude has ordered from the cosmic kitchen,* I thought, *I want some!*

I got so excited about the work they were doing that I showed up on HeartMath's doorstep on my spring break and volunteered to help.

They put me to work transcribing all their research. With my medical background, it was perfect. I sat at the computer, my jaw dropping in amazement as I typed. All the symptoms I'd been struggling with for the last eight years were explained succinctly and concretely by HeartMath's research.

The explanation? Stress. While doctors looked for brain parasites, tropical viruses, and bacteria, they'd ignored my experiences in the war zone: machine-gun fire, being kidnapped, and most significantly of all, abandoning the children I had come to love so dearly. It never occurred to anyone that my symptoms could be explained by emotional stress causing erratic heart rhythms, which were throwing everything else in my body out of balance.

My friends at HeartMath showed me that the first step to recovery was to transform my guilt over leaving the children into gratitude for having known them at all. My care for the children had gone off the rails and turned into "overcare." Being in a state of distress and guilt to the point of illness wasn't love—it was a distortion of love. To heal myself I had to reconnect with the true and healthy love underlying the distortion. At HeartMath, they taught me some effective, simple techniques to do this.

At first I didn't notice many changes in my health from using these techniques. But two weeks was the tipping point. After fourteen days of turning my guilt and grief into daily meditations of appreciation and love, all my physical symptoms reversed—quite literally overnight—and they have never returned. Finally healthy and freed from the burden of overcare, my life began to flourish.

Twelve years after leaving Nicaragua, I was living in Santa Monica, California. One day the phone in my apartment rang. When I answered, a man's voice asked me, "Do you remember Julio, Ana Raquel, and Jorge?"

After a moment of stunned silence, I burst into tears. "*Remember them?* Of course I remember them!"

The man said, "Would you like to talk to Ana Raquel?"

Before I could answer, she was on the line, and we were laughing and crying, both of us trying to talk at the same time. They had tracked me down via an internet search! Somehow they'd managed to keep the little slips of paper with my name and my phone number for all those years even while they'd been living on Nicaragua's streets.

Jorge, by then a grown man of twenty-five, had used the money I'd sent him to go to high school and college, eventually becoming a psychologist. He told me he was the director of an orphanage that housed thirty children. He was married and had given his first daughter the same middle name as mine: Christina.

A year later, I took a trip to Nicaragua to see my "street kids" again. Jorge greeted me at the border. I threw myself into his arms and we hugged each other for a long time, me crying for joy, Jorge grinning from ear to ear. After our initial excitement, Jorge bought a mango from a street vendor for us to share. Then he pulled a Swiss Army knife out of his pocket to cut the fruit and I recognized it at once. It was the knife I'd given him thirteen years before. When Jorge saw me looking at the knife, he stopped peeling the fruit.

"Chevita," he said, "there were so many times when I was tempted to go into drugs, crime, or prostitution to get food to survive, but then I'd think of this knife in my pocket, and the beautiful flowers that had grown from the seeds you gave me, and I'd tell myself, 'No! I have a mother in Canada, a mother who cares about me, and someday I'm going to find her again and make her proud of me.'"

I couldn't speak. I could only shake my head in disbelief, the tears streaming down my cheeks once more.

I now understand that every act of care, every act of love has an impact and generates a ripple effect far beyond what we know. We don't always get to see the result, but if we're wise, we give whatever we can and know that's enough. Because however much we may want to be superheroes, able to solve all problems in a flash, in reality we're humans, able to give whatever we can and take great joy in the giving. That is the true gift of love, for those we care for, and for ourselves.

♥　　♥　　♥

How often do you take giving love for granted, without considering the impact you may be having? Over and over I heard from the Love Luminaries about the extraordinary life-changing power of giving love—

in any and all amounts. When you remember this, you begin to look for more opportunities in your everyday life to express your appreciation, to be a little kinder than you might otherwise be, and to do what you can to help, whatever it is.

Heart Overboard: When Care Turns into Overcare

The Sun Never Says

Even after all this time
The sun never says to the earth,
"You owe me."

Look what happens with
A love like that,
It lights the Whole Sky.

—Hafiz, fourteenth-century mystic poet

As Sheva learned, genuine care can easily turn into overcare if you don't pay attention to your own well-being. Here are three easy ways to make sure you don't fall into the trap of overcare:

1. **Let go of being attached to a specific result:** When you're not attached to a particular outcome, you give freely and it's more enjoyable and energizing. Whenever I give, I remind myself of a helpful formula I once learned: "High intention, low attachment." Give with enthusiasm and let the universe take care of the results.
2. **Don't expect anything in return:** Dr. Stephen Post told me he learned a valuable lesson from the champions of compassion he's interviewed over the years. "We can get hung up on keeping score of reciprocal responses, and that really limits us. It keeps us from being free to love in a way that is uncalculating. We just need to do what a mother I once interviewed tells her son to do, 'Love, and forget about it.'"
3. **Make sure that your giving does not stress, drain, or weaken you:** Healthy giving makes you feel good. Unhealthy giving, when

you're giving too much to others, will push you out of heart rhythm coherence and, over time, will take you from overcare to no care. The symptoms of no care, according to the Institute of HeartMath, are burnout, depression, resignation, or cynicism. Paying attention to the signals your body is sending will help you to recognize and reverse these symptoms before they take their toll on you.

When good intentions are taken too far, they get in the way of the good you're trying to do. But when caring overflows from unconditional love, it keeps you in the healthy giving zone.

I'm Sorry. Please Forgive Me. Thank You. I Love You.

The holiest place on earth is where an ancient hatred has become a present love.

—*A Course in Miracles*

Another trigger that puts the heart into hibernation is feeling hurt by others. When we feel wounded, we withdraw and put up defenses against being hurt again. This blocks the heart and shuts down giving (and receiving), sometimes for a long, long time.

Almost everyone has a wound they're holding on to from the past and someone they haven't fully forgiven. No matter what the magnitude of the "wrong" we feel, in order to *give* freely, we have to *for-give* first.

Nelson Mandela, who spent twenty-seven years in prison, is my inspiration for forgiveness. I've heard the story told of how he decided to love his jailors because he knew that if he didn't find a way to love someone or something, the imprisonment would kill his spirit. Mandela practiced forgiving his guards, even those who were cruel to him. This had a profound effect on both Mandela and his guards. The guards kept having to be replaced, because Mandela's love softened their hearts too much and sapped their toughness. One of his former guards even sat in the first row at Mandela's inauguration as South Africa's first black president.

I've never faced a challenge of that magnitude, but cultivating forgiveness has helped me in situations in my life, both large and small. It doesn't matter who's at fault; holding on to resentment only hurts me by shutting down my heart. Forgiving someone is easier when I remember that it doesn't mean I'm condoning their behavior. It means I'm letting go of my resentment, which frees me to feel love and compassion, no matter how they behave.

A number of years ago, I learned a simple technique called Ho'oponopono, an ancient Hawaiian kahuna practice of reconciliation and forgiveness. The technique consists of sitting quietly and mentally repeating, *I'm sorry. Please forgive me. Thank you. I love you*, over and over. It's based on the principle of taking total responsibility for everything that happens to you. It doesn't matter whether you are the injured party or the person who did the injuring; when you shift your own energy, it shifts the energy of the relationship. Ho'oponopono allows you to bring the vibration of pure forgiveness into any situation.

Love Luminary Joe Vitale, the author of many best-selling books, including *Zero Limits: The Secret Hawaiian System for Wealth, Health, Peace, and More*, which he wrote with Dr. Ihaleakala Hew Len, master teacher of modern Ho'oponopono, has brought this ancient system of healing to the attention of millions of people. When I asked him how it worked, he said, "Ho'oponopono works on the inside of you to create a change in the outer world that you perceive. These four sentences clear out unconsciously accepted beliefs, thoughts, and memories that you don't even know are holding you back, and return you to a state of love—which is the natural state of the Divine and of the world."

While writing this book, I had a perfect opportunity to use Ho'oponopono. A very dear friend of mine I'll call Tracy had gotten mad at me for something and had stopped talking to me. I was feeling indignant; I didn't think I'd done anything wrong and I felt I was being misunderstood and mistreated. After a few months of getting the "silent treatment," I was scheduled to get together with a group of friends to move one of them into her new apartment, and Tracy was going to be there. I was worried that the silence between us would be really uncomfortable as we worked together in the small apartment, unpacking our friend's things. But I was *not* going to be the one to break the ice. After all, I thought I was the one being "wronged" by her treatment of me.

Sure enough, we got off to an awkward start that day. After two hours, both of us were still being silent ice queens, so I left for a few minutes to go sit in my car, feeling angry, hurt, and discouraged. But Mandela's story popped into my mind and I thought, *If he could love and forgive in the face of prison and beatings, I can certainly love and forgive in this situation.*

So I sat in my car and practiced Ho'oponopono, sending forgiveness and love to the whole situation. After about fifteen minutes of this, my heart softened, and I realized that Tracy wasn't just mad at me for what had happened a few months earlier; I could also see ways in which I'd caused her pain over the years of our friendship. I felt deep compassion for her and my resentment dissolved.

I went back into the apartment feeling openness and warmth. Within two minutes of my return, Tracy came over to me out of the blue and said, "Let's go unpack the boxes in the kitchen together." I was shocked; I hadn't said anything to her and yet she was treating me as though there hadn't been a problem. A little while later at lunch, she offered me her fresh mango slices, which I knew she adored, and said, "Marci, I know you like these, so have mine." The change in energy was like night and day.

Later I pulled aside another friend, who'd witnessed the whole thing, and asked her what she'd said to Tracy while I was gone to change her behavior. She said, "Marci, nobody said anything to Tracy. What did you do?"

Forgiveness unblocked both of our hearts and let us give again.

And thank goodness that happened. The friend we had helped move passed away in a tragic car accident less than a year after that incident. Once again Tracy and I were back at our friend's apartment—only this time we were clearing out those same kitchen cabinets that we'd set up together. I hate to think what it would have been like if I'd held on to my anger and resentment. Life's too short to keep our hearts closed.

In the last decade, a lot of research has been done on the ways forgiveness affects our health. It reduces chronic pain, lowers blood pressure and heart rate, cuts the risk of alcohol and drug abuse, and alleviates symptoms of anxiety and depression.

When you hold a grudge or nurse resentment or blame, you place painful limits on your heart's capacity to love. Forgiveness frees you from those limits and allows you to give to others.

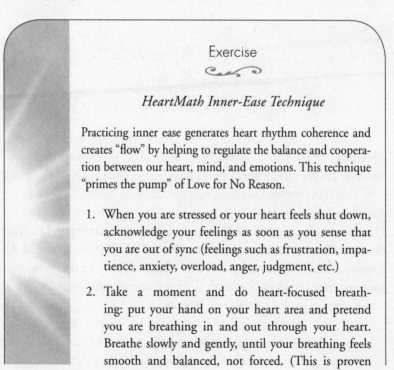

Giving love is a big part of our job description (Love Theme #2). In fact, many consider it our highest and best legacy to the world—including Love Luminary Beth Nielsen Chapman, Grammy-nominated singer and songwriter who Carol and I were delighted to be able to interview. She told us that love—in all its forms—is the main source of her creative inspiration. The last lines of her song "How We Love" sum up perfectly my thoughts about giving: *"All that matters when we're gone / All that mattered all along / All we have that carries on / Is how we love."*

The following exercise is a great way to keep your heart "in shape" for healthy giving.

Exercise

HeartMath Inner-Ease Technique

Practicing inner ease generates heart rhythm coherence and creates "flow" by helping to regulate the balance and cooperation between our heart, mind, and emotions. This technique "primes the pump" of Love for No Reason.

1. When you are stressed or your heart feels shut down, acknowledge your feelings as soon as you sense that you are out of sync (feelings such as frustration, impatience, anxiety, overload, anger, judgment, etc.)

2. Take a moment and do heart-focused breathing: put your hand on your heart area and pretend you are breathing in and out through your heart. Breathe slowly and gently, until your breathing feels smooth and balanced, not forced. (This is proven

to help create coherent wave patterns in your heart rhythm.)

3. During the heart-focused breathing, imagine with each breath that you are drawing in a feeling of inner ease and infusing your mind and emotions with balance and self-love from your heart. (Research from the Institute of HeartMath has shown that radiating love and self-care through your system activates beneficial hormones and boosts your immunity.)

4. When the stressful feelings have calmed, affirm with a heartfelt commitment that you want to anchor and maintain the state of ease as you re-engage in your projects, challenges, or daily interactions.

Used by permission of the Institute of HeartMath, www.heartmath.org

Love Key for Openness #2:
Let Love In

Do you remember the song "Let the Sunshine In" from the sixties rock musical *Hair*? (Am I giving away my age?) The chorus plays in my mind whenever I think about the idea of letting love in. Letting love into your heart is as essential as letting sunlight into your home. Without it, life is dark and dreary.

I spoke at an event not long ago where I shared the stage with Dr. Brian Weiss, the Yale-trained physician and author of *Many Lives, Many Masters*. During his talk, he shared the following anecdote about receiving love that he'd heard from Dr. Elisabeth Kübler-Ross, the great psychiatrist best known for her study of death and dying:

Elisabeth, who was a professor at the University of Chicago and a brilliant woman, once told me a story about her mother. One summer,

Elisabeth took a vacation back to her native Switzerland to visit her aging but still healthy mother, Emmy. Emmy, a vigorous, outdoorsy person, was a very loving and giving woman, unselfish, perhaps to a fault. She would give anyone anything—but would never accept anything in return. She was a completely independent woman.

On that particular visit, Emmy took Elisabeth aside and said, "Elisabeth, if I ever become a vegetable, please give me something to put me out of my misery."

Elisabeth was taken aback. "Mother, I can't do that."

Her mother pressed her, "Yes, you can. You're my only daughter who's a physician. You can give me something."

Elisabeth shook her head, "No, I can't. But don't worry, it's not going to happen. Strong women like you live to be a hundred. They don't go like that."

But it seemed her mother was having a premonition, because a month after Elisabeth returned to Chicago, Emmy had a massive stroke. Though she still had her mind, she lost motor function, becoming what she considered "a vegetable." She had to be fed, taken to the bathroom, and bathed by nurses, friends, aides, and family.

This was terribly difficult for the independent Emmy. She hated having to rely on other people to attend to all her physical needs. Emmy lived this way—without regaining significant function—for four years, and then passed away.

Elisabeth had been deeply distressed by her mother's incapacitation and saddened at her death. One afternoon, soon after her mother's death, Elisabeth sat down to meditate. As she closed her eyes and settled down, she was suddenly rocked by a strong voice inside her head. Elisabeth wasn't one to hear voices, but she said this cosmic voice shook her whole body, asking, "Elisabeth! Why are you so angry at me?"

She answered the voice in her mind. "Because my mother—my beautiful, caring mother—who gave everything and didn't ask for anything in return, lived four years in that miserable, helpless condition before she died. It makes no sense to me!"

The voice answered her back, "Those four years were a gift to your mother—a gift of grace—because love must be balanced. Elisabeth, if nobody were to receive love, who could give it?"

Emmy hadn't been able to receive love, and in those four years, she had learned how. Understanding this, Elisabeth was able to let go of her anger over her mother's fate.

Receiving from others is an act of love and connection that opens your heart—and benefits your body too. Research shows that when you receive, your levels of serotonin—the neurotransmitter of well-being and happiness—rise just as much as when you give. To receive, you have to let down your shield and any protective armor that might stop the free flow of love.

Tear Down the Walls

As you read in chapter 6, one of the main blocks to receiving love is feeling unworthy. But there are other blocks to letting love in—especially our limiting beliefs and fears.

Most of us believe what we were taught as kids: it's better to give than to receive. So we shy away from receiving because we don't want to seem self-centered or selfish.

This widespread, mostly unconscious belief needs to be adjusted. Yes, it's good to give, but that doesn't mean you shouldn't receive. (After all, the givers have to give to somebody!) It's not an either/or equation. People with open hearts can give and receive equally well.

Fear is another huge block to receiving. You may be afraid of being burdened with a sense of obligation or having to give something back. Or perhaps, like Emmy, you're afraid of becoming dependent or appearing weak or needy.

To break the grip of your underlying beliefs and fears, you have to first become aware of them. This awareness creates more breathing space for you to make different choices.

Singer Melissa Etheridge is a shining example of the power of receiving. I've enjoyed Melissa's music for years, so I was thrilled when I had a chance to hear her speak last year at the inaugural meeting for the Global Alliance for Transformational Entertainment. In between performing a few beautiful songs, Melissa recounted the following story, and I knew I had to interview her for this book. She is clearly a Love Luminary who lives the message of Love for No Reason.

During our interview, Melissa had me hanging on every word—I had "God bumps" (my term for goose bumps that are divinely inspired)—as she told about her "hero's journey" of waking up to love. I'm as inspired by her life as I am by her music.

Melissa's Story
Fearless Love

Some of us are looking for that lightning bolt of awakening— *ta-da!*—where one minute we're asleep and the next we're fully awake, but it doesn't always work like that. My awakening was a journey; it didn't happen in one moment. It took time—months and months of breaking through my biggest fears, the ones that were holding me back from truly feeling love for myself and all things.

This journey began one night in 2004 when I was playing at a casino in Ottawa, Canada. I was backstage before the show, sitting in a room with my drummer and my guitar tech in that lull time when you're hanging out, waiting to go on stage.

I was feeling sort of lost, and I remember saying to the guys, "I don't know what's happening anymore. I've been to the top of the mountain; I've been famous and I've made money, but it's all kind of blank and dark and empty." I looked up at the ceiling and said, "Okay, universe, what do you want from me? What's this all about? I'm ready for whatever, but I don't know what it is."

The very next morning I found a lump in my breast. I knew it was the universe's way of saying, "Okay, Melissa, you're ready. Here you go."

The moment I received the diagnosis of cancer, I felt like I was walking through a wall. I had the thought *I'm going to crash! This is going to hurt!*

Then *boom!* I walked through it, it dissolved away, and I was on the other side—a person with cancer. There was still a thread of the old me inside, the way I'd always been, but as time went by, I began to feel different—though not in the way I'd feared; instead of losing myself, I actually began to wake up.

In the months that followed I was able to let go of many things I didn't even know I was holding on to. First and most important, I let go of the constant chatter in my head. During some stages of chemotherapy I was forced to sit still and do absolutely nothing because it hurt to do anything else.

At first, I sat with my mind going a thousand miles a minute. But after I'd gone through my life two or three times in my head, the tape finally ran off the player. I just stopped thinking. My mind quieted. And in that quietness was an incredible light, energy, spirit, and love, which I knew was my own higher self. When I connected with that, all fear went away.

In that stillness, I understood that I had cancer and was on chemo for a reason—to connect with love, to connect with my higher self, and then walk my life in that love from there on out. I experienced that I couldn't feel love and fear at the same time. They were like magnetic opposites. The love pushed all my fears away, and once they were gone, I could see how small they really were. The fear of how I look, how old I am, whether I have enough money—all the usual yardsticks that we measure ourselves by in this material reality—they just broke away, and there was a deep sense that "I am enough." I thought, *I could just sit here in this chair and be completely enough. I don't need anything else.*

This experience of *being* love has changed everything—including every relationship I have, with loved ones, strangers, people I work with, my children, and myself. In fact, it starts with myself: I wake up in the morning and my first thought is *I love myself.* I look in the mirror and see that I am beautiful, I am sexy, I am strong, I am good. It starts right there.

My mind is constantly making choices, and my higher self helps my mind make the love choice rather than the fear choice in everything—what I eat, where I go, which piece of clothing I put on. It's a constant conversation with myself.

And when I start from love, I understand that whatever issues the people I interact with are going through, whatever they project onto me, has nothing to do with me. I don't take it personally; I look at them with love. And that changes everything in my whole day.

Soon after I became clear that I was going to choose to live my life from love, my higher self gave me an opportunity to exercise that choice. I got a call from the organizers of the Grammys inviting me to sing Janis Joplin's "Piece of My Heart" at the awards ceremony—which was great, except that the event would take place right when I was finishing my chemo treatments. I'd be bald in front of hundreds of millions of people worldwide!

I had made the claim that I wasn't going to choose fear anymore, so the universe was asking me, "Do you really mean that? Because we have an opportunity for you here."

I had to say, "Okay! I'm not going to be afraid of how I look, or of scaring other people with how I look." I had to say yes, because that was the deal I'd made with myself: from here on out, it's about love, and it's about saying yes.

So I said yes, and I got up on that stage, bald as can be, and sang my heart out. And the rewards and the reverberations of that choice are still coming back to me, more than five years later. People are constantly telling me, "Oh, that performance you gave at the Grammys changed my life. My mother was going through this, or my sister was, or I was . . . and watching you I realized, 'Hey, if she can do it, I can do it too.'" That loving embrace comes back to me constantly from friends and from strangers to this day.

And that experience has helped wake me up to the second great shift in my life, after choosing love over fear: I realized that it was okay to receive other people's love and support.

Going through cancer and five courses of chemo and radiation was a lesson in letting myself be taken care of in a way that previously might have made me feel weak. I grew up in the Midwest, where you're supposed to work hard, be nice, and take care of other people. I started making my own way when I was eleven or twelve years old; I've always taken care of myself, and I've always been "fine."

But when cancer knocked me down, and then the chemo knocked me down, I saw that letting people give to me was more healing than if I were to say, "Oh, no, no, I can take care of myself." It was healing for me and healing for them. Receiving their loving care deepened my relationship with everyone around me, because I was finally able to say, "You know what? I need help. Let that love come in."

That choice is something I still live with every day. Receiving love is a big thing, especially for women. It can be hard sometimes when the old patterns of guilt and shame come up, but if I choose to drop those patterns, the love flows in and out freely.

Living the truth of who we are—beings of light and love, not of fear—comes down to a simple matter of commitment, of making the choice, each and every moment. As I say in my song "Fearless Love,"

> *I want to live my life*
> *Pursuing all my happiness*
> *I want a fearless love*
> *I won't settle for anything less.*

A Grateful Heart

Wake at dawn with a winged heart and
give thanks for another day of loving.
—Kahlil Gibran, twentieth-century Lebanese American author

Like Melissa, you can experience a "fearless love" when you practice fully opening your heart to receive love. One of the most powerful ways to do this is through gratitude and appreciation.

I learned a lot about gratitude and appreciation from my mom. Though she didn't start out a gratitude expert, in her later years my mom became my role model. For most of her life, she was the glass-half-empty type, but about five years before she died, Mom went through a complete turnaround and became the most positive and grateful person I've ever known. She saw the bright side of every situation, and she was constantly saying what a wonderful life she had. She was a total joy to be around.

A year before she passed away, my mom had a long and difficult surgery. In the recovery room, tubes jutted out of her arms, mouth, and nose. As she was waking up, my sister, brother, and I were standing next to her bed, and I leaned over and whispered to her, "How are you, Mom?" She opened her eyes and looked at me, put a big smile on her face, tubes and all, and said, "Oh, honey, I'm happy for no reason."

I thought, *Mom, you got it! I'm so proud and delighted that you passed the toughest test in the world: how to find love and happiness in the face of life's challenges.*

Start your own gratitude practice by consciously registering and savoring all that you're receiving right now. This "rewires" your brain to develop the habit of noticing the many gifts that come into your life.

The scientific research on the benefits of gratitude could fill a book—which it has many times over. Gratitude triggers a parasympathetic nervous system response—the opposite of stress—and creates coherent heart rhythm patterns, which generate a cascade of positive effects. Being grateful improves overall health, helps you sleep better, lowers the levels of stress hormones in your blood, reverses stress damage to your heart, and much more.

I often say that gratitude is the fast track to love. Over twenty years ago, I started a daily gratitude practice of listing five things I was grateful for at the end of each day. It turned my life around, opening my heart at a time when it felt broken. I still do it every day.

While writing this book I decided that I would supplement my daily gratitude practice with a forty-day receiving practice. The idea for this came one day when I called my friend Christine Arylo, the queen of self-love you met in the last chapter. She told me that she was going to spend the next forty days consciously looking for ways that she could become more open to receiving love.

"I'm in!" I told her and together we embarked on our receiving adventure. Knowing Christine and I would be comparing notes regularly motivated me to keep going.

For me, the main practice was actively allowing people to do things for me—like letting someone hold the door open, accepting a friend's offer to share her lunch, allowing a colleague to go out of his way to help me. This was hard at first; I was so conditioned to say, "Don't bother, I can do it."

I realized I'd been going around with a shield that prevented people from giving to me—from even offering to give. I'd made a point to always do it myself, because I didn't want to bother others or take up their time. My I-can-do-anything-Superwoman persona was really just Cootie Girl in disguise.

The next time I caught myself slipping into my old way of behaving, I took a deep breath, smiled, and said, "Thank you," while receiving the gift fully by feeling appreciation in my heart. The forty days have been over for a long time, but receiving love and support from others has become a way of life for me.

Love Luminaries in Fur Suits

Another great way to practice receiving is to hang around with masters of the skill. I'm talking about our furry or feathered animal friends. Pets are world-class receivers. Have you ever seen a dog refuse a belly scratch because he didn't want to inconvenience you? Or a cat move from her sunny spot on the couch because she was afraid of seeming selfish? Pets naturally let in love 24/7 with an innocence and enthusiasm that's worth emulating.

And the love pets dole out is pure Love for No Reason. Many of us get our first taste of unconditional love from our family pet. Pets love you just because. Whether you're having a good day or a bad day. Whether you finished running the Boston Marathon or just blew your diet. (And maybe just a little more when they know it's dinnertime.) All that unconditional giving helps you practice receiving.

Having a pet isn't a guarantee you'll be a loving person, but for most of us, living with an animal companion seems to soften our hearts. You don't have to live with a pet to experience their heart-opening power. Even just looking at pictures of animals can stir the Love for No Reason inside, which explains why the most popular YouTube videos and emails circulating in cyberspace usually feature animals. Carol's favorite website for a quick Love for No Reason pick-me-up is called Cute Overload. It's got "Aaaawww"-inspiring photos and videos of cats, dogs, kittens, puppies, hamsters, horses—you get the idea.

Of course, not everyone's heart responds strongly to animals. For you, it may be photos of nature or gorgeous architecture, quotes from inspiring people, or uplifting music that tickles your love-body and induces the vibration of love in you. It doesn't matter what it is. Practice opening to receive love using whatever makes your heart sing.

Searching for a Heart of Gold

Certain cultures place greater emphasis on opening the heart than others. Those that do, know that an open heart is extremely precious—worth its weight in gold.

I learned about a unique method to open and heal the heart from my massage therapist, Love Luminary Cathy Korson. Cathy, an American-born Buddhist nun who lives half the year in a monastery high in the mountains of Burma (Myanmar), is reviving the ancient Burmese art of healing with gold.

One day during a massage session, Cathy placed a two-inch square of very, very fine gold leaf on my chest, in the area of my heart, and gently pressed it onto my skin, while saying a Burmese blessing of lovingkindness. She told me that this was special gold foil that monks had prayed over and blessed. In Burma, this traditional healing remedy is believed to physically open the ventricles of the heart and allow for increased circulation as the gold leaf is absorbed through the skin.

In our interview Cathy told me, "Besides its healing properties, gold placed on the heart is a powerful symbol. It reminds us that the heart, like gold, is pure and untarnishable."

She went on to say, "Love for No Reason is our natural state, clouded only by our greed, anger, and delusion. To be able to love unconditionally is to liberate your heart; it's the path to perfection."

I loved the Golden Heart Healing experience so much that I asked her to bring back some gold-leaf squares for me from Burma the next time she went. Now I apply the gold at least once a week and enjoy the sweetness, softness, and warmth it produces in my heart. (See the Resources section for more information on Golden Heart Healing.)

The Transformation of Love: Turning Love for Good Reason into Love for No Reason

*However your mind wanders, wherever you journey, return
to savoring the luminous space of the heart. Again and again
return to where the breaths meet, fuse, and transform into each
other. Rest the attention in your blessed core as you practice this
and continually be reborn into the thrill of a new world.*

—The Bhairava Tantra Sutras

As you've seen, learning to receive can start with focusing on something or someone you love for good reason: feeling gratitude and appreciation for a special person or pet, a favorite place, or a fulfilling activity; melting at the sight of natural beauty or of overwhelming cuteness; zeroing in on the gifts that come to you each day. All these stimulate the heart to flow in love for a specific reason and initiate the vibration of the energy of love.

To turn that directed love, or Love for Good Reason, into Love for No Reason, you simply unhook your focus from the outer object and bring your attention to the love itself. You ride the love back to its source, or as Love Luminary David Spangler put it, "Once love begins to flow from me, I can follow that flow back to its wellsprings." Then you can experience the love that's reverberating in your heart—that state of love the Love Luminaries call "an ocean of love."

You did this very thing in the exercise in chapter 1 to help you understand the difference between Love for Good Reason and Love for No Reason. Love for No Reason doesn't depend on anything outside you being a certain way. Your heart is wide open—just because. Then unconditional love fills you and flows through you into the world.

♥   ♥   ♥

There are so many great meditations for the heart! One of my favorites is the one below. I've adapted it from the Adorata Meditation I learned from Tiziana DellaRovere, who has developed a fabulous method of directly connecting with the experience of unconditional love. I've worked closely with Tiziana, and I love her practice of "bringing the presence of the Divine Feminine and the Divine Masculine into sacred union in the heart." This meditation helps you open your heart and let love in.

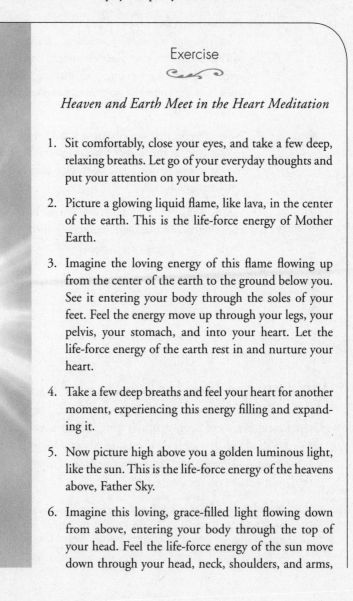

Exercise

Heaven and Earth Meet in the Heart Meditation

1. Sit comfortably, close your eyes, and take a few deep, relaxing breaths. Let go of your everyday thoughts and put your attention on your breath.

2. Picture a glowing liquid flame, like lava, in the center of the earth. This is the life-force energy of Mother Earth.

3. Imagine the loving energy of this flame flowing up from the center of the earth to the ground below you. See it entering your body through the soles of your feet. Feel the energy move up through your legs, your pelvis, your stomach, and into your heart. Let the life-force energy of the earth rest in and nurture your heart.

4. Take a few deep breaths and feel your heart for another moment, experiencing this energy filling and expanding it.

5. Now picture high above you a golden luminous light, like the sun. This is the life-force energy of the heavens above, Father Sky.

6. Imagine this loving, grace-filled light flowing down from above, entering your body through the top of your head. Feel the life-force energy of the sun move down through your head, neck, shoulders, and arms,

and into your heart. Let this luminous energy of the heavens rest in and nurture your heart.

7. Take a few deep breaths and feel your heart for another moment, experiencing this energy filling and expanding it.

8. Picture these two energies that are both resting in your heart, merging together into oneness, creating a sphere of radiant golden love. Feel the merged energy of the earth and the sky relaxing and melting your heart open. Let the sphere of golden love expand throughout your body.

9. Now imagine that your heart is a golden bowl open to receiving all the love and blessings that are coming to you today. Sit for a few minutes experiencing this openness and love.

10. Gently bring your attention back to your body, wiggle your fingers and toes, and then slowly open your eyes.

© Marci Shimoff 2010

Summary and Love for No Reason Action Steps

Giving from a state of fullness and letting love in without resistance are the keys that unlock the Doorway of Openness. Use the following action steps to increase the flow of love through this all-important energy center:

1. Do at least five acts of kindness every day. These can be heartfelt wishes or actions you take. Giving to others will improve your health and open your heart.

2. Beam love or give mental hugs to people you come in contact with over the course of your day. Notice the boost of love, energy, and joy it brings.

3. If you're holding on to any resentments or grudges—past or present—they're blocking your ability to love. Use the kahuna technique of Ho'oponopono to release and forgive. (I'm sorry. Please forgive me. Thank you. I love you.)

4. To make sure giving doesn't leave your love tank on empty, be aware of the symptoms of overcare. Replenish yourself at the first sign of stress that comes from unhealthy giving.

5. When you feel stressed or your heart feels shut down, practice the HeartMath Inner-Ease technique to generate heart rhythm coherence and bring more flow into your life.

6. Cultivate gratitude by acknowledging five ways that your heart was opened during the day. Consciously savoring the many gifts you receive trains your brain to take in the good.

7. Practice being open to receiving. The next time someone offers you a gift—whether in the form of a present, a compliment, or some assistance—graciously receive it. Look to your pets for inspiration on how to let love in.

8. To help open and heal the heart, use the Golden Heart Healing process.

9. Turn the experience of conditional love into Love for No Reason by following the feeling of love back to its source. Bask in the ocean of pure love that resides in your own heart.

10. Use the Heaven and Earth Meet in the Heart Meditation to experience the fullness of love and cultivate your receptivity.

CHAPTER 8

The Doorway of
Communication:
Coming from Compassion

There are men who would quickly love each other if once they were
to speak to each other; for when they spoke they would discover
that their souls were only separated by phantoms and delusions.
—Ernest Hello, nineteenth-century French philosopher

Picture the scene: It's 7 p.m. I'm in the middle of dinner and the phone rings. It's the inevitable telemarketer.

For years, I'd get annoyed. I'd either grit my teeth, trying to ignore the ringing phone, or answer with a tone that made it clear I was angry the caller was interrupting my meal. Then I'd unceremoniously hang up on the person. But doing this always left me feeling crummy. I didn't like being so rude.

When the no-call list was launched, I signed up immediately, but I continued getting calls that kept me out of the love zone. Then one day I began thinking about the people on the other end of the line, calling to sell me something. I pictured them with families at home, trying to feed their kids and pay their bills, just like everybody else. My heart began to soften, and I decided to change my approach.

Now, as soon as the caller starts to rattle off their sales spiel, I gently interrupt them and say, "Thanks for calling. I'm not interested in this, but I wish you really great luck for the rest of the evening."

And it's true—I *do* wish them luck for the rest of the evening. I find that this attitude totally and completely disarms them. They never start over or say "But, but, but . . ." or try that second line of attack on me. They just stop. They recognize that somebody has been nice to them, has wished them something kind, and has spoken the truth. They always say, "Thank you so much," and we both hang up feeling good.

This new approach keeps my heart open, opens up the telemarketer's heart, and gets my desired result—getting off the phone—but leaves me in the energy of love.

Speaking from the heart doesn't mean acting like a Goody Two-shoes—forcing yourself to talk like Glinda, the Good Witch of the North, when you really feel like erupting, volcano-style. You don't suppress your anger or try to sugarcoat it. Instead, you do what I call "leaning into the better-feeling speech," which is a variation of the concept of "leaning into the better-feeling thought."

Leaning into the better-feeling thought simply means giving more attention to the thought that increases your experience of love. So for example, when you're having a negative thought about a situation, find an *equally true* thought about the situation that makes you feel better, and deliberately lean into it. This concept is what positive psychology pioneer Dr. Martin Seligman calls "learned optimism." Though the glass is half empty, it's equally true that it's half full. Getting into the habit of consciously favoring the thought that leads to more love will keep your heart open.

The same applies to speaking. When you lean into more loving, yet equally true, words, you communicate love. Now, after telemarketing calls, I actually go back to the dinner table with a smile on my face. I feel I've connected with another human being on the other end of the line instead of making that person my dinnertime enemy.

There are ways to speak and listen that open the heart and there are ways that don't. Harshness, yelling, and critical speech constrict our energy, as does withholding our truth, being phony, and not voicing our needs. Listening defensively—or not listening at all—also stops the heart's flow.

When the Doorway of Communication is open, you speak and listen in a way that increases compassion and connection. You authentically share what you're thinking and feeling, instead of editing yourself or saying things you don't mean to win approval. You listen empathetically to hear the feelings and needs beneath the words people are saying.

When this center is blocked, you feel frustrated and misunderstood; you can't express what's really true for you, and you have a hard time hearing what's true for other people as well. When you're not speaking from love or listening with your heart, you'll have more conflicts with people in your life.

When this center is open, you become a full-time conduit for Love for No Reason.

The Chimney of the Heart

The communication center is traditionally referred to as the fifth or throat chakra. Associated with the throat, mouth, neck, and ears, this energy center influences your ability to express yourself fully and hear others with openness. Our heart communicates through this center, which is why it's sometimes described as the "chimney of the heart." It's a good metaphor. When a chimney's working well, smoke floats up and out into the world, and fresh oxygen gets drawn in via the flue. This easy exchange in both directions allows the fire to burn hot and strong.

In the same way, when the "chimney" of your throat chakra is open, it keeps the fire of your heart burning brightly by allowing you to express your feelings honestly and listen to other peoples' words with understanding and empathy.

But if you push down your true feelings, you stifle the love and communication coming from your heart. Imagine stuffing a bunch of damp rags down a chimney: the fire would go out within minutes!

The communication center is a channel between our inner world of thoughts and feelings and our outer world of experiences and relationships. To keep that channel clear, you need to speak authentically and listen without judgment.

Building Bridges

Often our communications separate us from others rather than connect us. When the pain-body—made up of our old fears and hurts—is driving the conversation, we inevitably create more fear and hurt. We get locked into repeating patterns of criticism, complaint, or misunderstanding that can be hard to break.

In my interview with Love Luminary Gay Hendricks, whom you've met in earlier chapters, he described the moment he first realized that his communication with his wife, Katie, was being driven by pain and fear instead of love. Here's how Gay described what happened:

About twenty years ago—during the first decade of our over thirty-year marriage—Katie and I were having an argument, and I had the thought, *Wow, this is not our five hundredth argument; this is our five hundredth run of the same argument!* I realized that a big source of our conflicts was that we weren't being honest with ourselves or each other about what we were feeling inside. Instead, we were blaming each other for our upset.

A few weeks later, I had a chance to see this dynamic in action. One Friday night, Katie got home forty-five minutes later than she'd said she'd be. When I opened the door, I saw that she had two big bags of groceries in her arms. That should have given me a clue as to where she'd been, but the first thing out of my mouth was a frustrated, "You were supposed to be home at seven thirty! Where have you been?"

Not surprisingly, this triggered an argument. In the middle of it, I thought, *I'm sounding on the surface like I'm angry and critical, but what I'm actually feeling is scared.* I was so startled that I stopped talking and put my attention on the fear.

As I tuned in to the feeling, I realized it was exactly what I used to feel as a little boy when my mother was late or forgot to come get me from school, which was quite often. I was projecting this old fear of being abandoned onto Katie by criticizing her for being late. But it was really about me still carrying around the feeling that I was always going to be abandoned.

I blurted out, "I realize that I'm criticizing you, but it doesn't have anything to do with you. I'm not really angry; I'm scared." We sat down on the floor, with the bags of groceries sitting next to us, and talked for a long time that night. We both saw how our ability to love and appreciate each other would skyrocket if we could be more aware of these underlying issues. From then on, we agreed that when things came up, we would check inside as quickly as possible and say, "What I'm scared about is . . ." rather than "What you did wrong was . . ." This honesty kept our hearts far more open than they would have been if we'd blamed the other person or told them what they needed to fix.

When Gay tuned in to his deeper feelings, he was able to communicate from an authentic place, describing what was really happening in his heart center. This opened up the possibility for understanding, helping him and Katie to bridge the gulf between them, little by little.

Katie and Gay made a commitment to each other those many years ago to completely eliminate criticism from their relationship and replace it with 24-hour-a-day appreciation. It took a few years of practice, but Gay says that he and Katie haven't spoken a word of criticism to each other for over fifteen years!

Are You an Agent of Love or an Agent of Fear?

Many Love Luminaries shared that each time we communicate with anyone—whether a partner, a stranger, or even an audience of hundreds—we're either an agent of love, creating understanding and connectedness in each encounter, or we're an agent of fear, creating distance and disconnection by being aloof, sharp, or defensive.

If you're an agent of love, your heart softens as you express yourself, which softens other people's hearts too. If you're an agent of fear, everyone's hearts harden like stone. The way you speak and listen determines whether you're an agent of love or an agent of fear. Agents of love still express sadness, hurt, anger, or frustration, but they do it skillfully and in the service of creating more love.

The following keys give you the skills to replace fear-based speaking and listening with love, unlocking the Doorway of Communication and fostering connection and intimacy in your life.

> ## Love Keys for the Doorway of Communication
>
> 1. Speak the Language of Love
> 2. Hear from the Heart

The Speaking Key helps you to express yourself with an open and vulnerable heart while maintaining your strength.

The Hearing Key teaches you to listen compassionately, creating deeper bonds of love.

Love Key for Communication #1:
Speak the Language of Love

The poet Samuel Taylor Coleridge wrote, "What comes from the heart, goes to the heart." When we speak directly from the place of unconditional love inside us, we touch that same love in the people we're speaking to.

On the surface, our words convey meaning, the message we want to communicate to others. But on a deeper, more significant level, they also carry a vibration, or energy, through the sounds they produce and the intention behind the words. To amp up the wattage of your love-body and have the most positive influence on the world around you, use words that transmit frequencies of love—not fear.

Love Luminary Fred Johnson is an expert in the field of sound healing. He told me, "Breath is the essence of love given to us from the Divine. God gives us the inhalation; how we use the exhalation as sound is our responsibility. The sounds that we move into the world are the manifestations of either the energy of love or the energy of fear. That's why we must be conscious of the way we speak to ourselves and how we speak to the world."

I first learned about the power of words from my parents. When I was a child, there were two phrases I wasn't allowed to say: "I can't . . ." and "I hate . . ." My parents knew that these words carried vibrations that didn't support love.

I would later discover the scientific basis for this wise rule. For the last twenty-five years, I've been demonstrating in my speeches a remarkable process called muscle testing, based on Educational Kinesiology (EK). We know that everything in the universe is vibration: food, people, situations, and our words. Using muscle testing, we can measure the effects of any of these vibrations on our bodies to see whether they strengthen or weaken us.

Here's how it works. I ask a volunteer from my audience to hold one arm straight out to the side. Then I gently press down on their wrist, asking them to keep their arm up, which they're able to do. Then I have them say a negative phrase such as "I can't . . . ," "I hate . . . ," or "I'm a bad person." Instantly, they lose muscle strength and are unable to hold up their arm. As soon as they make affirming statements, such as "I can . . . ," "I love . . . ," or "I'm a good person," their arms regain strength!

This exercise demonstrates the power of our words in action: if we're going to keep the Doorway of Communication open, we need to start noticing our old habits and unconscious use of words that weaken us. Watch, for example, how many times a day you say, "I hate"—whether it's "I hate traffic," "I hate Brussels sprouts," or "I hate that politician." These phrases—and the inherent negative energy contained within them—are like poison to our minds and bodies, draining our energy and often leading to illness.

In his groundbreaking book *The Language of the Heart*, psychologist and researcher James J. Lynch points out that speaking has a dramatic effect on our cardiovascular system. His pioneering research conducted in the 1980s showed that speaking had a direct impact on blood pressure and that people who consistently spoke negatively had a higher incidence of heart disease. So, your words can actually hurt you, but they don't have to if you learn to use them correctly. Becoming aware of the way you speak is the first step.

Pay special attention to when you use what wisdom traditions say are the two most powerful words in the English language: "I am." Anything that comes after those words is magnified many times, so it's important to use words of love and peace, such as "I am radiant," "I am abundant," or "I am loving." Avoid reinforcing negative states and emotions; whatever we say, our subconscious minds believe. When we say, "I am . . . ," we summon tremendous creative power and the universe responds. It's like Captain Picard in *Star Trek* commanding his crew to "Make it so!"

Let Your Heart Shine

One way to speak the language of love is by appreciating others. This strengthens your love-body and contributes love to the people around you too. There's a wonderful story about the power of appreciation that I've told in my speeches for years. It's based on the work of Helice "Sparky" Bridges whose organization, Difference Makers International, has designed blue ribbons that read, *Who I Am Makes a Difference.* Their goal is that 300 million people worldwide each receive one of these ribbons by 2020.

The story is about a teacher in New York City who heard about these blue ribbons and decided to use them in an "appreciation ceremony" one afternoon with her high school seniors. She honored each student one by one, telling them what she most appreciated about them and then presented them with a ribbon.

She then gave each student three more blue ribbons to pass along in acknowledgment of others to see what impact it would make in their community. One student gave a ribbon to his work supervisor. From there it ended up in the hands of his boss, a busy executive who decided to give the ribbon to his fourteen-year-old son. That night, the executive sat his son down on the couch and said to him, "My days are really hectic and when I come home I don't pay a lot of attention to you. Sometimes I scream at you for different things. But tonight, I just wanted to let you know that you do make a difference to me. Besides your mother, you are the most important person in my life. You're a great kid and I love you!"

Hearing this, the son began to sob. He went over to a drawer, opened it, and took out a gun. Still crying, he looked at his father and said, "Dad, I was going to commit suicide tomorrow because I didn't think you loved me. Now I don't have to. Please take this gun from me."

I've told this story a thousand times, and it still makes me cry. *That's* how powerful expressing appreciation can be. Imagine what a different world we'd live in if people more regularly used their words to appreciate and affirm one another.

Try it yourself! The Appreciation Practice is something Carol and I started doing together each day while we were writing this book. We'd tell each other three things we appreciated about the other. The result was that we could work together with more open hearts. You can do this with your family, coworkers, or friends. Even a simple statement of appreciation for the cashier—"You've got a great smile!"—as you check out at the grocery store can make a difference in someone's day.

Love Luminary Johnny Barnes is a shining example of the power of the loving word. I came across Johnny quite unexpectedly while attending the semiannual meeting of the Transformational Leadership Council, which is a group of speakers, authors, coaches, and visionaries that I'm honored to be a part of. At our meetings, we share ideas and brainstorm ways that we can support each other's efforts to make a difference in the world.

In 2009 our spring meeting was held in Hamilton, the capital city of Bermuda. While I was there, I heard an intriguing story about an elderly gentleman named Johnny Barnes, who's become a national icon in that country with his unusual claim to fame: for over a quarter of a century, Johnny has stood beside a busy city roadway, waving and saying "I love you" to all the people going by. Talk about a Love Luminary! I knew I had to interview him for this book.

Johnny was the perfect ambassador for Love for No Reason. In the interview, we could feel the genuine love and happiness he radiated right through the phone! What follows is Johnny's story of speaking the language of love.

Johnny's Story
This World Was Made for Love

G ood morning! Have a good day! God bless you!"

I can't count how many times I've said those words.

I'm eighty-six years old, and for the last twenty-seven years I've spent a quarter of my waking hours standing on the side of a busy road in Bermuda calling out a greeting and waving to people as they drive by. Sometimes I even blow kisses.

Now, that may sound crazy to you, but after all this time, it's become the most natural thing in the world for me.

You see, I love people, and I love telling them that I love them. Each morning, while it's still dark, I put on my big straw hat, pick up the bag lunch my dear wife makes me, and head for my spot at the Crow Lane roundabout, a circular intersection right in the middle of downtown Hamilton.

When I get there, I put down my sack, raise both my arms, and begin. A smile straight from my heart spreads across my face as I wave, blow kisses, and start calling out my greetings: "Good morning! God bless you! You know I love you, darlin'! Have a good day!"

Most of the people who go by smile and wave their hands in return. A lot of them tell me they love me back. Some people have even stopped and brought me flowers!

I consider it my personal mission in life to spread joy and love whenever, wherever, and however I can. The seed was planted by my mother over eighty years ago, when I was just a little boy of about five or six years old.

One day, my mother sent me on an errand to take a message to someone who lived nearby. On my way, I passed the elderly woman who lived next door to us walking on the street. I looked at her and she looked at me, but I didn't say anything. I just kept on with my errand.

When I got home, my mother made certain that I had delivered her message, and then asked me, "Johnny, who did you see on your way?"

I told her that I'd seen the lady who lived next door.

"And did you speak to her?"

"No."

My mother didn't like that answer one bit! She disciplined me firmly, saying, "Johnny, everyone you see, you speak to! Reach out to people; we're all in this together. Each of us has a bit of God inside us."

And that is how I started saying a little something to all those I met—no matter who they were.

The idea to wave at people from the side of the road came later, when I was a young man working as an electrician on the railway in the early 1940s. The impulse popped into my head on my lunch hour one day. I was sitting on the wall in front of the rail yard eating my sandwich, and I just threw my hand up in the air and started waving at all the passersby—in cars, on bicycles, walking by me on the sidewalk—everybody. It felt so good that I began coming in a half hour before my shift every morning to do it some more. I'd sit on the wall and greet folks on their way to work. Some people thought I was nuts, but I didn't care. It made people happy.

A few years later, I started standing on the roundabout where I am now, and my morning half hour of waving stretched into an hour. I did that every day before work for thirty years. When I retired in 1983, I kept getting up in the morning and going to the roundabout to greet people, but started staying a little longer. And then a little longer. And a little longer. Today I leave my house at three thirty in the morning, get to the roundabout at twenty minutes of four and stay until ten a.m., five days a week. That's six hours of spreading love every morning. I can't think of a better way to spend my time.

You'd be surprised how many people are out on the roads early in the morning; there are truck drivers, people heading to the office, others going to work at the hospitals, joggers and cyclists getting in their morning exercise. I especially enjoy seeing the faces of the children as they wave back at me from the cars on the way to school. They call out, "Hi, Johnny, I love you." Sometimes, if the children come around and I've got my back to them greeting somebody else, they make their parents drive around again so that we can wave to each other.

Of course, there are some people that frown and shake their fists at me, but it doesn't bother me. I just smile and keep waving. One man came up to me and told me he wanted to get me off the roundabout. I said, "I love you, my brother. I still love you." He came back a couple of days later and said the same thing about wanting me off the street. I told him again that I loved him anyway. The next time he passed me, he said, "You know? You're a pretty good fella." I still see him from time to time.

God gives us all something to do. If you can bring joy and happiness to others, you keep on doing it. People seem to like my staying power. I just keep showing up day after day, and year after year; they kind of count on it now. In fact, not long ago the city actually put up a life-sized, bronze statue of me, wide-brimmed hat and all, doing my two-handed wave! It stands on the opposite side of the roundabout from me and keeps on spreading love after I go home.

After I finish at the roundabout, I work in the garden. I love getting back to the soil and growing things. I eat my dinner in the late afternoon, and in the evenings, I don't watch TV, I go to bed early.

I have a wife, Belvina, whom I've been married to for over fifty years. I put a lot of honey on her and keep her sweet. She doesn't mind sharing me, though she sometimes worries about my health. I remind her that I may look like an old man, but I still feel like a little boy. Doing what I do feels wonderful. Tired? What's that?

The way I see it, this world was made for love. When the good Lord wakes me up mornings, puts a song in my heart, joy in my soul, and a smile on my face, I just have to give it away.

♥   ♥   ♥

The same day that I interviewed Johnny, I was leading a group coaching call. One of the women participating happened to mention she was from Bermuda. (I *love* those "coincidences.") "Oh," I said, "do you know Johnny Barnes?"

"Of course," she said. "He waved at me this morning!"

We all marveled at the synchronicity.

She sees him daily as she rides her bike to work. She said, "I do believe that his presence there every day is being felt on some level by all of us who pass by, and I'm sure we're all the better for it. Johnny reminds me that I truly am loved—at all times, whether I know it or not."

Speak Your Truth as an Agent of Love

Another important way to keep your communication center open is to speak your truth—how you really feel about things. You may be wondering, "How do I speak as an agent of love, when how I really feel isn't exactly loving?"

What many of us do in this situation—stuff our feelings, bite our tongues, or say only what's appropriate or polite—shuts down the communication center and closes our hearts.

Yet saying what you feel at every moment isn't the answer either. Speaking your truth isn't an excuse to fly off the handle or dump your "garbage" on someone. That's equally damaging to your heart.

So, when you're feeling upset, what can you do instead? Chill— Communicate *Heart-Informed Love Later.*

Wait until the emotional "charge" has passed before blurting out something you'll regret later. Take a deep breath and remind yourself that your pain-body is up to its old tricks—urging you to insult, blame, or tell someone off and create more pain, because pain is what it feeds on. Remove yourself from the situation until your pain-body calms down. Use the tools that you've learned in earlier energy centers chapters: feel your feelings, own your triggers, and have compassion for yourself. Then, after some time has passed, you'll be able to say what you want without creating more pain.

For example, I recently got an email that really pushed my buttons. I immediately wrote an angry reply, but realizing that my "truth" was nothing more than a knee-jerk reaction that wouldn't serve anyone—least of all me—I stopped myself from clicking send. A few hours later I rewrote my response without the venom or emotional charge. The next morning my doorbell rang and I opened the door to find a flower deliveryman holding a beautiful vase of roses from . . . guess who? Yep, the very same person who'd sent that button-pushing email.

Chilling isn't the same as stuffing your feelings; you're going to express yourself at some point. But waiting until you can speak with less negative charge increases your chances of connecting with the other person in a more loving way.

The Magic of Nonviolent Communication

Waiting to express love later is a good first step, but we also need to know how to express ourselves in a loving way *and* still get our needs met. It's possible to do both, through an extraordinary, world-renowned communication method called Nonviolent Communication (NVC).

NVC, developed by Marshall Rosenberg, PhD, is a simple four-step process: observing, feeling, discerning needs, and making requests. It helps you speak with respect and compassion, honestly expressing your needs and feelings without using blame, criticism, or demands.

NVC is based on the premise that negative feelings are the messengers of unmet needs. Feeling angry, hurt, or anxious means that somewhere deep inside you, you feel like you need something you're not getting. NVC shows you how to identify the needs behind whatever you're feeling and turn them into requests. Then you can ask for what you want without anger or fear.

The process starts with observation. Instead of going into instant reaction, which is what we usually do, you bring your attention to what's actually happening in the moment that you don't like. You stick to the facts.

Next, you get in touch with the feelings that come up in relation to the situation: Are you hurt, irritated, discouraged? You name the feelings you're experiencing.

Then you ask yourself why you feel the way you do. What need of yours isn't being met?

Once you have gotten that far, the next step—making a specific request for a concrete action—isn't very hard. You include the information from the first three steps into your request. For example, if I'm a working mother who walks into the kitchen after supper and sees that the dishes aren't done, instead of blowing up or doing them and feeling martyred, I could say to my husband or children, "When I see that the dishes aren't done, I feel angry because I'm working really hard and need to feel that we're all supporting each other. Would you be willing to do the dishes tonight?"

Whether they agree to your request isn't the point here. When you check in this way to your true feelings and then voice them in a nondamaging way, you're keeping the communication center open.

The Nonviolent Communication exercise at the end of this section will walk you through this process step by step.

Singing, Music, and Sound

Communication doesn't just happen on the level of speech. Though we're focused so far on the spoken word, there are other powerful ways to unblock the doorway of communication. Music, singing, and chanting have been used across all cultures for eons. From Gregorian chants to Indian *bhajans* (devotional songs) to *tuvan* (Siberian overtone singing), sound has helped people heal their bodies, minds, and souls.

One of the most heart-opening activities I can do is to sing. Okay, it may not be as heart-opening for the people around me—I can barely carry a tune. Even so, I set aside my vanity and sing whenever I can: in the shower, driving down the road, cleaning the kitchen. Whenever I do, I feel alive, free, and connected to the joy in my heart.

When I interviewed Love Luminary and world-famous musician Deva Premal, a woman whose angelic presence and singing transport me to another realm, I asked her about the relationship of singing to the heart. Deva said, "You can't sing with a closed heart. You just can't do it. And if you try, as soon as you start singing, your heart just naturally opens more and more."

Singing is particularly heart-opening when people do it together in community. In my childhood, I spent two weeks every summer at Girl Scout camp. My favorite memories are the evenings when we'd sit under the stars and sing together around the campfire. (I'm sure the s'mores added to the singing high.) These days, I love to sing Christmas carols with others or spend an evening at a gathering of people singing and chanting.

All sound and music—including singing—is vibration, and all vibration affects our love-body. There are sounds that close down the heart: think of how you cringe and contract when you hear nails on a chalkboard. Now think of how you relax and open when you hear a beautiful symphony or the gentle waves of a calm ocean.

According to Love Luminary and expert in the music/mind-body connection David Ison, "Music can be composed specifically to open the heart and to alter the body and mind. Each chakra has an optimal rate of vibration. When you listen to music that matches the vibration of a chakra's optimal frequency, it resonates with your chakra to open it."

David has developed a series of therapeutic programs called the Musical Body that combine sound, vibration, and meditation with his beautiful music. The National Institutes of Health has found that David's sound vibration therapy can slow the pulse, lower blood pressure, and significantly reduce a number of physical symptoms, including tension, fatigue, headache, and depression.

Extensive research has shown that music can help create the relaxation response—a deep state of rest that improves our response to stress. This allows a person to become more receptive and open their heart. Deva says, "Music is a transcendental tool that can connect us to the huge invisible energy of love. But listening to music is just like taking in food: there's food that's good for you and food that's not. Negative or angry music can make us feel more stressed and shut down. Music that uplifts us will always open our hearts and have a positive effect on mind, body, and soul."

A striking example of the effects of different music can be seen in Japanese researcher Masaru Emoto's famous photos of water crystals. Dr. Emoto exposed water to various types of music, including classical and heavy metal, then froze the water and photographed the resulting crystals. The crystals formed by water that had been exposed to Bach's *Goldberg Variations* were beautiful and symmetrical (similar in shape to the crystal formed from the water that love and appreciation were directed toward).

But the pattern that emerged in the frozen water exposed to the heavy metal music wasn't crystalline at all. Asymmetrical and unremarkable, the other frozen sample it resembled most was the one of the water that had been repeatedly called, "You fool!" (You can draw your own conclusions from that last similarity. I just know what CD *I'll* be reaching for.)

According to the traditional knowledge of the chakra system, each chakra has specific sounds that are associated with the vibration of that energy center. For example, the sounds *ah* and *ha* are related to the heart.

Well, *that's* interesting—notice what sound we make when our heart melts looking at an adorable baby: *aaaah*. And what's the sound we make when our hearts are opened in laughter? *Ha, ha, ha*. And what about the joyous sound of *hallelujah!* The next time you want a quick love lift, try laughing or vocalizing a big, full *aaaaahhh*. Your heart will thank you.

Everyone Smiles in the Same Language

Smiling, which also affects the communication center, falls into a category all its own. Though not speech or sound, it directly connects us to our hearts. Thich Nhat Hanh, the Vietnamese Buddhist monk, spiritual teacher, and author of *True Love*, talks a lot about how important smiling is for experiencing love and happiness. He says, "Sometimes your joy is the source of your smile, but sometimes your smile can be the source of your joy."

And smiles can add to others' joy too. They're so contagious. Talk about a universal language: smiles open up hearts and communicate love better than almost anything else on the planet.

There's loads of research showing the power of smiling to improve your physical and emotional well-being. When you smile, you're flooding your system with positive neurochemicals such as endorphins, serotonin, and the "love hormone," oxytocin. Studies have shown that even deliberately putting a smile on your face has many of the same effects as a spontaneous smile. Which is why I had to smile when Love Luminary and qigong master Chunyi Lin told me that *SMILE* stands for "*Start My Internal Love Engine*." Ladies and gentlemen, start your engines!

I was first introduced to the Nonviolent Communication (NVC) process by Love Luminary Peggy O'Neill. Peggy, who stands only three feet eight inches tall, is an inspirational speaker and the author of *Walking Tall: Overcoming Inner Smallness No Matter What Size You Are*. I consider Peggy a master of communication from the heart. When she raved to me about NVC, I begged her to teach it to me. The following exercise is what she shared.

Exercise

❧

Nonviolent Communication: Speaking

NVC is often referred to as the "language of the heart" because it awakens empathy for yourself and others. The next time you're upset with someone, use this four step NVC process to concisely describe your observations, feelings, needs, and requests. It will help you honestly express yourself, calmly and clearly.

1. **Observation:** Take a few deep breaths before talking to help calm your emotions. Speak in a clear and audible voice, using short, succinct statements. Using "I" statements, describe what you observed—as though you've watched the event on a video or listened to it on an audio tape ("I saw" or "I heard"). Tell just the facts. For example, you might say, "I saw you come in the door and drop your coat on the floor," or "I overheard you tell Dan that you're going to fire me at the end of the month."

   Don't embellish your statements with what you felt, conjectured, or assumed about the situation. Omit name-calling or blame. For example, *don't* say, "You're such a slob. You're always leaving a mess around here!" or "I can't believe you're going to fire me!"

2. **Feelings:** Now share the feelings that arose in response to the observed event. For example, "When I saw you come in the door and drop your coat on the floor, I felt frustrated and disrespected." Stick with direct feelings such as fear, sadness, anger, hurt, or hopelessness. Avoid feelings that describe your desire to attack, accuse, or shame someone, such as "When I saw you walk in the door and drop your coat on the floor, I felt like smacking you."

3. **Needs:** Now state the need that is underlying your feeling. An example of sharing a need: "What I need is order in our shared space." Or "I need to know if it's true that you're planning to fire me soon."

4. **Requests:** Now make a request for a concrete action. Requests work best when they are realistic and clear, such as "I ask that you hang up or put away your things when you come home." Or "Would you be willing to lower my pay rather than fire me?"

     Requests that do not work well are ambiguous, open-ended, and nonspecific, such as "I request that you always keep this place tidy." "Always" requires too open-ended a commitment, and "tidy" may mean something different to you than it does to the other person.

When you become experienced with the process, you can combine all four steps into two sentences: When I observe (see, hear, etc.) _____, I feel (emotion or sensation) _____, because I need (something I value) _____. Would you be willing to (concrete action I would like taken) _____?

Bravo! You have just communicated without creating hurt or violence on the planet. This is really something to celebrate.

For more information, go to www.NonviolentCommunication.com

Love Key for Communication #2:
Hear from the Heart

The first duty of love is to listen.

—Paul Tillich, twentieth-century theologian and philosopher

The flip side of speaking from the heart is, of course, hearing from the heart. Have you ever talked to people who act as if listening is just the annoying pause before they get to speak again? Those people are *not* hearing from the heart. Hearing from the heart means listening in a way that melts any blocks between you and the other person. It keeps you both in the energy of love.

In his book *Nonviolent Communication: A Language of Life*, NVC originator Marshall Rosenberg shares the following story about the power of hearing from the heart no matter how emotionally charged the situation:

> I was presenting NVC to about 170 Palestinian Muslim men in a mosque at a refugee camp in Bethlehem. At the time, the prevailing attitude in the Arab world toward Americans wasn't favorable. As I spoke, a wave of muffled commotion went through the audience and a man suddenly leapt to his feet. Facing me squarely, the man hollered at the top of his lungs, "Murderer!" Immediately, a dozen other voices joined him in chorus, "Assassin!" "Child-killer!" "Murderer!"
>
> Rather than reacting, I focused my attention on what the man in front of me was feeling and needing. In this case, I had some clues. On the way to the mosque, I had seen a number of empty tear-gas canisters that had been shot into the refugee camp the night before. Clearly marked on each canister were the words: *Made in U.S.A.* I knew that the men in the room harbored a lot of anger toward the United States for supplying tear gas and other weapons to Israel.

I spoke to the man who was standing, "Are you angry that my government is using its resources in the way it is?"

The man responded that of course he was angry. "Our country doesn't need your bombs or tear gas. We need housing. We need education."

I acknowledged the man's anger and his desire for support in improving his living conditions, but the man kept railing at me, "Do you know what it feels like to know that your children are going to a school that has no books? My son is sick from playing in an open sewer because there is no playground! Do you have any idea what it's like for us?"

I told him I could understand how painful it was for him to raise his children in these circumstances. "It sounds like you want more Americans to be aware of the suffering you and your family are experiencing."

"That's right," he shot back. "I want the human rights you Americans talk so much about. Why don't more of you come here and see what kind of human rights you're bringing here?"

The conversation went back and forth like this for another twenty minutes—the Palestinian man talking about his pain and me listening for the feeling and need underlying each statement. I didn't agree or disagree with him. I received his words, not as attacks, but as gifts from a fellow human willing to share his soul and deep vulnerabilities with me. Once the man felt understood, he was able to hear me explain my purpose for being at the camp.

An hour later, the same man who had publicly called me a murderer was inviting me to his home for a Ramadan dinner.

Speaking from the heart requires getting clear on *your own feelings*. Listening from the heart requires getting clear about *another person's feelings*.

During a conversation, wouldn't it be nice to be able to read subtitles that spelled out what the other person really meant? The spoken words might be "You were supposed to call me!" but the subtitles would say, "I was worried sick about you."

If you only listen to the words spoken, rather than the underlying intention, you may wind up feeling blamed or attacked. This triggers a natural defense response, or worse, makes you attack the other person: "What are you? My mother? Do I have to call you every ten minutes and tell you where I am?" Things usually escalate from there, and the chances of communicating from the heart plummet.

But when you learn to read the subtitles, you may be inspired to respond quite differently—to what's underneath the words, not just to the words themselves. You might say, "It sounds like you were worried, honey."

Imagine how this kind of response would steer the communication on quite a different course! In my interview with Love Luminaries Jim and Jori Manske, who've developed a program called Radical Compassion based on the principles of Nonviolent Communication, they told me, "We can remain in a state of love when we recognize that everyone is doing the best they can to get their needs met."

In the story that follows, Jim describes a pivotal moment in his relationship with his father, when compassionate listening saved the day and let love grow.

Jim's Story
Listening with Love

As a young man, sometimes I had a hard time communicating. I habitually kept my lip zipped, motivated by the fear that if others knew what was going on in me, I'd be ridiculed, bullied, punished, or rejected. I wasn't always a great listener either. At times I was distracted by my own internal dialogue and tended to react badly to what I perceived was criticism.

Wanting to increase my communication skills attracted me to learn

and practice Nonviolent Communication (NVC), which I've been studying and teaching for more than ten years. Long practice of these principles
has enabled me to communicate compassionately—to consciously choose
when to open my mouth and when to keep it closed and listen—so that
everyone involved ends up feeling closer to one another and there's more
love flowing in our lives.

This ability to speak and listen with love made all the difference two
years ago, when my mother was gravely ill and my father and I were put
to an extreme test. Mom had suffered for years with emphysema and then,
a few weeks after her eighty-first birthday, she caught a cold that quickly
turned into pneumonia. Her condition deteriorated and she had to be
rushed by ambulance to the hospital. By the time she arrived, she'd lost
consciousness. She was immediately admitted into the intensive care unit.

Dad and I spent the following days in her room, waiting, waiting,
waiting—looking for any sign that she would emerge from her coma. Each
day for the next week the doctors and nurses briefed us on her condition
and the options available to her. The report was always the same: she wasn't
improving and there was nothing more they could do.

As those terrible days went by, it became clear to me that the only
thing sustaining my mother was the machinery of modern medical
technology—tubes, needles, and drugs. I felt intense anxiety and distress
all week, wishing I could find a way to contribute to her well-being but
feeling helpless and losing hope that any strategy would work.

At the end of ten days, the doctors told my father and me that it was
doubtful that my mother would ever regain consciousness or breathe on
her own again; her brain had been damaged beyond repair.

I sensed the awful truth of this. I could feel that Mom was gone, even
as the machines continued to breathe for her and the drugs regulated her
heartbeat. I had no doubt as to what Mom would have wanted. She had
expressed her wishes to me several times before she got sick, and I knew
she would not want this.

I voiced my anguish to my father, expressing my concern for Mom's
wishes and for a sense of dignity and completion for her life. He responded,
"I could never live with myself if I made the decision to remove her from
life support."

Hearing the first word of Dad's response, "I," a surge of anger came up in me. I thought, *This isn't just about you, Dad. What about Mom? What about the rest of the family? This affects us all.* But thankfully, my NVC training kicked in and I was able to keep quiet and remain present enough to be aware of the strong emotions racing through me. I recognized the underlying judgment I was feeling: it seemed to me that Dad was being self-centered.

Being self-centered was definitely not okay in our family. If someone took care of their own needs at the expense of another's, they were judged to be self-centered and selfish. I had internalized that judgment and was quick to disapprove of anyone, including myself, who I thought erred in that direction.

At the same time, I knew my judgment of my father was crazy—and highly ironic. There are few people in the world more self-sacrificing than Dad. He was born in the twenties, served in World War II, and worked long hours to provide for his family all through my growing-up years. Yet even after a hard day at work, he'd often make the time to connect with me. We played ball and later rode motorcycles together, and I loved those times we shared.

Now, in this highly charged emotional situation, I'd gotten triggered and gone into reaction mode. Fortunately, because I'd practiced NVC for so many years, instead of going off on an angry tirade, I was able to make the choice to stop and breathe, to be quiet for the moment, and to begin NVC's empathetic listening process.

First, I just noticed what was going on in my body as the anger moved through me. My teeth were clenching; my eyes were tearing; my heart was racing.

Next, instead of trying to push these physical reactions away, I gave myself permission to have this experience. In just a few moments it passed, and as I turned my attention toward my dad, I realized that he was feeling just like me—upset! He was devastated by his helplessness to make his wife of sixty-two years well again and by the dreadful reality he was facing. I felt his predicament and saw that he was doing the best he could to do the right thing for Mom and also meet his own needs. A stream of empathy and compassion flowed from my heart to his.

Remaining silent, I thought, *You're feeling scared. You want to protect Mom and yourself from the current agony and from future suffering. You need clarity and acceptance.*

Eventually I gave voice to the empathy I felt and said, "Dad, it sounds like you can't imagine living with yourself if you make that kind of decision. Are you feeling scared and needing clarity about what would best support Mom?"

He nodded silently, tears in his eyes. The moment passed.

I sensed that he could best find that clarity on his own, so I remained quiet after that. I felt peaceful inside. A little while later, my wife, Jori, and I went to get some lunch, leaving Dad alone with my mom.

When we walked in the door about an hour later, Dad was sitting with Mom in the dimly lit room. The machines continued their relentless humming and whirring. Nothing had changed outwardly, but I could tell that something had happened. My dad looked up at us, and there was a quality of tenderness and openness toward me and a sense of peace in him that hadn't been there earlier.

Dad pulled me aside and said quietly, "Jim, call the family." That was his way of saying, "There's no point in prolonging the situation. I'm ready to let her go."

Tears of relief, compassion, and grief flowed for both of us and we hugged long and hard.

Something shifted that day for my dad and me. Our relationship, and my sense of connection with him, deepened.

Today Dad and I are closer than we've ever been. Even though we live thousands of miles apart, I call him every day and I know he looks forward to our talks. We even read the same books and discuss them—our own private book club. I treasure the opportunity to visit whenever possible.

Dad is still in a lot of pain with grief and depression, as well as his own health challenges, and every day when I call, I know I'm likely to hear about his struggles. Even so, there is *nothing* on God's green earth that would keep me from calling. I want to be there for him and listen to him talk about whatever he wants to, whether it's to share his sadness or just to comment on the weather. I have a total willingness to be with my father, wherever and however he is. Listening is still the best gift I give to him— and to myself.

Compassionate Listening

*When love overflows and is expressed through every deed,
we call it Compassion. That is the goal of religion.*

—Mata Amritanandmayi Devi (Ammachi), spiritual leader
known as "The Hugging Saint"

As Jim found, something magical happens when we listen with compassion. When you hear from your heart, your body's fear system shuts off and you stop seeing the other person as an enemy. Instead you see the person's humanity and how alike the two of you are. The dynamics of the situation change. Rather than being adversaries—figuratively sitting on opposite sides of a table and arguing with each other—you and the person you're listening to *both* sit on the *same side* of that imaginary table and work together toward a positive outcome.

My marketing director, Shelly Roby, shared a tip that she uses to hear with compassion. She said, "When I listen with my heart—especially when I'm having difficulty—I actually picture a beam of light connecting my heart with the other person's heart. I focus my attention on that visual image, and it always helps me."

Compassionate listening works in all your relationships. Try it with your coworkers, children, other family members, friends, and even people you have a hard time with. Being a listening presence is a gift we give to other people, allowing them to feel more open, heard, and loved.

A wonderful technique for hearing from the heart is called Compassionate Listening, codeveloped by Love Luminary Leah Green. Leah is the cofounder of the Compassionate Listening Project, which teaches programs all over the world that specialize in helping people speak and listen from the heart—even in the heat of conflict. Leah's work grew out of twenty years of on-the-ground peacemaking with Israelis and Palestinians.

220 *Love for No Reason*

Exercise
Compassionate Listening

1. Quiet your mind and become fully present to the other person, genuinely seeking to connect with their heart—their "core essence."

2. Silently anchor yourself in the core of your being by breathing into your own heart. It is here that you will access compassion and the spaciousness to hold the other's feelings and experiences—their pain, fears, and judgments—with care and respect.

3. Maintain eye contact and an open, relaxed posture. Avoid trying to control the situation. By withholding your own thoughts, judgments, interpretations, or advice, you remain in service to the speaker.

4. Stay open and present. Imagine yourself creating a sacred space for the other person to freely explore their inner landscape. They are finding their own pathway through the terrain.

5. Allow silence. This helps the speaker to hear themselves more deeply, and to touch the feelings under the surface.

6. Let your facial expression match the feelings being expressed. The speaker will feel "heard" by the empathy in your eyes.

7. If you find yourself distracted by your own thoughts or judgments, simply notice and release them, just as in a meditation practice, and return as fully as possible to the speaker. As you become more skilled and present, the speaker will feel safe to explore at deeper levels.

8. Offer only reflection. When people hear the details of what's important to them reflected back, or their own feelings, a whole new world of awareness and understanding opens up, and oftentimes solutions or "next steps" naturally emerge. Take care to offer pure reflective listening! Interjecting your own interpretations, advice, or analysis is not helpful.

Used by permission of Leah Green, www.CompassionateListening.org

Summary and Love for No Reason Action Steps

Speaking the language of love and hearing from the heart are the keys that open the Doorway of Communication, making you an agent of love rather than fear. Use the following action steps to increase the flow of love through this energy center:

1. Use the Appreciation Practice to become more fluent in the language of love. Each day, share with family members, friends, and coworkers at least one thing that you love and appreciate about them.

2. When someone triggers strong emotions within you, rather than reacting in the heat of the moment, CHILL. Take time to deal with your feelings, and Communicate Heart-Informed Love Later.

3. Remember that your subconscious mind believes every word you say, particularly if those words follow the statement "I am." Use the power of words to affirm love.

4. Use music, singing, and chanting to open your heart and elevate your mood. For an instant love lift, make a deep, full *aaaahhhh* sound.

5. Throughout the day, remember to smile—Start My Internal Love Engine. Doing this will flood your body with feel-good chemicals.

6. To express yourself in a way that keeps you in the love zone, use the four steps of the Nonviolent Communication Speaking exercise: observing, feeling, identifying needs, and making requests.

7. When in conflict, imagine yourself and the other person sitting on the same side of the table and working together toward a positive outcome. Or try visualizing a beam of light connecting your hearts.

8. Use the Compassionate Listening exercise to create a safe space for others to communicate with you. Be sensitive to the unspoken feelings and needs that underlie people's words.

CHAPTER 9

The Doorway of Vision: Seeing with the Eyes of Love

If the doors of perception were cleansed,
everything would appear to man as it is, infinite.
—William Blake, eighteenth-century British poet and artist

What if you could see with the eyes of love, so that everything looked radiant and left you open-hearted? You'd be seeing beyond the surface of things, not with X-ray vision like Superman, but by catching glimpses of the deeper reality of life. My wise and wonderful coauthor, Carol, writes about her experiences of this as a child:

> When I was a little girl, I used to go into the bathroom, climb up on top of the closed toilet lid, and look into the medicine-cabinet mirror. I'd stare at my reflection, taking in my blond hair, hazel eyes, and pint-sized nose, and think, *How weird. People think that's who I am.*
>
> I knew that the face in the mirror, and the body that went with it, was me, but it wasn't *really* me. The real me was riding around inside this girl everyone called Carol. Even as a child I saw that there was more to life than met the eye.

This idea was reinforced when I was around eight and my older brother's wife, Diana, told me a story about a woman she'd met at work. Diana worked in the campus library of the college she and my brother went to. Her coworker, although very nice, was a terrible dresser. Her hairstyle was unflattering, her clothes neat but frumpy, and she never wore even a trace of makeup. Though Diana was more interested in books and ideas than in fashion, she found this woman's complete disregard for appearance a little strange and wondered why she didn't make even a small effort to be more stylish.

She got her answer one day when the woman's husband came to walk her home after work. He was blind! Diana said it was clear that the man adored his wife and that his wife felt the same way about him. Seeing this, Diana said she felt humbled. She told me, "I learned not to judge someone for something so superficial."

This story struck me very deeply. I remember it almost forty-five years later, because it made me think long and hard about what true beauty is.

When the Doorway of Vision is open, you move through your life seeing not only the bigger picture, but the biggest picture there is: everyone is made of one essence and that essence is love. I know, I know, this is a platitude you've heard so often that it slides right off your brain, but when this doorway opens, these words become a factual description of the world as you see it.

You're able to see that people are more alike than different and that what we all have in common is our underlying essence of love. Love dominates your vision.

You develop what some spiritual traditions call celestial perception: you're able to see the beauty in everything—even in what appears to others as ugly. I call this having "mother's eyes." A mother sees beauty in even the most homely of children. Mother Teresa saw beauty in the lepers in the street. When you see with mother's eyes, you see the spirit that's inside everyone.

Your attention is drawn to what's right, happy, and uplifting more than to what's wrong, depressing, and discouraging. It's not that you don't see what's in front of you. You do—warts and all. It's that your eyes and mind aren't hijacked by the flaws and faults present in everything. You look on the world with a kind eye.

According to Love Luminary Arielle Ford, who speaks and writes on this subject, the Japanese call this *wabi-sabi:* seeing the perfection lurking in the imperfect. A friend's crooked smile, your grandmother's wrinkled face, the macaroni necklace a beloved child makes for you are all examples of how perfectly heart-opening imperfection can be.

When this doorway is open, your mind functions at a higher level. You go beyond being smart and you become wise, relying on the intelligence of both your mind and your heart.

But when this doorway is blocked, you get stuck in your head. We all know people like that—hey, you might be one of those people yourself (or married to one)—people with strong intellects that analyze, discriminate, and reason with the skill of a surgeon wielding a scalpel, slicing through extraneous details to get to the facts. This laser-sharp approach comes in handy in many situations, but if you only have a scalpel, how will you stitch up the incision you've made? Life works a lot better when you can find connection and harmony in the world around you, as well as being able to analyze and reason.

When your intellect is out of balance, you become critical, judgmental, and trapped by your limiting beliefs. You ignore your internal compass and doubt your intuition. The bottom line: too much brain and not enough heart make life feel flat and dry.

But when the mind and heart work together, love infuses your perception and thinking. You experience Love for No Reason within you and around you; it's everywhere you look.

Keep Your (Third) Eye on the Ball

The sixth energy center, or the vision center, is traditionally called the third eye or brow chakra. This chakra is located in the space between your eyebrows, and its energy field includes the center and sides of your head. It's connected to the pineal gland, the tiny and mysterious part of the brain that's activated by light and influences your body's biorhythms. The philosopher Descartes called the pineal gland "the place where all our thoughts are formed," and mystics say it's the gateway to our psychic or clairvoyant (French for "clear seeing") abilities.

The third eye chakra influences the eyes—both the physical apparatus of sight and the inner faculty that lets you "see" the spiritual reality of life. It also governs the mind and intellect: your thinking, ideas, and reasoning ability.

This chakra is also linked to your "sixth sense," the inner wisdom that shows itself through flashes of insight or whispers of intuition. Throughout history, people have given this inner vision as much importance as outer vision. But since the dawn of the Age of Reason, objective rationality and logical thinking have become so dominant that insight and intuition are often discarded.

Now, I'm not suggesting that you give up discernment. There's nothing wrong with reason or logic; it's just that they need to be balanced with the heart's love and wisdom. The intellect has been hogging the stage for too long; it's time to bring in the heart for a duet.

When the vision center is healthy, the heart and mind work together and both inner and outer vision are enhanced.

Unlocking the Doorway of Vision: The Two Love Keys

During many of my interviews with the Love Luminaries, I was struck by how they perceived the world differently from most other people I know. They had a compassionate perspective on life that shaped the way they saw people, events, and situations.

The French novelist Marcel Proust said, "The real voyage of discovery consists not in seeking new landscapes, but in having new eyes." To see with your own "new eyes," get in the habit of looking for the essence of love and truth in others and paying attention to the wisdom within yourself. Here are the two keys that will wake up your vision center to heart-based seeing.

Love Keys for the Doorway of Vision

1. Look for the Beauty
2. Trust Your Inner Wisdom

The Beauty Key helps you release the judgments and beliefs that keep you stuck in criticism and faultfinding. It lets you see beyond the surface of things to the deeper truth and beauty in people and situations.

The Trust Key puts you in touch with your intuition. When you follow your internal guidance, you strengthen the connection between your heart and mind.

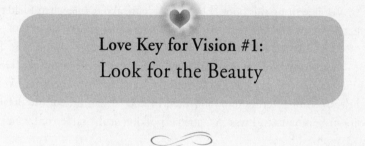

Love Key for Vision #1:
Look for the Beauty

We become what we look at most.

—Hugh Prather, author and minister

When I say beauty, I'm not talking about just aesthetic loveliness. I mean beauty in the deepest sense of the word. The kind of beauty the poet Keats was describing when he wrote his famous line "Beauty is truth, truth beauty." When you experience the beauty that's interchangeable with truth—and which also encompasses the highest love—you've reached the pinnacle of human life. Finding and living this beauty/truth/love is the spiritual equivalent of winning the lottery, finding your soul mate, and being given the Nobel Prize all rolled into one. Which is why it's worth looking for.

So how do you find it? You start by knowing where to look. (Hint: It's not always on the surface.) You have to go beyond your past impressions, likes and dislikes, and tear down any walls you may have built to shut yourself off from the world. Then you can meet each experience with the innocence and openness of a child.

In some spiritual traditions, novice monks are initiated into a monastery with the help of a gazing process. The new monk sits opposite an older monk and looks steadily across at him, letting his gaze settle on finer and finer levels of the older monk's face. At first he notices the older monk's physical appearance, then as he continues to gaze, he may observe something of the older monk's personal essence or character, and then after a while he may perceive a finer level still, the spirit or the glow of the divine deep within the other man. In this way, the new monk sees truths beyond the surface appearance, layer by layer, until he arrives at the greatest truth of all: under all the apparent differences, we are the same.

While writing this book, I heard an identical message when I had the great honor of meeting with His Holiness the Dalai Lama.

The Dalai Lama has always been a great source of inspiration for me—both for who he is and for being such a happiness advocate. (He is at the forefront of much of the scientific research on happiness.) For years I'd dreamed of meeting him, and then in 2009 I had one of my dream-come-true moments. I was in Canada speaking at the same conference as my happiness hero!

After listening to his address to the general conference, I learned that a small group of people had been invited to participate in a private meeting with His Holiness. Literally two minutes before this meeting began—and much to my surprise and delight—I was also invited to attend.

We were ushered into a rather small room with a few rows of chairs arranged in a semicircle. A few minutes later, His Holiness walked in and sat down directly across from me.

Just sitting within ten feet of this great spiritual master was transformational. His presence was incredibly calming, bathing the entire room in an aura of quiet, unconditional love.

The Dalai Lama graciously welcomed us to the meeting, and before taking our questions, he shared a few words that put us instantly at ease. He said whether he is addressing the president of a nation or a homeless person on the street makes no difference to him, because he treats everyone the same.

"Differences in religious beliefs, politics, social status, and position are all secondary," the Dalai Lama explained. "When we look at someone with compassion, we are able to see beyond these secondary differences and connect to the primary essence that binds all humans together as one."

He added that when we are in this state of being, we feel love for ourselves and for others, not because of what we do, but simply because we are.

Listening to his remarks, I couldn't help but smile to myself. *He's describing the state of Love for No Reason*, I thought. When we love for no reason, we accept ourselves, others, and the conditions around us without expectation. We see the same pure love that we're experiencing inside us in everyone else—even if they aren't aware of it themselves.

But it takes awareness and practice to make a habit of seeing beyond appearances to the Love for No Reason that we all share.

Training Our Eyes

The actual act of seeing takes place in the brain: the eyes collect the data and forward it to the brain's visual processing centers. To make sense of the barrage of real-time information streaming in, certain brain structures sort and filter the incoming perceptions, looking for signs of danger, potential pleasure, and useful information.

One of these filters is called the reticular activating system (RAS). It's the mechanism that alerts you to anything in your environment that has significance for you. Have you noticed that when you buy a new car, you suddenly notice all the other cars of that same make on the road? Or how in a noisy restaurant, the sound of your name being spoken cuts through the surrounding chatter? Your RAS locks on to information that otherwise might be ignored as "background noise."

Here's the fabulous part of this—you can actually program the RAS to alert you to whatever you want. Having the intention to look for love and beauty puts your RAS on notice and starts the ball rolling. Once your attention is brought to the love or beauty in front of you, the next step is to register it through appreciation. Doing this over and over will create the unconditional love groove you want to form in the neural pathways of your brain.

For maximum experience of Love for No Reason, each day remind yourself to look for love's radiance and the *wabi-sabi* beauty in your family, friends, and coworkers. Search it out in your physical environment and in each situation. It may feel strange at first—Pollyannaish and uncomfortable—but it gets easier and more natural as time goes by.

The Divine in Me Bows to the Divine in You

One of my favorite ways to keep my attention focused on the truth/beauty of the world and of myself is to use the Sanskrit greeting *namaste.*

Pronounced *NAH-mah-stay*, it's often translated as "The divine in me bows to the divine in you."

The word *namaste* is usually accompanied by a gesture: you place your palms together at your heart and bow your head slightly. In India, people often make this gesture of reverence for each other in silence, but it still has the same heart-opening effect.

There are some who consider *namaste* a spiritual practice. Holding the hands palm to palm is a specific *mudra*, a hand position that's used to positively influence the energies of the body or mind. And either speaking or thinking the word *namaste* acts as a mantra, a sound that creates a powerful beneficial effect on your awareness. According to the ancient texts, this greeting increases the flow of pure love in your energy system.

You don't have to say *namaste* out loud or do the hand gesture to get the benefit. When I want to practice strengthening the vision center, I look around at whatever is in my field of vision: a friend, a tree, the ocean, a beautiful painting. Sometimes I just picture someone or something with my inner eye. Then I think the phrase, "The divine in me bows to the divine in you," and I feel that in my heart. I let the quiet appreciation this creates sink in for a moment or two. This immediately helps me see things more deeply and lovingly, and it gently opens my heart.

Believe me, seeing with the eyes of love changes everything. It feeds the love body, and it's the single best tool for transforming a dreary gray world into a gorgeous multihued extravaganza.

Love Luminary Yvonne Pointer knows all about the heart/vision connection. An author and activist, Yvonne has received many national awards for her work creating safer communities for children and teens. Her story, which follows, illustrates the power of looking for the beauty in everyone.

Yvonne's Story

Love's Disguises

*W*hen my fourteen-year-old daughter, Gloria, was raped and murdered, it felt as if my life was over too. My heart was like a tomato that someone had crushed in their hand, spilling out all the seeds, and leaving a smashed and broken mess.

The day my daughter died, she'd left for school saying good-bye and carrying her books; she was excited because she was going to get an award that day for perfect attendance. But she never made it.

It was three days before I saw her again. She had been so severely beaten, it took the undertaker that long to make her presentable.

When they told me they were done, I went to the funeral home and stood for a long time over her casket. I was so filled with pain, I could hardly breathe. I remember saying, "This will not be in vain. This is not just going to happen and nothing be done about it."

At first I tried to make sense of it: Could I have stopped this? What was I not paying attention to? But I kept coming back to the thought, *There's a murderer loose in this city.* The man had not yet been found; in fact, he hasn't been found to this day. I started worrying about all the other children who were walking around and living in jeopardy because that killer was out there, unsuspected.

I had to find a way to protect those kids, to make sure what happened to Gloria didn't happen to anyone else. My first idea was to get someone famous to speak out about what we could do to keep our children safe. I didn't think anyone would listen to a mother like me from Cleveland's inner city; it needed to be a celebrity, somebody important.

I began a letter-writing campaign to find someone to come to Cleveland and help save the children. This was in 1985, so I started with Mr. T, the popular TV actor with the Mohawk haircut and big muscles. I wrote to the president. I wrote to Michael Jordan. I wrote to everybody I thought could help. But nobody came.

So I decided I'd have to do it myself. I thought, *Until that famous person arrives, I'll just do what I want them to do: go into schools and clubs and tell the children not to get into cars with strangers and that sort of thing.*

I did that for about four years, and it felt like I might be doing some good, but it didn't help my pain. My heart was still crushed; I didn't even know if I had a heart. Everything seemed gray. Everything. The trees, the grass, the sky—I was just walking around in a gray world. I was so numb I couldn't see the love that existed in the world around me.

I remember exactly where I was when the color came back to my life.

I was driving down the street, my head so heavy with depression it was hard to hold it up. I stopped at the traffic light and leaned back in my seat. Looking to my left, I saw a run-down apartment building, part of the city's low-income housing projects. The yard in front of the building was nothing but dirt, but there was one tree that was surrounded by all these flowers. I thought to myself, *Well, that's an unusual sight. Who would plant flowers in that dirt yard with no grass? And such bright flowers, all yellow and red and . . .* "Oh, my God!" I gasped with surprise. "I can see color again!"

I began to weep. Knowing that someone had braved the dreariness and the despair of living in a project with a yard of dirt and still had enough love in their hearts to actually plant flowers—it changed something for me. Just like that, the color came back into my life. I began to feel alive again.

I went back to work with a broader perspective. Now it wasn't only about saving the children; I also wanted to find people who felt as hopeless as I had felt, and tell them, "Hey, you can overcome this thing! You can get your life back."

So that's how the Positive Plus Women's Support Group got started. Our mission was restoration, taking broken lives and giving hope where there had been none. Many of the women in the group had lost a child to violence like I had. We helped each other heal—recommitting to our own forgotten goals and dreams in the process.

In addition, I continued my work of educating communities to better protect children, but as time passed, it seemed to me that the solution required going back to the source of the problem—the people who were hurting the children.

So, about six years after Gloria died, I started going to prisons to speak to the inmates. I didn't go in with a judging eye. I knew that wouldn't be useful. Instead, I went in with a deeper vision of their true essence and I tried to help them see their better natures. To find the love in their own darkness—the color in their own gray world.

I'm still visiting prisons today, twenty years later. When I talk to a group of prisoners I start by saying, "I came to tell each of you this: you are a hero." Hearing that, the room always goes dead silent.

Knowing I've got their attention, I say, "There's a hero that lies within you; you've just got to take off all of the extra stuff."

I tell them, "You're not rapists. You're not murderers. That's your disguise, the 'stuff' you've put on. You've got to shed all those things that are not who you were born to be, and get to the person you truly are." I remind them that Clark Kent had to take off his suit before he could be Superman.

The inmates tell me that I give them hope. I pray that that hope leads them to love. Because if I had to sum up my journey from despair to where I am today, it would be in these words: love lifted me. From the moment of my daughter's death, I just kept putting one foot in front of the other until a path of love unfolded before me. And seeing the love around me—even in unexpected places—helps others see it too.

♥ ♥ ♥

The part of Yvonne's story that made the deepest impression on me was when she stood in a room full of prisoners, some of them murderers and rapists—the very man who killed her daughter could even have been one of them—and yet she told them they were heroes. The love in her reached out to the love in them. Only the most open heart and mind could be capable of experiencing such an unconditional state of love in a situation like that. But we all can take a page from Yvonne's book: part of seeing through love's disguises is learning to release your judgments of people.

Releasing Judgments

A peach is not its fuzz. A toad is not its warts. A person is not his or her crankiness. Your assumptions are your windows on the world. Scrub them off once in a while or the light won't come in.

—Alan Alda, actor and author

One of the biggest blocks to experiencing Love for No Reason is being judgmental, which is different from exercising good judgment or voicing an opinion. Being judgmental is condemning another person or situation, which creates tension and separation in our relationships, effectively cutting off the flow of love.

Our pain-body is responsible for our judgments and their kissing cousin, criticism. These constrict our vision and our heart, which gives rise to more judgment and criticism, which constrict us even further, and on and on. This vicious cycle is the pain-body's way of accomplishing its goal to create more pain; that's what it lives on. Breaking the cycle of judgment and constriction requires awareness—very much like owning your own triggers did in chapter 6.

The brain's neural processes are partly to blame for our tendency to rush to judgment. Every perception, thought, memory, and idea we have is made up of neurons firing in a certain sequence. If they fire often enough in a particular sequence, a neural pathway is formed. So far, so good— except that, once established, these pathways can interfere with your perception of reality.

In their excellent book *A General Theory of Love*, psychiatrists Thomas Lewis, Fari Amini, and Richard Lannon write, "the neural past interferes with the present. Experience methodically rewires the brain, and the nature of what it *has* seen dictates what it *can* see." In other words, once your brain begins to perceive something, it scans its memory banks for a similar initial experience. If it finds one, it often continues the remembered experience— *whether or not that's what's really going on in the present!* This means that your memories can distort how you see the world. When you understand this, you can take your own judgmental and critical reactions less seriously.

Questioning your own thoughts rather than automatically accepting them as the gospel truth supports unconditional love—*and* happiness. In my book *Happy for No Reason*, "Don't believe everything you think" was one of the twenty-one fundamental Happiness Habits I uncovered when I interviewed more than one hundred unconditionally happy people. When you stop letting your old patterns of thought call the shots, you can see what's more deeply true for you.

There are some wonderful techniques for releasing yourself from the grip of judgments and limiting beliefs. My favorites include the Work developed by Byron Katie, the Sedona Method by Hale Dwoskin, the Lefkoe Method by Morty and Shelly Lefkoe, TAT (Tapas Acupressure Technique) by Tapas Fleming, and the Option Method, which I learned from my dear friend Love Luminary Lenora Boyle. (You'll find an exercise using the Option Method at the end of this key.) I've interviewed each of these people and they're all great examples of unconditional love. I recommend you learn one or more of these tools. (They're all listed in the Resources section.)

When you view the world through eyes that are unclouded by past limiting beliefs, your life will get much simpler. What people say and do, and the things that "happen" to you, can simply be viewed as "happenings"— no more, no less. Without all the added layers of story, you're free to respond with increased compassion and humor—and to stay in a Love for No Reason space more of the time.

Optical Illusions

I'm sure you've seen at least one of the optical illusions that have been circulating for years: the young lady and the old crone, the two faces and the chalice, almost any M. C. Escher drawing. In these mind-bending pictures, you often first see the image one way and can't see it any other way. Then suddenly your perception shifts and you're looking at what appears to be a completely different image. Once you've seen both images, you can usually toggle back and forth between the two. You have the freedom to choose one or the other.

The technique of reframing—or seeing the events in your life in a different context—is like suddenly seeing the optical illusion you've been staring at in the new way. Based on the work of noted psychologist Virginia

Satir, reframing works by changing the frame you put around the things that happen to you. For example, if you break your leg before a summer vacation, one way to frame the event is as a disaster: all your plans are ruined, you can't go to the beach, you can't work in your garden, and so on. Another way to frame it is as an opportunity: now you can do something enriching, but sedentary, that you'd never normally make time to do, like reading *War and Peace*, putting together a photo album, or writing a blog. The same event: a broken leg. Two different frames: disaster or opportunity.

One young college student who was faced with this exact scenario spent his summer vacation learning to play the guitar. It was something he'd always wanted to do but had never had the time to pursue. As the summer progressed, the young man found that he loved playing the guitar and was even pretty good at it. Back at school, he changed his major and his life goals, deciding to become a professional musician. The young man's name? Julio Iglesias. The famous Spanish singer reframed his broken leg into an opportunity and ended up with a spectacular career doing something he loved. Julio has said, "Breaking my leg was the best thing that ever happened to me!"

Like Julio, you can choose a frame that closes your heart or one that instantly allows compassion, expansion, and connection to flow. We talked about a similar idea in chapter 4: you can sense your support if you look at anything that happens to you as being for your enjoyment, growth, or both. This is another great example of reframing.

Reframing invites you to put on a different pair of glasses: one that directs your attention to the underlying spiritual beauty in people and the higher truth of the events in your life. I recently started a new practice that I suggest you try: stop labeling anything that happens to you as bad. No more, "I had a bad day." "What bad news." "It's so bad that I lost my job." In the face of everyday hassles—traffic jams, getting chewed out by the boss, or relationship hiccups—looking for the Beauty/Truth brings you back to unconditional love.

Exercise

Dissolving Limiting Beliefs with the Option Method

Dissolving limiting beliefs will shift your perception and open you to greater love. Ask the following questions for any belief that limits your love or hurts you in some way.

1. Write down a negative judgment or limiting belief that keeps you stuck or blocks your experience of love. A belief is a *perception* of reality or a conclusion that you've come to, based on past conditioning. Some examples are "I'm not good enough" and "I can't do it."

2. Write the following questions on paper. After you ask the question, notice your first thoughts, body sensations, images, then write your responses without editing.

   • *Do you believe that?* Even if you believe it just "sometimes," it's still affecting every decision you make.

   • *Why do you believe that?* You have some reasons you've used in the past to build your case, trying to prove the belief is true. Explore those here.

   • *Do you know if it's true?* Ask yourself why might you believe something that you don't know is true.

   • *What might concern you if that belief were gone?* This is a crucial question to answer. In other words, *What might happen that you wouldn't like if that belief were gone?* There's a concern about the belief's being eliminated, otherwise it wouldn't be there. The belief is serving you in some way. Let this question sink into your heart and it will awaken you.

3. If another limiting belief is uncovered during this process, then begin with step 1 again and question a new belief.

Simply questioning your limiting beliefs—and the reasons you may have been holding on to them—allows those limiting beliefs to start dissolving automatically. When you realize a limiting belief is no longer true, you feel freer, happier, and more open to love.

Used by permission of Deborah Mendel and Lenora Boyle,
www.ChangeLimitingBeliefs.com

Love Key for Vision #2:
Trust Your Inner Wisdom

Have you ever known something—known for sure it was true—but didn't know how you knew it? That sense of clarity and certainty *for no apparent reason* is what I mean by inner wisdom, inner knowing, inner guidance, or intuition. It's an inner light that can illuminate your way—if you give it a chance.

It's not that some people have intuition and others don't; we all have it available 24/7. The problem is that we've stopped looking for and paying attention to it.

Your intuition, sometimes called your sixth sense, links you to your inner world. When you know something through intuition—from the inside out—it may not always be logical or make sense intellectually. You just "know" it. This is why so many people dismiss intuition as woo-woo or flaky.

Since logic and reason have been the top dogs in our culture for so long, we've been trained to ignore or dismiss what we can't prove, including guidance from within. We just don't trust our inner wisdom.

Don't get me wrong, a lot of great things have come from the reign of the intellect—hair dryers and indoor plumbing come to mind. But there's also been a downside: a shift away from listening to our inner voice that's resulted in a massive disconnection from our heart.

Yep, the voice of intuition is directly connected to your heart. Research conducted by the team at HeartMath has demonstrated the heart's intuitive intelligence. In one study, participants were shown a series of images. Most of them were peaceful, such as landscapes, trees, and animals, but there were also disturbing images randomly interspersed among the positive ones.

The subjects were monitored before, during, and after the viewing for changes in respiration, skin conductivity, brain waves, heart rate variability, and more. The researchers found that significant changes in heart activity consistently occurred five to seven seconds *prior* to the appearance of the disturbing images on the screen. The heart somehow knew what was going to happen on the screen before it happened and reacted differently to the disturbing images than it did to the pleasant ones.

The ancient sages would probably smile at these scientific attempts to pin down the third eye experience. By nature it's mysterious and until now has evaded measuring and proof. But what HeartMath's astounding data suggests is that although the brain has classically been viewed as the exclusive processor of information, the fact is that the heart receives and responds to intuitive information *before* the brain.

These findings confirm that your intuition is the prompting of your heart. Dr. Rollin McCraty, who led this study, told me, "Intuition is the voice of the higher self coming through the heart to the brain." That's why intuition can be insistent, nagging, and even unsettling. It's your heart wanting to overturn the applecart, so that you take a risk and move more boldly (or less boldly) than your rational mind might allow.

And while it might seem like intuition is guiding you off the map, making you turn left when others are turning right, what it's actually doing is showing you your essential nature, the larger truth of yourself: you know more than you think you do. You can follow your own vision.

Following your intuitive guidance puts you in harmony with the unseen workings of the world. Synchronicities occur when you act on intuitive flashes. Connections happen. Whatever's best for you gets thrust into your awareness like a firework exploding in the night sky. It's only there for a second. The question is, do you have the heart to follow it?

Many of the Love Luminaries spoke of intuition as the promptings of Higher Love—hearing the whispering of their heart's wisdom inside. They trust this inner wisdom and allow it to guide their choices, instead of letting the intellect alone decide how they live their lives.

This heart-centered way of decision making can lead to some surprising choices. Love Luminary Allison Stillman, a talented aromatherapist and author, told me the following anecdote about what life is like when you listen to your heart:

> Since childhood, I've paid attention to my heart's instructions, not in the "what feels good in the moment" kind of way, but by doing what I know, deep inside my soul, is for my highest good. And while many of the decisions I've made have left my family and some of my friends scratching their heads and thinking I was nuts, each of those choices has led me into a deeper, more loving relationship with my life.
>
> In 1998 a friend of mine who was starting a litigation software company approached me and asked if I would work with him. I told him I didn't know anything about software technology or litigation, but he convinced me that my people skills would be an asset. So I set my aromatherapy practice aside for a time and dove in.
>
> After a steep learning curve, I became the marketing director of the company. For the next six years, I traveled to corporate boardrooms and some of the largest law offices in the country, meeting the power players in the world of corporate law. Still, I let my heart lead the way. I saw each encounter as an opportunity to find the deeper human qualities in everyone I met and to connect from that level.
>
> In the sixth year of my marketing career, the CEO of my company accepted an infusion of cash from an investment banking firm to take the company to the next level. To safeguard their investment, the banking firm sent one of their executives to work with us. The executive, whose favorite description of herself was "bitter and twisted," spent the next few months following me around and learning the business.

Then one Friday at 5 p.m., she called me into her office. "Allison," she said, "I've been observing you for four months now and I've never seen anything like it. Your sales team, senior management, your clients, the support staff—everyone loves you! Clearly, your priority has been keeping this lovefest going and it's worked.

"Well, today is the day that ends. I need you to take that same energy you've given to cultivating relationships and direct it to the bottom line. Can I count on you to do that?"

It took a nanosecond for my heart to inform me, "It's over." But I only said, "Let me think about it over the weekend, and let's talk about it on Monday."

Over the weekend, my mind catalogued all the reasons that I needed this job. I'd just bought a new house; I had car payments and bills that required a salary. I had stock options, health insurance. But it didn't matter . . . I knew what was right in my heart and what was true for my soul.

On Monday morning I walked into the executive's office and gave her my notice. I stayed to train my successor and then followed my heart's promptings out the door.

After that, contrary to my logical mind's prediction of financial ruin, my life unfolded in wonderful ways I could never have imagined. I found part-time consulting work—which led me to meet the man who would later become my husband—resumed my aromatherapy anointing practice, and wrote and published a book. Today I am rich in all the ways that matter to me.

The company, however, didn't fare quite as well. Ms. Bitter and Twisted's "bottom line first" campaign effectively removed the heart of the business. And we all know what happens when you take the heart out of any living organism. Over the next two years, the company died a slow and painful death.

The real bottom line? In business and in decision making, people try to keep the mind and heart separate, but they work best as a team. The same thing is true in life, and I'm grateful that my heart's always there to offer its own wise intelligence.

Tuning In

The question I'm asked most often about intuition is "How do I know whether that voice inside is coming from my inner wisdom or from my fears and emotions?" It's a great question, and it's important to learn how to distinguish between the two. Intuition is a deep level of wisdom that always leads you to your greater good. You can tell when you're in touch with your inner knowing because it's always accompanied by peace, a sense of lightness, and a calm certainty. You just *know*. There's no emotion or drama involved.

When you're guided by your emotions, you "do what you *feel* like doing." You may feel like doing something out of fear, anger, sadness, or pain, but those impulses aren't coming from intuition. They're reactions, based on old patterns of thinking and feeling. When you act on an emotion, it may or may not be good for you in the long run. (Most likely, it won't be.) And it's certainly not a reliable path to Higher Love.

For that, you have to trust your inner wisdom. It may not be linear— it may urge you to do things that are inconvenient, move you into unfamiliar territory, or even require a leap of faith—but it always takes you to a more expanded state of Love for No Reason.

Trust Your Vibes

Love Luminary Sonia Choquette, spiritual teacher, chakra expert, and the author of many best-selling books, has spent her life listening to her inner knowing. Her message to the world is "Trust your vibes."

In our interview, Sonia explained that your vibes come from your heart/spirit, which is the most intelligent part of you because it's a piece of the universal Spirit that's animating and guiding everything. "Spirit navigates whales across oceans, sends fish swimming upstream to spawn, takes monarch butterflies from one continent to the next and brings them back to the exact same branch. It knows what the intellect can never know."

When you pick up on those vibes and—here's the important part— *trust* them enough to allow them to direct your course, your heart and your spirit join your intellect, and together they guide your life in ways that serve your highest good. The benefits of trusting your vibes range from avoiding traffic jams (you get an inner signal to take a different route) to avoiding heartbreak (you know immediately that someone is trouble and keep your distance) and beyond. But most important, according to Sonia, when you trust your vibes, life becomes a graceful dance; stress dissolves and your heart expands in love.

When I met Sonia, I was struck by how alive and filled with enthusiasm and joy she is. Trusting her vibes makes her truly vibrant. In the following story, Sonia describes how, by keeping her in touch with a deeper reality, her inner guidance helped her overcome apparent obstacles to love.

Sonia's Story
Led by Love

*I*n my family, intuition wasn't the sixth sense—it was considered the first! My parents would never have met and married without it. At seventeen, my dad left the farm to join the Army and serve in World War II. When he returned, he brought back with him my mother, a fifteen-year-old war bride.

Mom had been a prisoner of war in a German prison camp. She had lost her entire family in the war and had never finished school. Neither she nor my dad was book-educated; the resource they relied on most was their intuition.

When making decisions, my parents never asked my siblings and me, "What do you think about this?" or "What did you read about that?" It was always, "What does your spirit say?" That was the absolute marker of truth and it was never challenged.

They weren't against education, not at all. They told us, "Go, learn everything you can at school. But when it comes right down to it, above all—no matter what you hear, no matter what's said, no matter how things appear—trust your vibes."

Trusting her vibes had saved my mother's life on many occasions during the war. When she'd been put into the POW camp at fourteen, she'd heard the people around her crying, "We're going to die." They had already given up. But something inside her had said, "*No!* I'm *not* going to die. Just pay attention and listen." The voices of doom all around her offered her no hope, so she grabbed on to the voice inside herself as a lifeline and began listening to it.

When the Nazis sorted the prisoners into groups, a fourteen-year-old girl on her own didn't really fit into any category. Not knowing what else to do with her, they put her with a group of people being sent to Odessa in the Soviet Union. Everybody knew that Odessa was the end of the line. My mother had no illusions about what was in store for her if she ended up there.

They herded her onto the train, where she found herself standing beside an open door. She could see guards holding guns outside, standing near the tracks.

The train began to move. As it gained momentum, she looked around and noticed that, at that moment, no one was watching her. In that split second, her spirit said, "*Jump!*" There was no time to think or evaluate; she went with it. As she flung herself out the door, she told herself, *At least if I die, it will be on my own terms.* She hit the ground, rolled in the dirt, and then waited for the train to pass.

She survived.

For the rest of the war, until she met the American GI who would take her to the United States, what kept her alive was listening to her internal GPS—and following her inner vibrations each step of the way. My father followed his intuition too. He was bold and had confidence that he would always be guided to do the right thing.

And so my six siblings and I got the message early on. As we were growing up, our parents encouraged us to look for opportunities to trust our vibes. Every day when we walked out the door to school, my mother called out to us, "Listen to your spirit! I expect to hear about it at dinner."

And every night at the dinner table, my mother and father listened attentively as the seven of us recounted all the intuitive experiences we'd had that day. We didn't watch TV or read magazines and we didn't miss them; we were happy just talking and sharing our stories. My parents created an atmosphere in which intuition was embraced as glorious wisdom.

I only became aware that listening to your intuition wasn't a common experience when I entered school. I saw that the more people were cut off from their spirits, the more fearful and isolated they became. I'd look around, puzzled, and think, *It's as if everybody has a paper bag on their head and then is crying, "I'm lonely."* I wanted to tell them, "Take that bag off your head and look around. If you did, you could see how much goodness there is, and how much love there is, because it's everywhere." When you listen to your vibes, you're led to love. You see and feel it.

As a kid, I was sometimes led by my vibes to love in unexpected ways. I went to a very small Catholic school that was directly across the street from the public school. The public school kids hated the Catholic school kids, and the Catholic school kids were afraid of the public school kids. Everyone was glad that our school let out thirty minutes before the public school did, so we could all run home and not have to meet "the bad guys."

The year I was in second grade, I decided there was something about this closed-heartedness I didn't fully accept. So one day after school, I hung around and then dallied on my walk home so I could actually meet the public school kids. I wanted to see what they were like. As I walked past the public school in my Catholic uniform, sure enough, a group of girls came running across the playground toward me, yelling, "Let's get her!" and "Let's beat her up!"

I froze. The voice of my fear said, "Run!" but another voice, the strong, calm voice of my intuition, said, "Sit down." I struggled for a moment about what to do: *Run or sit down?* I sat down.

The girls came to an abrupt stop a few yards from me and stared. They didn't know what to do with me, because they'd expected me to run away from them. One girl said, "What are you doing?"

I smiled and said, "Well, I'm sitting down because I wanted to meet you."

They looked at me with confused faces. But one of the girls asked, "What do you mean, you want to meet us?"

I said, "I just wanted to say hi because I think you're cool."

That floored them. They went from going in for the kill to sitting down with me and playing instead. We talked, awkwardly at first, and then more and more easily as we all played jacks together.

I really did think they were cool. They didn't have to wear uniforms like we did. Mine was blue and had a skirt that went down past my knees and had about forty thousand pleats. Plus, I had to wear white anklets and black shoes. I hated it. I remember one girl had on saddle shoes, knee socks, Bermuda shorts to the knee, and a cute round-neck top with short sleeves and bright little flowers on it. I looked at her in admiration and said, "I like your clothes; they're so beautiful." Her name was Vicki Sue and she became one of my best friends.

After that day, the public school girls and I agreed that I would wait and meet them after school, so we could all walk home together.

Trusting my vibes paid off big that time. Not only did I make some new friends, but I also became the coolest kid in my school: I'd met the bad guys and lived to tell the tale.

In the years since then, I've had many similar intuitive experiences—some minor, some major. They've all reinforced my conviction that my parents had it right: listen to your intuition and you'll be led to love.

At seven years old, Sonia had already skipped a few grades when it came to trusting her inner wisdom. Today, she says, it's this wide-open sixth sense that helps her perceive love in all its forms and expressions.

Opening yourself to inner guidance is like building a muscle. With practice it gets stronger and stronger. In her classes, Sonia guides her students to coax the sixth sense out of hiding by playing a guessing game she calls "I Wonder." To play, take that phrase into your day and have fun with it. Ask yourself, "I wonder what color shirt my boss is going to wear to work?" "I wonder what surprising thing will happen today?" Pay attention to your answers.

Sonia's playful prescription opens your heart, because wonder aligns you with love rather than fear. She told me, "If you invite intuition in, you will fall in love with life very fast."

Life becomes interesting instead of scary. When you wonder, you put your judgments and intellect to the side and approach the people and situations in your life with curiosity and a positive, even friendly attitude. Seeing the world with wonder keeps your inner wisdom alive.

A Gift from the Heart

I've had a strong intuitive sense throughout my life, but I had the most dramatic and moving experience of intuition as I was writing this chapter. It's had a profound effect on me and shown me another role intuition can play in our lives.

I was in San Diego with Carol on our writing retreat, so I hadn't seen my mother in a few weeks. One night, as I was drifting off to sleep, I suddenly said out loud, "My mother is going to die tomorrow." This outburst completely shocked me. I had no idea where those words came from. Confused and alarmed, I tried to reassure myself, *That can't be. She just had a physical two days ago. The doctor said she was fine.* Eventually I fell asleep, feeling unsettled.

As I was waking up the next morning, the thought flashed through my mind, *Mom's going to die today.* Concerned, I decided I'd call and check on her. But strange as it sounds, in the next instant the thought flew out of my mind and I forgot all about both incidents for the rest of the day.

Later that afternoon, around 6 p.m., as Carol and I were working on the book together, I got a phone call from my sister. As soon as I heard her voice, I knew what had happened. My mom had just passed away. The immediate wave of grief was intense, but I remembered my earlier premonitions, which brought me some comfort. I believe that those intuitive warnings were what kept me from being totally overwhelmed by the unexpected and heart-wrenching news. They also gave me a "big picture" perspective, helping me to see the divine orchestration that guided the unfolding of events. My heart had given me notice—two little cushions—to help break my fall. Sometimes your intuition's guidance isn't about doing something but is simply a loving gift from your heart.

Love Luminary Doc Childre, the founder of HeartMath, says, "The heart's intuition brings the freedom and power to accomplish what the mind, even with all the discipline in the world, cannot do if it's out of sync with the heart."

People who live in unconditional love are not only in touch with their intuition, they live by it. Their inner wisdom is the light they see by, leading them to lives of true freedom.

Love Luminaries David and Kristin Morelli, hosts of the transformational radio show *Everything Is Energy*, are bright lights who help people release their blocks to experiencing a life of love, fulfillment, and ease. They shared with me this powerful exercise that allows you to bring your heart's wisdom into your daily life.

Exercise

Inner Chamber—The Heart of Intuition

1. Close your eyes and receive a few deep breaths. Imagine gathering all the bits of your attention, focus, or energy into the center of your head behind your third eye (between your eyebrows).

2. Gather any of your attention that's on your past, and bring it to the present . . . right here, right now. Gather your attention back from the future . . . bring it to the present. Bring that and any other scattered attention into the "still point"—a point of light in the center of your head. Breathe.

3. Imagine sliding down a tube from the center of your head into the space of your heart. Look around and find a door. This is the door to the inner chamber of your heart (a space reserved just for you and your essence; some call it Spirit, God, or Higher Self).

4. Open the door, enter, and then close the door securely behind you. Look around at this inner space and notice how it looks. Move to the center of this space and allow a golden light from above to connect into you.

5. Feel the walls of your personality melt away, allowing only inner truth and insight to remain. Experience for a moment the "real" you.

6. What important question do you have? Ask it. Allow your deep answers to emerge. Let yourself be surprised. Answers can be feelings, thoughts, images, or a knowingness. When you listen long enough (open to the space and allow), answers will come out of the silence. What insights do you get? Rest in this space as long as you'd like, asking other questions too.

7. When you feel complete, say, "Thank you," then exit the chamber, closing the door behind you. Be sure to bring your answers with you as you go back up the tube to the center of your head.

8. Take a moment to let the wisdom of your heart fill your mind, and then open your eyes slowly. You may want to write your answers down.

Used by permission of David and Kristin Morelli. For an audio version of this exercise, visit www.EverythingIsEnergy.com/love.

Summary and Love for No Reason Action Steps

Looking for the beauty in people and situations and trusting your inner wisdom are the keys that open the Doorway of Vision. Use the following action steps to increase the flow of love through this energy center:

1. Develop "mother's eyes" by looking for the underlying spirit that connects all living things and by finding perfection in the imperfect.

2. Program your reticular activating system to bring your attention to beauty in all its forms. This practice will create the neural pathways of love in your brain, causing this refined perception to become second nature.

3. Don't believe everything you think. Learn a technique for releasing yourself from judgments, like the Work, the Sedona Method, the Lefkoe Method, or TAT.

4. "Reframe" the circumstances of your life in a way that opens your heart and generates feelings of compassion, expansion, and opportunity.

5. Use the Option Method exercise to dissolve limiting beliefs, shift your perception, and open yourself to greater love.

6. "Trust your vibes." Remember that sometimes the most magical journeys are launched by an intuitive hunch.

7. Play the "I Wonder" game to strengthen the muscle of your sixth sense. Ask yourself "I wonder" questions throughout the day and pay attention to the answers.

8. To bring your heart's wisdom into your daily life, access your intuition by using the Inner Chamber exercise.

CHAPTER 10

The Doorway of Oneness: Connecting to Wholeness

We live in succession, in division, in parts, in particles. Meantime within man is the soul of the whole; the wise silence; the universal beauty, to which every part and particle is equally related, the eternal One.

—Ralph Waldo Emerson, nineteenth-century author and philosopher

When I learned to meditate as a teenager, the instruction I received was to "Let go. Take it as it comes," and just do the simple technique that was designed to let my mind settle down to the source of thought: pure being.

I remember the first time I touched that silent place. It felt like coming home. I forgot my body and my thoughts. I felt spacious, peaceful, whole—as if I were part of the vast tapestry connecting all life.

As I came out of that state, and before I started having my usual thoughts again, I noticed that this spaciousness didn't feel empty: it was filled—with love. I wasn't Marci, I wasn't sixteen. I was just Love.

I continued meditating daily. A few years later I became a teacher of meditation, and I taught my ninety-two-year-old grandfather to meditate so he could have that love-filled experience too. My grandfather was a short, round, cherubic-looking old man with a kindly face. He found the process so easy. As he sat meditating for the first time, he looked peaceful, smiling slightly, with his eyes closed. When he was finished, I asked him how he liked it. He laughed and said, "This is just like talking to God. I already do that every day."

Talking to God, meditating, praying—all these spiritual practices are ways to connect to what Emerson called the "wise silence, the eternal One," and what I call "the Divine." When you make a practice of connecting with this wholeness, whatever name you give it—God, Nature, Higher Power, Universal Spirit, or something else—you're opening the Doorway of Oneness and laying a strong foundation for Love for No Reason.

Throughout history and in all traditions, there have been accounts of spiritual experiences opening people to unconditional love. Saint Francis of Assisi, the great Sufi mystic poet Rumi, the "Little Flower" Saint Thérèse of Lisieux, and the great rabbi Baal Shem Tov are just a few of those people whose spiritual awakenings made them so "intoxicated" with God's love that they couldn't help but radiate that love to everyone and everything.

There are also modern-day "saints," people whose deep connection to Spirit grounds them in Higher Love 24/7, like the Dalai Lama and Ammachi, an Indian woman referred to as the "hugging saint." These spiritually awake beings are conduits for pure unconditional love to be expressed in the world, and that's why just being around them opens your heart.

When the oneness center is open, you tap into the silence that lies at your core: that expansive stillness under all the thoughts and feelings.

Anchored to that peace inside, you let go and surrender to life's flow, trusting that there's an inspired intelligence coordinating all events and experiences for you. Some people sense a loving presence with them at all times—a combination divine parent/best friend/guardian angel, riding shotgun and giving them helpful advice. But whether palpable or subtle, your connection to a Higher Power creates more serenity, ease, and expansion—a sense that you are connected to something larger than yourself.

When this center is blocked, you feel disconnected from spirit and the deeper meaning and purpose of life. Life feels like a repeating loop of eating, drinking, sleeping, and working. You know something's missing but you're not sure what. This sense of emptiness and futility, what philosophers call existential angst, is often buried beneath the hustle and bustle of our day-to-day activities. But it's there. It's what fuels those 3 a.m.-and-still-awake moments when you're plagued by the feeling that nothing really matters.

When you strengthen the oneness center, the qualities of spiritual meaning and universality flourish in your life. Then Divine love enriches your human experience of love.

Your Crowning Glory

The oneness center is traditionally called the crown chakra and is the uppermost of the seven energy centers, located at the crown of the head. Its role is to open you to the higher realms of spirit and divinity, connecting you to the aspects of life beyond your mind and physical body.

Also known as the "thousand-petaled lotus flower," the crown chakra acts like an antenna or, as Love Luminary Janet Sussman calls it, "a satellite dish for Spirit." It receives the "signals" of pure consciousness or divine energy. Many spiritual and religious traditions consider this cranial center a hotline to God. Have you ever noticed that statues of the Buddha include a bump on the top of his head? That bump is called the *ushinisha,* and it's not a topknot hairdo but a symbol of the Buddha's highly developed crown chakra and continual union with God.

Wearing turbans and coiling the hair on the top of the head—in the style of Indian holy men—are also nods to the power of the crown center. Both are believed to help one maintain a spiritual focus.

The Islamic practice of bowing to Allah, called *sujud,* is said to activate the crown chakra.

In the Jewish tradition of Kabbalah, *Keter,* which means "crown," is the topmost center of the Tree of Life, a symbolic representation of the ten interconnected centers of energy in the human body. In the Kabbalistic view, *Keter* is where we make direct connection with *Ein Sof,* or pure transcendent light or Divine energy.

In Christianity, the depiction of halos of light around the heads of Jesus, saints, and angels is a common way to portray their holiness—that is, their connection to wholeness!

And on a more earthly plane, royals through the ages have tried to claim this golden-headed glory by wearing jewel-encrusted gold crowns.

In many traditions the crown chakra is associated with the Divine Father or Father Sky—the mirror image of the root chakra's association with the Divine Mother or Mother Earth.

When the crown chakra is open, it takes in the light of the Divine. A river of life-giving energy fills and illuminates the body and all other energy centers, and enriches our experience of love.

We Really *Are* All One

*One day when I was sitting quiet, it came to me: that
feeling of being part of everything, not separate at all.
I knew that if I cut a tree, my arm would bleed.*

—Alice Walker, American novelist and poet

Warning: The next paragraph is one that you may be tempted to dismiss out of hand, thinking you've heard it before and it's hopelessly idealistic and abstract. Please don't. Just thank your mind for sharing its opinion and keep reading.

When the Doorway of Oneness is open, you experience your oneness with all creation. Not as a sentimental idea but as a concrete reality. Everything is as precious to you as your own self, because you experience that everything *is* your own self.

Developing this energy center causes your identity to shift. You identify less with your individual personality, with its habits, fears, likes and dislikes, and more with the pure awareness underlying your personality— what many people call God or Divine love.

This underlying reality—God, Divine love, what I call Love for No Reason—is the fundamental essence of everything, the stuff of life itself. We're back at Love Theme #1: Love is who we are! Love is the substance that makes up the building blocks of everything in our lives. Our very molecules are formed from love. We have the capacity to experience oneness because everyone and everything is made of one thing: love.

Love Luminary, author, and journalist Lynne McTaggart has written a groundbreaking book called *The Field* about the scientific evidence supporting the existence of this fundamental oneness, in particular the discovery of the Zero Point Field—a massive web of energy connecting all matter. In our interview Lynne described it this way: "This field is a teeming maelstrom of subatomic particles oscillating between wave and particle, popping into being and just as quickly popping back out into pure potential energy.

"For years scientists have known that we live in a quantum 'sea of energy.' Subatomic particles send information back and forth, constantly, like a little game of basketball. So when you get right down to the basics of matter, there's no separation. We're all part of this energy field; we're just another knot in this rope.

"The problem is that until fairly recently we defined the universe as this collection of separate objects that operate according to fixed laws in time and space. So we define everything out there as other than us. My work is educating people that we're not actually separate. We're all in unity. Living in the experience of this oneness really is the essence of love."

Your Brain on Oneness

With all the new technology we have for seeing exactly what's going on in the brain, scientists now know that subjective experiences of oneness have very real and distinct neuronal correlates. Andrew Newberg, MD, an assistant professor at the Hospital of the University of Pennsylvania and the coauthor of *How God Changes Your Brain*, is considered one of the pioneers in the field of neurotheology, the study of what happens in the brain during religious and spiritual experience. Many of Dr. Newberg's studies involve taking brain scans of nuns, monks, and experienced meditators while in prayer or meditation.

A brain scan gives a "snapshot" of your brain's activity with red areas indicating more activity and blood flow, and blue areas, less activity and blood flow. Brain scans done during experiences of oneness show a unique pattern of brain functioning: brilliant red in the frontal lobes of the brain, linked to attention and focus, and a deep blue in the back of the brain, in the area of the parietal lobes—the brain structures associated with the ability to orient ourselves in space and time and to distinguish boundaries. It's this decreased activity in the parietal lobes that appears to be most directly related to the experience of oneness.

The parietal lobes are responsible for your sense of "me" and "not me" and enable you to function in the physical world. They help you walk, put on clothing, and type on a keyboard because they let you perceive where your body ends and the floor or T-shirt or computer keys begin.

But when you meditate, the parietal lobes quiet, and the boundaries of your individual self fade, till eventually you feel no separation—just peace, expansion, and unity.

These experiences of oneness come in all different flavors—mystical union with God, unbounded compassion, divine ecstasy, and deep silence—and each appears to have a slightly different neurological component. In my interview with Love Luminary Dr. Zoran Josipovic, research scientist and adjunct professor at the psychology department and Center for Neural Science at NYU, he told me that in a study he'd conducted, when meditators reported reaching a state of "nonduality" (another way of saying oneness), he found that the brain's two main networks began functioning in a more connected and harmonious way.

These networks—one running the inward, reflective thinking and the other the outward, task-oriented thinking—normally operate in opposition to each other. When one is more active, the other is less. "But when we experience nonduality," Dr. Josipovic said, "they come into greater balance, and functional integration and harmony is revealed." This is a unique and optimal state of brain functioning that's characterized by inner peace and contentment.

There are many other brain structures involved in these peak experiences of oneness: the insula, the anterior cingulated cortex, the thalamus . . . the list is long. Some of these same brain structures are also correlated with the experience of unconditional love. The important point to take away is that experiences of oneness, like experiences of unconditional love, can no longer be considered wishful thinking or fantasy: they're valid brain states, with measurable parameters.

In fact, when scientists showed Carmelite nuns the images of their brains that had been scanned during the nuns' experiences of profound union with Christ, the nuns smiled and lit up with joy. The scans showed that something physiologically significant was happening to them. Thus science had confirmed that their otherworldly experiences weren't just imagination or desire but something very real.

It turns out that experiences of spiritual oneness have powerful "this-worldly" benefits too. Dr. Newberg found that connecting to wholeness through prayer, meditation, and other spiritual practices reduced stress and anxiety, increased compassion and empathy, and improved mental clarity. So your brain on oneness is actually a pretty good idea.

Unlocking the Doorway of Oneness: The Two Love Keys

Because our lives are more fragmented and frantic than ever, experiencing oneness can seem like an impossible dream. Something, perhaps, for cloistered nuns, priests, monks, or saints, but not for the average person. Dealing with bills, bosses, and bulging inboxes doesn't seem like a recipe for spiritual bliss.

But you don't have to renounce the world to develop the oneness center. Based on the scientific research and on my interviews with the Love Luminaries, I've found that the following keys are two of the best ways to connect to wholeness.

Love Keys for the Doorway of Oneness

1. Plug In to Presence
2. Surrender to Grace

The Presence Key helps you experience the depths of your own inner stillness through a daily practice of silence, meditation, or prayer.

The Surrender Key invites you to let go of your need to control everything and allow a Higher Power to direct your life. When you do, grace—another name for divine, unconditional love—flows in, providing solutions, blessings, and unexpected joy.

Love Key for Oneness #1:
Plug In to Presence

You need not leave your room. Remain sitting at your table and listen.
You need not even listen, simply wait, just learn to become quiet, still,
and solitary. The world will freely offer itself to you to be unmasked.

—Franz Kafka, twentieth-century Austrian author

Plugging in to Presence is a way to go beyond the busy-ness of your daily life and find peace, joy, centeredness, and unconditional love. There are many ways to plug in to Presence, but silent meditation and prayer are the ones that have been shown to specifically light up the oneness center.

When you become still, the noise of your everyday life slips away and you glide down into the silent space that is your sacred center. You switch on the satellite dish of the oneness center and begin to pick up broadcasts from the Divine.

Why don't we tune in to those broadcasts more often? For most people, the problem is time. We simply feel we don't have enough bandwidth to add anything more to our already overscheduled lives.

While it seems as though time is the problem, the real problem is our inability to prioritize what we do with our time.

My first meditation teacher used to say, "If you're too busy to meditate, you're too busy!" He knew that some things we do in life eat up energy, while others give us energy. Think of it this way: if we're so busy driving from place to place that we don't make time to stop for gas, we're going to eventually end up stranded on the side of the road with no way to get where we want to go.

When we make time for the things that fill up our tank—like spiritual practices—we can handle everything else in the day more effectively, while also staying connected to the source of love inside.

Meditation: Take a Dive into the Sea of Love

There is a life-force within your soul, seek that life.
There is a gem in the mountain of your body, seek that mine.
O traveler, if you are in search of That
Don't look outside, look inside yourself and seek That.

—Rumi, thirteenth-century Sufi poet

In the past few decades, extensive research has shown the benefits of meditation. Immune functioning, blood pressure, productivity, relationships—you name it, meditation is good for it. Regular meditation practice has become universally accepted as an effective way to manage stress and anxiety and to improve mental, emotional, and physical health.

According to Love Luminary Dr. Dean Shrock, the reason meditation is so good for you on every level is that it connects you to the state of unconditional pure love. Dr. Shrock, who is a psychologist and the author of *Why Love Heals*, has spent years developing wellness and stress-reduction programs. He says, "Meditation allows you to access the quantum field of energy, which is essentially a field of all-pervasive love. You could define stress as anything that makes you forget your connection to this omnipresent, all-powerful force of the universe. So when you're resonating in harmony with love, you experience the least amount of stress or resistance and health is a natural consequence. That's why I say that love heals. And meditation heals by leading you to love."

Love Luminary Janet Attwood, coauthor of *The Passion Test*, has been a friend of mine for thirty years and has one of the biggest hearts in the world. Janet is committed to helping people let love flow in their lives by living their passion and purpose. In 2003 Janet sat down to get clear on her own passions and realized that one of them was to spend time with the enlightened saints and sages of the world.

So she spent the next two years traveling the globe interviewing more than seventy of the wisest souls on the planet, most of whom had spent long years in meditation. When I asked Janet what she'd learned, she answered, "What they each told me in one way or another is that love is the glue of the universe. Love is what brings you back to yourself, to realize that your limitations are an illusion. Your real nature is infinite, unbounded love."

This infinite, unbounded love—Love for No Reason—blossoms through regular spiritual practice. It's the quintessential love-body workout.

Tuning the Satellite Dish to the Divine

Prayer: Wireless access to God with no roaming fees.

—Sign outside a church

Prayer is another way to plug in to Presence, which is why it's a part of every spiritual tradition. At its most sublime, prayer is an experience of communion between you and the Divine. You open to Presence, and when that connection is made, you're plugged in to the pure vibration of love.

Prayer doesn't have to be tied to organized religion. We humans have been praying ever since the cosmic starting gun went off—even if it was only to send an urgent SOS to the powers that be asking that we make it to the cave before the tiger caught us!

Sri Sri Ravi Shankar, a spiritual teacher and humanitarian, says that prayer happens spontaneously in two situations. "One is when you are utterly grateful, and second is when you are utterly helpless, nowhere to go." When you're figuratively brought to your knees, by great joy or great sorrow, you naturally turn to God.

For example, we may feel grateful to God when we marvel at the majesty of a mountain bathed in late afternoon light, or are transfixed by the beauty of a painting, or are moved by a particular piece of music. At times like these, awe and appreciation undo us, and through that opening, our love pours out.

When life overwhelms us with grief or fear, we cry out to God for help. The Bible is full of references to the Divine as a source of strength and comfort, "The Lord is my rock, my fortress, and my deliverer . . . in whom I take refuge." (Psalm 18:2).

Opening to Presence isn't a one-way communication. Tuning your satellite dish to the Divine creates a channel for the energy to flow both ways. While some people think of prayer and meditation as a way to "talk *to* God," it's also a way to "*listen* to God," to *receive* signals from the universe or your Higher Power.

That's what happened to my extraordinary friend and guardian angel, Love Luminary Bill Bauman, who after years of opening to the Divine, was literally and permanently overtaken by Higher Love. I always describe Bill as "the enlightened Mr. Rogers." With humility, humor, and unbounded kindness, he has spent the last thirty years guiding people to experience the truth of who they are—unconditional love.

Bill's Story
Opening to Higher Love

My life has always been guided by a search for love—not the usual hearts-and-flowers kind of love, but a bigger-than-life, all-encompassing kind of love that for a long time I wasn't sure even existed.

But it *does* exist. I know because I found it. My search came to an end one February day over twenty years ago.

My longing for love started early on. I spent most of my childhood looking for a sense of security and just trying to survive. My parents didn't abuse me, but they didn't give me a feeling of safety or welcome either.

My chance to break away from this life came at the age of thirteen. One day out of the blue I heard a voice inside me say, "Bill, I want you to be a priest." It scared me to death! But it was also exciting. We were Catholics, so I knew that this was a calling, and that a calling was a very big deal. I had never even felt average, and now this voice was asking me to do something decidedly above average.

I answered the call. Right after my fourteenth birthday I left home to attend a seminary a thousand miles away. There I found the security I'd always craved but never had at home. At the seminary, we were taught that if we just obeyed the rules, a great reward would come to us. This gave me a sense of control over my life that was very satisfying.

Yet even though I was studying to be a priest, I wasn't very religious in the "organized religion" sense. Still, as a seminarian I spent a great deal of time in prayer—which for me was silently opening to greater love. As time went on, I started to see that being a follower of Christ truly is all about opening one's mind and heart to love. When I eventually became a priest, I enjoyed spending my life talking about God's love and helping people find that love.

But the same structure of rules that had given me security ended up being the reason I decided to leave the priesthood at the age of twenty-seven. Over time it had become clear to everyone that I favored following my heart over following the rules.

Being on my own was freeing, and when I met Donna, my wife to this day, it opened me to a different kind of love. For the first time in my life, I had found a human being who loved me for who I was—unconditionally.

But life wasn't all roses. I was happier, but there was something more I wanted—a bigger love—that continued to elude me. I kept having this feeling, *Is this all there is?*

One day after we'd been married a while, Donna, who was always honest with me, said, "Do you realize how pessimistic you are?" It came as a shock, because I just assumed everyone woke up in the morning and immediately began thinking about everything that could go wrong in the day ahead, felt huge anxiety about it, and then started planning what to do to defend themselves against it all. I had been good at preaching love, but I wasn't very good at living it.

Donna's wake-up call prompted me to begin identifying the things in my personality that separated me from love and find the ways to overcome that separation. I found this so intriguing that I wanted to help others do it too. So I went back to school to become a psychotherapist and, to my delight, discovered even more tools to heal my own life. Little by little, I began working at resolving all my childhood wounds and issues.

As time passed, I added more spiritual tools and practices to my repertoire. I recommitted to opening myself to God each day, meditating, working with energy and light, and always striving to experience people through loving rather than judgmental eyes. I found myself becoming a blend of psychotherapist and spiritual teacher. I seemed to have a knack for guiding people to reach inside themselves to find their own spiritual strength. After many years of working in this way, I began giving seminars based on my own mix of spiritual and psychotherapeutic processes.

Which brings us to that February day two decades ago, when searching turned into finding.

It was the last day of a three-day seminar on personal empowerment I was giving to about eighty people. I had been feeling kind of queasy for a couple of hours, and as we stopped for our usual afternoon break, a really strange sensation came over me. I told my assistant, "I'm going to lie down here on the stage. If by chance I'm not up in ten minutes, just go ahead and have the group practice the exercises we learned this morning."

I lay down and instantly went into a state of paralysis. I couldn't move a muscle. But it didn't feel like a medical emergency; it felt like something otherworldly was happening. I stayed with it, not having the slightest idea where it would go. Then, in a matter of minutes, "Bill Bauman" vacated the premises. It was the oddest feeling I'd ever had in my life.

I had no rush of panic about what was happening—just a deep sense that it was something highly significant. With "Bill Bauman" gone, I just stayed for some time in this absolutely nowhere space, my mind just present enough to notice that nothing was there.

I don't know whether I was in that state for ten seconds or ten minutes, but at some point, something else came in to take the place of "Bill Bauman." That "something else" could be called many things by different people: my higher self, the Divine, pure Being. But, to me, it felt like Love.

I stayed in that state for two to three hours. When I came out of it, I knew something profoundly life-changing had just happened, something way too big for me to grasp. The former "Bill Bauman" was still gone—he never did come back—but I could function normally, or even better than normally, because everything seemed to be an effortless flow.

I walked around for two or three days just being in this frictionless state before I fully recognized what had changed. Before, I'd felt like an individual human being—limited by my own small perspective—having an experience of life. Now there was only Love having an experience of life through me. Love was breathing, Love was seeing, Love was eating a sandwich. Judgments about myself and others were gone; anxieties about what might take place were gone; there was only Love.

Since that day, I've been privileged to help others experience their own version of what happened to me. Though I had sought the experience of Love with a capital *L* all my life, ultimately what happened to me that day was not something I created through my own human will. It was a gift given to me by God, or the universe or my Higher self—whatever name you use for the infinite source of blessings.

And yet I know that what set the stage for that gift of grace were the many years of opening myself quietly, sincerely, with gratitude and awe, to the wholeness of love inside me.

❤   ❤   ❤

Bill's story shows that when you keep consciously opening yourself to wholeness, your "spiritual wealth" accumulates. Although you may not reach a single tipping point the way Bill did, your life is still steadily enriched by your practices. When wholeness is your income, the outcome will be love.

Forget the Coffee, Try a Morning Cup of Connection!

Marianne Williamson, a Love Luminary extraordinaire, is a leading voice of transformation in the world, bringing wisdom and the message of unconditional love for our personal and global healing. I've been inspired by Marianne's words since she first began teaching in 1983, and I'm deeply grateful for her friendship and guidance in my life.

Recently she and I were speaking at the same conference, and in her talk, she emphasized the importance of spiritual practices, especially as a way to start our day, "Every serious spiritual, philosophical, and religious path that I know of stresses the importance of the morning, because that's when our minds are most open to receive new impressions.

"Most people get up in the morning and pick up a newspaper or turn on the TV or radio. They get a full report of all the disasters happening, and then they add *caffeine*! They saunter out into the world and are mystified that they're depressed by noon.

"So what's the alternative? When you wake up in the morning, don't you take a bath or shower? Of course you do, because you don't want to go out into the day with yesterday's dirt on your body. But if you don't meditate and pray every morning, you're carrying yesterday's stress into the day."

Love Luminary and physician Dr. Dharma Singh Khalsa seconded Marianne's view. Dr. Dharma, as he likes to be called, is an expert on brain longevity and the author of *Meditation as Medicine*. In our interview he said, "Doing meditation or sitting in prayer first thing each morning is what I call 'starting your day in a positive way.' When you do this, you're energizing your body and getting the positive neurotransmitters in your brain going. This creates a baseline of calm to go back to. It's also a form of behavioral conditioning, like Pavlov's dog and the bell. If you become stressed, you can close your eyes for a minute or two, and *boom*, your whole brain functioning begins to shift, because it's been conditioned by regular practice to have that response."

This is important because you don't just meditate (or pray) for the sake of the experience you have while you're doing it, although it can often be the high point of your day. Spiritual practice, whatever time of day you choose to do it, brings a state of inner wholeness to your everyday activities, adding a spiritual element to the rest of your life.

So, invest a little time each morning to recharge your batteries and set up a baseline of Love for No Reason for the rest of the day. I know, it's another thing to do, but it will make everything else you have to do easier, more enjoyable—and more meaningful.

Some people like to get a double dose of wholeness. Love Luminary Paul Scheele, author of *Natural Brilliance*, told me that he likes to meditate every morning to prepare himself for a dynamic day *and* meditate every night to prepare himself for a profound sleep. At night, he uses a practice called *yoga nidra*, which puts him in a state of conscious sleep: his body is asleep while his mind experiences a deep awareness. He says the following statement internally with conscious intention right before sleep: I now return to the expanded nature of love that I am.

Neti, Neti: **Not This, Not That**

If you're not sure about all this meditation and prayer stuff, there are other ways to connect to wholeness. You can start from exactly where you are—it doesn't matter what you believe or don't believe—and mentally peel away all the parts of yourself that hide your deeper nature. Jack Canfield, my wonderful mentor, told me about one way to do this.

Jack, the cocreator of the *Chicken Soup for the Soul* series and the author of *The Success Principles*, is one of the world's "bright lights." He radiates consciousness, humor, and love, which makes him a Love Luminary for sure! When Carol and I talked to Jack about Love for No Reason, he told us that there are many different ways to access that state of unconditional love in addition to meditation and prayer, including centering, calling in the light, and a process he teaches called the Disidentification Exercise.

Developed by the great Italian psychologist Roberto Assagioli, the Disidentification Exercise is a psychosynthesis exercise that Jack says, "helps you set aside your identifications with your accomplishments, roles, body, personality, emotions, and thoughts and recognize that who you truly are is a pure center of awareness and choice. And from that center you can choose to reidentify with your higher self, which is where all the higher qualities like unconditional love, joy, compassion, and courage emanate from. Like other spiritual practices, this exercise helps you identify with the infinite, the One, the Universal Consciousness that you are."

To do the Disidentification Exercise, simply repeat the following statements slowly and thoughtfully (silently or out loud): "I have a body, and I am not my body. I have emotions, and I am not my emotions. I have a mind, and I am not my mind. I have many roles that I play, and I am not my roles. I am a center of pure self-consciousness and will." This exercise is most effective if you practice it daily, ideally shortly after waking up in the morning; think of it as a symbolic second awakening. You can also repeat it several times during the day, returning to the state of disidentified "I" consciousness.

In the Vedas this process of finding out who you are by finding out who you aren't is described as *neti neti*, a Sanskrit expression that means "not this, not that." *Neti neti* allows you to gently let go of your small self and discover your big Self, which is all about love.

Love Luminary Arjuna Ardagh, the author of *The Translucent Revolution*, uses a similar process of inquiring into and recognizing the truth of who you are when he guides people to experience this inner state of love. He says that cultivating "genuine active curiosity" in this way has kick-started thousands of his clients to new spiritual awareness. "The first thing you discover is a kind of emptiness, a silence, a presence which doesn't seem to have content to it, like looking up at a limitless sky. That boundary-less place inside you is your own consciousness, your awareness. It may seem to be empty or nothing at first, a disappointment. But when you relax into it, you realize that it's also full—it is everything."

When you experience this presence as a simple pure state, then you begin to notice that it's the ground of all your other states. According to Arjuna, "You realize this presence is what you really are: Love."

Love Luminary John Douglas is a master of spiritual healing and guiding people to their own connection with Divine love. He calls his program "spiritual bodybuilding," and Carol and I both experience that our love-bodies are in better shape when we do his practices, like the one that follows.

Exercise

Meditation for Oneness

This meditation guides you through all the energy centers of the love-body so that you can experience greater love and expansion of consciousness. Combining gratitude and the power of your attention, you activate, cleanse, and develop each of the centers, which connects you to wholeness.

1. Sit comfortably and close your eyes. Take a few slow, deep breaths.

2. Place the tip of your tongue on your upper palate.

3. Say an opening invocation or prayer to connect you to Presence. Use whatever feels meaningful to you.

4. Be aware of your crown chakra (oneness center). Say silently, *Let me be a channel of Divine energy. Thank you for being my center of Divine connection and illumination. Namaste.* Take a moment to feel your gratitude for this center.

5. Be aware of your third eye chakra (vision center). Say silently, *Thank you for being the center of my inner world and empowering my higher knowledge. Namaste.* Take a moment to feel your gratitude for this center.

6. Be aware of your throat chakra (communication center). Say silently, *Thank you for being my center of communication. Namaste.* Take a moment to feel your gratitude for this center.

7. Be aware of your heart chakra (openness center). Say silently, *Thank you for being my center of love, mercy, and compassion. Thank you for the love for all that is. Namaste.* Take a moment to feel your gratitude for this center.

8. Be aware of your solar plexus chakra (self-love center). Say silently, *Thank you for being the center of my power and will to align with my soul and Divine will. Namaste.* Take a moment to feel your gratitude for this center.

9. Be aware of your sacral chakra (vitality center). Say silently, *Thank you for being my center of vitality and creative power. Namaste.* Take a moment to feel your gratitude for this center.

10. Be aware of your root chakra (safety center). Say silently, *Thank you for being my center of abundance, supply, and power of the earth. Namaste.* Take a moment to feel your gratitude for this center.

11. Sit quietly for a few minutes before opening your eyes.

Used by permission of John Douglas. For the audio version of the meditation this exercise was adapted from (called Meditation for Power Development), go to www.spirit-repair.com.

Love Key for Oneness #2:
Surrender to Grace

Grace isn't a little prayer you chant before receiving a meal. It's a way to live.
—Jacqueline Winspear, author

Surrender. For most people the word conjures up images of white flags, defeat, and failure. But the surrender I'm referring to couldn't be more different. Surrendering to grace means letting go, relaxing your body, mind, and heart, and trusting that your life is unfolding exactly as it should. As you go about your daily activities, you experience a greater sense of ease despite life's ups and downs. You begin to trust that the universe cares for you (that it's friendly) and will respond to your needs.

When I'm able to surrender and move through my day with the simple faith that I'll get what I need, I'm always amazed at the way things seem to flow: I'm in the right place at the right time, the person I have to contact just happens to call, a piece of information I need just drops into my lap. These synchronicities make life feel effortless and "grace-full." I feel as though I'm receiving gift after gift. This experience matches the traditional Christian understanding of grace, which is "the free and unmerited favor or beneficence of God."

Grace is the Divine in action. It has only one goal for you: to allow you to experience Higher Love. So when you surrender to grace, you can trust that you're heading for more love in your life—no matter how it looks at the moment.

Sometimes it's a crisis that drives us to surrender, to "let go and let God." Often people say the gift of the challenge they faced was that they had to just let go. And that act put them in a bigger flow of energy, of intelligence, of love. I call this trusting the cosmic GPS; you're still the one driving the car, but you let someone with a greater knowledge of the terrain do the navigating.

Many sages have said that living our lives ruled solely by our small individual minds is like being in prison. It limits our experience of the truth of life. In my interview with Love Luminary Stuart Mooney, a spiritual teacher and the founder of Stuart Mooney Spiritual Therapy, he told me that according to scientists, the sensory apparatus of the brain takes in about 400 million bits of information a second, but out of that we register only two thousand and call that reality. We wonder why we're depressed and nothing makes sense; it's because we block out so much of the total reality! When we surrender to grace, we open up to a much larger reality. We become free.

According to Stuart, it's up to us to create the conditions for grace to flow. "The door out of our prisons has only one lock—on the inside. It has to be opened by us, and we have to ask for help from something larger than ourselves. It's as if we were drowning in the ocean and trying to save ourselves by pulling up on our own shirts. No matter how hard we pull, we're still in the ocean. We need something bigger than ourselves, outside the ocean, to come and pluck us out of the water. God does this and then puts us over His/Her shoulder, holds us tenderly, and whispers in our ear, 'I'm so glad that you're here. You are so beautiful, just the way you are, and I love you.'"

Rev. Cynthia Bourgeault, Episcopal priest and writer, addresses the question of grace from a Christian perspective. This Love Luminary told me that "the path to grace is an unclenching, like opening your hand to loosen your grip on how you want life to be. You can't separate Jesus' teachings on love from his teaching on non-attachment. He always said, 'Go forward, don't cling, don't hang on to your physical possessions or your titles. Just let it all go.'

"All the great paths take us through this same eye of the needle, of letting go of clinging and attachment to the little self in order to begin to discover this huge web of reciprocity and interdependence that actually holds us up. I want to emphasize that this isn't a revelation that comes to mystics or some special type of people; it's the fruit of just putting one foot in front of the other on a path that starts right on your own doormat."

And if you can't see the entire path? Just take a step. One step in the direction of Divine love will bring that love one step closer to you.

Love Luminary Deirdre Hade is well acquainted with the path of Divine love. Deirdre is a spiritual teacher and gifted healer; her Four Chambers of the Heart Meditation is one of my absolute favorite meditations! (See the link to this meditation in Deirdre's Radiance Healing listing in the Resources section.) She's also one of the most committed people I know when it comes to her own spiritual practices. The results are visible: she's got light shining from her eyes and looks ten years younger than she is. (If only she could bottle that, I'd buy a case!) She simply exudes radiance.

I've heard Deirdre tell the following story numerous times, and each time I'm inspired and entertained. When it comes to surrendering, she does it in style.

Deirdre's Story
Coming Home

One day in the early sixties, when I was around six years old, I walked all the way to the end of the country road that passed in front of our home in North Carolina.

There, in the middle of nowhere, was this little house with a white picket fence all covered with roses. Sitting in rocking chairs on the porch were Edna Mae and Myrtle, two bright-eyed sisters in their nineties, whose parents had been slaves. We became good friends, and I'd go visit them all the time. I remember that they had lace curtains and a huge stand in the middle of the living room with an enormous Bible on it. They'd serve tea and talk to me about God.

Edna Mae and Myrtle were always so loving and kind, but I could see that they were very poor. I once asked, "Don't you feel bad living in this small house at the end of the road and not having any money?"

Edna Mae said to me, "Oh, no, child. We live in the mansion of God's love! That's our real home."

I thought about that comment for years. As I traveled my life's road, which took me through some pretty bleak patches, I often wondered, *What would it be like to live in the mansion of God's love no matter where I was?*

As a teenager, I saw deep suffering up close and personal. My mother was diagnosed with breast cancer when I was fifteen. They had to do a radical mastectomy. In those days, there was no psychological support, no counseling, nothing to help you cope, and my mother went into a horrific depression. The stress of all this aggravated my father's severe chemical imbalance, and his mental illness went into high gear. He was a genius, but he was bipolar and had a multiple personality disorder. I was the oldest child, so it was up to me to hold down the fort.

The doctors gave my mom a year to live. One day not long after that prognosis, I sat by her bed and asked her, "How long do you want to live?"

She said, "I want to see you and your little brothers grow up."

I told her, "We can do it." I don't know how I thought I could make that happen, but I was determined to try.

Mom and I spent a lot of time in prayer together. I would go to her bedroom, sit in the chair by her bed, and ask God to heal her. When I did this, she said a great light would come in and fill her. And then I started seeing angels, beings of light, appearing as real to me as anything physical, and I thought, *Okay, mental disorder runs in the family! Whoops. Better keep this one under wraps.* So my mother and I had this secret club with the light and the angels. A few saints came to visit too.

Within six months, my mother stopped looking sick and started looking younger and younger. Soon her cancer went into remission.

After that, I went back to focusing on my own life. At sixteen, I started dancing professionally with a regional dance company, which I loved, but along with that came terrible eating disorders, bulimia and anorexia. Trying to maintain a dancer's perfect body combined with feeling the pressure to perform sent me straight into a place I called "the pit," and I stayed there for a long time. I was always fighting to stay out of that dark place, but there were days when I'd wake up and feel a huge weight pressing me down. I couldn't move. I'd think, *Well, I'm just going to lose my mind too.* But there was always some light inside me that let me know, *I don't have to live like this. My mind does* not *have to break and not come back.*

My mother knew that I was suffering, and now she was too. She had been in remission for six years, but the cancer had returned, metastasized so deep in her bones that she was bedridden and couldn't move. The doctors kept telling us, "We don't know how she's alive. It's a miracle." But I knew what it was; one day she said to me, "I can't go until you're free."

I told my mother, "Okay, Mom, I'm going to do it. I'm going to get free." So I dedicated myself to finding the hand of God and getting myself out of the pit. I went on the search. I studied everything there was to study. I spent hours in meditation and prayer, and I found many beautiful teachers—all of them gifted.

And it helped. I wasn't on the mountaintop, but I had climbed out of the pit by the time my mother passed away. They'd given her one year to live, but she had ended up living fourteen more!

The years went by. My father passed away. I got married, had two kids, and got divorced. I had continued all of my spiritual practices and developed a lot of awareness. But that weight in my heart kept coming back. So I prayed and I prayed and I prayed. "God, if you can just lift this last weight off of me. I'll just do anything you ask. I promise, anything."

Not long after that, I was praying and meditating one night when a brilliant light appeared. I thought, *Oh my God. What is this? An alien attack? Okay, now it's finally happening. I really am losing my mind.* I had never seen a light like that. It was the middle of the night, but it shone like spotlights right in front of me and then it came pouring into me. I went into an altered state. All of a sudden I was aware of being completely one with all of creation. I didn't understand the concept of separation anymore. I felt that every particle of my being was in the outer reaches of the universe and right here, at the very same time.

By morning, the weight on my heart that I'd struggled with for so long had lifted. The darkness in me, the pit—it was just gone. Nothing looked the same. Nothing smelled the same. Nothing felt the same. I was in a state of consciousness I had never experienced before; there was nothing but love, nothing but God. Every night for the next four months the light kept coming in, and I kept moving into more and more expanded states of oneness with all creation.

Then one morning, after the kids had gone to school, I sat at the breakfast table, and said to God, "Fine, I'm one with all creation, but guess what? I don't have any money." A lot of people think that when you feel one with God, you'll suddenly have a Mercedes in the driveway. (Sorry! It doesn't work like that.)

I hadn't worked outside the home while I was married, and now my alimony was coming to an end. I said, "I can't pay the rent next month. I have to get a job. What should I do?"

And the knowingness in me—the voice of that huge, unbounded Oneness I call God—said, *Remember when you agreed that you'd do anything I said?*

I said, "Yeah, what do you have in mind?"

God answered, *Tell people you're a healer and start healing people.*

And I said, "Oh, no-no-no-no-no. I'm not going to be like one of those fruit loops. You don't understand. I have an image to protect."

And God said, *Do you want to pay the rent or not?*

I did.

God said, *Make a flyer. Do sessions all weekend. You'll have your money.*

I groaned, "God, you're going to kill me." But I asked my friend Sheila if I could borrow her office in Beverly Hills to do healing sessions.

She said, "*Really?* I didn't know you were a healer."

I did *not* say, "God told me to do this." Sheila was a psychiatrist, and I knew how crazy that would sound. Instead I said, "Oh, it's something I did when I was younger. I figured it was time to bring it on out."

So I had the place. I made the flyer. Then I asked God, "So how am I going to get the people to come? Stand on a street corner?"

God said, *Yes.*

I groaned again. "God, this is *too* hard. Make it easier. I am *not* standing on the street corner, passing out flyers."

God said, *Oh yes you are. It's called humility.*

It was the scariest thing I'd ever done. But I handed out those flyers to the people going by, and I asked them, "Do you want a healing session?" And guess what? Quite a few people said yes! I couldn't believe it. My schedule filled up, and I saw that I'd make my rent in two days.

But what was I actually going to do when the people showed up? I thought of the healing work I'd done with my mother. Bringing in the light wasn't exactly a formal system of healing I could use. The morning of my first appointment, I said, "Okay, God, what do I do?"

Bring your crystals, tuning forks, and essential oils. When you get there, put your hands over the people and I'll tell you what to do.

And so, at my first appointment, I stood over the young woman lying on the massage table and did what I'd done for my mother: I brought in the light. I opened to the vastness of the love and let it stream into me.

Then God said, *Use this crystal. Now that tuning fork. Now . . .*

At every step, I felt grace flowing through me and I just kept out of the way. Afterward, when the woman stood up, I said, "Well?"

She looked at me, her eyes glowing, and said, "Oh my gosh! I feel great."

I only smiled, but in my head, I said to God, *Thank you for letting me serve.*

It just took off from there. Soon I was able to support myself and my kids *and* be an instrument of healing. Being a conduit for love is a fantastic way to spend your time. The love that comes through me lights me up as well.

I feel blessed to have received so much grace. I opened myself to God, and kept opening and surrendering, and grace came. Grace held me and contained me when I felt nothing could hold or contain me. Then it healed me. It was only through grace that I found my way home.

Conversations with God

Many of the Love Luminaries feel they have a personal relationship with God, and for them, prayer is more of a dialogue with the most loving friend/parent/counselor imaginable. Having "conversations with God" like Deirdre did is one way to surrender to grace: you pose a direct question and then wait for the answer to be revealed, knowing that you'll be guided to the most loving result for everybody involved.

Other people prefer to pose more open-ended questions, like Love

Luminary James Keeley, whom you met in chapter 4. James says the way he surrenders to grace is to sit quietly and offer an invitation for it to flow. He says to God, "If there's anything you'd like me to know right now about how you're caring for me, I'm interested in finding that out. If you have a vision to share with me, I'd love to see it. If there's a feeling you want to put in my heart, it's all yours. I'm literally waiting, like a television plugged into the cable channel. I'll watch whatever you broadcast." Then he stops talking, and he listens.

Love Luminary Cynthia Lane, a healer and writer, told me about what happened to her once when she forgot about the listening part of divine communication. A student of Native American wisdom, she had made a trip to Bandelier National Monument near Santa Fe, where there are kivas, ancient Pueblo ceremonial structures, built directly into the cliffs. Climbing up to one of the kivas, Cynthia sat down inside to pray. She started by silently offering thanks for a long list of things for which she was grateful. All of a sudden, words showed up in her awareness, a kind of knowing rather than a voice. *Will you please be quiet? How are you going to hear what we have to say if you go on and on like that?* She knew this was the voice of Spirit and of the rocks themselves. Now when she sits to pray, she says, she just sits in silence and listens.

Whichever way you prefer to surrender—direct question or open invitation—what's important is letting go of the need to control the outcome. When you do, you create a space for universal love to flow in and direct your life.

The exercise below is a combination of two processes that I've found very useful: grace points and the Divine Grace prayer. I learned about the grace points from Ellena Lieberman, author of *The Principles of Dynamic Manifestation*, during a wonderful consultation I had with her. The grace points were introduced by Edward Conmey, based on his work with the Akashic Records, which are believed to contain the record of each soul's journey. The Divine Grace prayer is an excerpt from one of the many Transformational Prayers developed by Love Luminary Connie Huebner.

Exercise

Invitation to Divine Grace:
Grace Points and the Divine Grace Prayer

Grace points are pressure points in the hands that when gently touched activate the energy meridians in the body that are connected to the heart. Consciously using intention or prayer while holding these points allows your body to relax and moves you into an open, receptive state of clarity and peace.

The grace points are found in the soft tissue of the hand (either right or left hand).

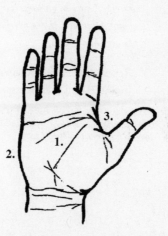

Point 1—Main Grace Point (middle of the palm)
Releases contracted energy so insights are clearly received; it also anchors positivity and brings greater peace.

Point 2—Body Release Point (center of the side of the palm)
Releases unmoving, stuck energy (issues, judgments, beliefs, emotions, pain, etc.) from the body.

Point 3—Ancestry (Genetic Lineage) Point (the web between the thumb and forefinger)
Releases issues, judgments, beliefs, emotions, etc., that have been passed down through the DNA or taken on through family connections.

Process

1. To begin, simply have the intention of inviting Divine Grace into your life.

2. Using the thumb of one hand, touch the main grace point (point 1) on the other hand. Hold that point for thirty seconds while repeating this prayer:

   I open to Divine Grace and allow it to fill me now. I am living in Divine Grace as I move through my life. I trust Divine Grace to give me everything I need. Divine Grace is holding me now. I am overflowing in the fullness of Divine Grace. And so it is.

3. Repeat the same process for the body release point (point 2) and the ancestry point (point 3).

Grace points used by permission of Edward Conmey, www.PeacePath.org. Excerpt of Divine Grace Prayer used by permission of Connie Huebner, www.TransformationalPrayer.com.

Summary and Love for No Reason Action Steps

Plugging in to Presence, the universal vibration of love that pervades all things, and surrendering to grace are the keys that open the Doorway of Oneness. Use the following action steps to increase the flow of love through this energy center:

1. Recharge your spiritual batteries by investing time each day in silence, meditation, or prayer. Tapping into this inner wellspring of spirit will connect you to the energy of unconditional love.

2. Set a baseline of peace by doing a spiritual practice each morning. This will nourish your love-body and keep you anchored to Spirit throughout your day.

3. Practice the Disidentification Exercise to peel away the layers of who you *aren't*—your body, your emotions, your mind—so you can discover the universal consciousness that you are.

4. Use the Meditation for Oneness to connect with all the energy centers of the love-body.

5. Surrender to grace and allow the cosmic GPS to guide you. Let go of your need to control everything and put yourself in life's flow.

6. Initiate your own "conversation with God" by posing a specific question and waiting for the answer to be revealed, or by quieting your mind and opening to the outpouring of Divine inspiration.

7. Invite Divine Grace into your life by using the grace points and the Divine Grace Prayer.

PART III

Living Love for No Reason Every Day

Dedicate yourself to LOVE. Decide to let Love be your intention, your purpose, and your point. And then let Love inspire you, support you, and guide you in every other dedication you make thereafter.

—Robert Holden, author and lecturer

CHAPTER 11

Ready . . . Set . . . Love!

It is not how much you do but how much
love you put into the doing that matters.

—Mother Teresa

Now that you've been through the whole Love for No Reason program, you have a better idea of what it would be like to live in this state on an ongoing basis. You've seen how it will bring you more freedom, openness, joy, and the deeper fulfillment we all want in life. The obvious next question is "How do I make it last?" The answer is by continuing to practice the new habits of unconditional love that change your body and brain functioning.

As Love Luminary and brain researcher Dr. Zoran Josipovic told me, "Turning a *brain state* into a *brain trait* is what makes any change permanent. A brain state is a temporary change in your brain that results from a deliberate action. Over time, if you experience that brain state enough, it becomes a brain trait." That's how unconditional love can become second nature. Practice is the granddaddy of all change. Just keep using the keys in the Love for No Reason program, and over time, it's certain you'll strengthen your love-body and see great results.

Love for No Reason grows steadily when Higher Love is your priority. It's a moment-by-moment choice you make by asking yourself, *What can I do right now, in this situation, that will open my heart?*

If you've read this far, it's clear that you've already made the decision to move in the direction of love. Now it's just a matter of using the Love Keys that you've learned in Part II to keep your heart open.

Here's a summary of the seven doorways to Love for No Reason and the Fourteen Love Keys that make up the Love for No Reason program. Ultimately, love is about feeling connected to life in all its different aspects. Unlocking each doorway removes the blocks and creates an effortless flow, connecting you fully to every area of your life.

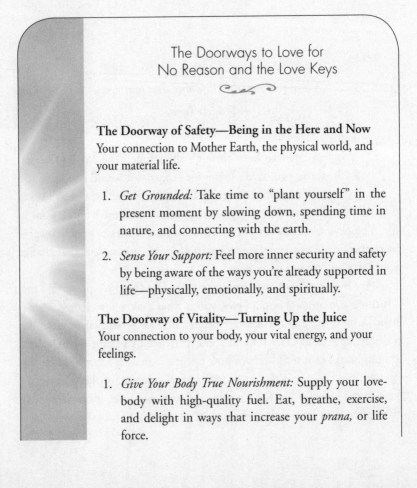

The Doorways to Love for No Reason and the Love Keys

The Doorway of Safety—Being in the Here and Now
Your connection to Mother Earth, the physical world, and your material life.

1. *Get Grounded:* Take time to "plant yourself" in the present moment by slowing down, spending time in nature, and connecting with the earth.

2. *Sense Your Support:* Feel more inner security and safety by being aware of the ways you're already supported in life—physically, emotionally, and spiritually.

The Doorway of Vitality—Turning Up the Juice
Your connection to your body, your vital energy, and your feelings.

1. *Give Your Body True Nourishment:* Supply your love-body with high-quality fuel. Eat, breathe, exercise, and delight in ways that increase your *prana,* or life force.

2. *Feel Your Feelings:* Experience your feelings directly and completely instead of suppressing or venting them.

The Doorway of Unconditional Self-Love—Loving Yourself No Matter What

Your connection to your sense of self, your will, and your authentic power.

1. *Love the Unlovable in Yourself:* Practice self-compassion, self-forgiveness, and self-acceptance to bring the vibration of love to your own being, just as you are.

2. *Honor Your Power:* Take responsibility for your own experience of life and of love.

The Doorway of Openness—Living with an Open Heart

Your connection to others and the world.

1. *Give from Fullness:* Expand your heart by being compassionate, kind, altruistic, and forgiving. Give what you have and not more.

2. *Let Love In:* Boost your ability to receive love through practice; make a habit of gratitude, appreciation, and opening your heart through awe and "*aaahhh.*"

The Doorway of Communication—Coming from Compassion

Your connection to your speech, your expression, and your ability to hear others.

1. *Speak the Language of Love:* Express yourself as an agent of love, communicating what's true for you, including your feelings and needs.

2. *Hear from the Heart:* Listen empathetically for the subtitles—what's really being said beneath others' words.

The Doorway of Vision—Seeing with the Eyes of Love

Your connection to your inner wisdom, your intuition, and Beauty/Truth.

1. *Look for the Beauty:* See the perfection in imperfection and recognize the same spirit in everyone.

2. *Trust Your Inner Wisdom:* Pay attention to your heart's promptings, which come to you as inner knowing or flashes of intuition.

The Doorway of Oneness—Connecting to Wholeness
Your connection to wholeness, grace, and the Divine.

1. *Plug In to Presence:* Tune your "satellite dish" to the Divine by making time for stillness. Meditate or pray each day—especially in the morning.

2. *Surrender to Grace:* Let go and trust the Cosmic GPS to put you in the right place at the right time.

You can take a covered wagon or the Concorde to a life of unconditional love. Using the keys, insights, tools, and techniques in this program is like riding in that supersonic plane—it will help you quickly and easily uncover the love that's already inside you.

Your Love for No Reason Tool Kit

Consider this book your Love for No Reason tool kit, with a variety of tools you can reach for to connect you to love, no matter what's going on. Try each of the techniques and exercises I've recommended and decide which ones work best for you.

As you use this program, here are a few important tips that will help you along the way:

1. Remind yourself regularly of the three Love Themes.
2. Treat yourself with love.
3. Surround yourself with people who support your commitment to love.

Here's how you can make the most of each tip.

Remind Yourself Regularly of the Three Love Themes

These three themes are the Love for No Reason mantras. Keep them in your mind and heart; they'll help you make the all-important paradigm shift that's the foundation of living a life of unconditional love.

Love Theme #1: Love is Who We Are. Love isn't just something we feel for others, it's who we are. It's the thread that makes up the fabric of our life.

When you stop looking for love in a certain form coming from certain people, and realize that you're surrounded by—actually composed of—love, you relax and your energy expands. You let go of the feeling, *There's a limit to love and I have to get mine.* Instead, you experience the ocean of love flowing within you to enjoy and give to others.

Love Theme #2: The Purpose of Life is to Expand in Love. If you ever feel unsure of what you're supposed to do in a situation, here's a good rule of thumb: always do what leads to greater love. Love is your job description— no matter what you do for a living. If you put giving and receiving love at the top of your priority list, you'll definitely experience more everyday success and raise the quality of your life.

Love Theme #3: The Heart is the Portal to Love. Your heart is your ticket to experiencing Love for No Reason. If it's open, love flows freely, both in and out. If it's closed, even with the best intentions, you'll have a hard time being loved or being loving. Try pouring water into or out of a jar if the lid is on. It's a simple case of physics.

Keeping this Love Theme in mind will help you focus your attention on what opens your heart. When your heart feels open, expanded, and light, then you know you're on the right track for greater love. When it's shut down, tight, or heavy, you know you're going in the direction of less love. Whenever you need to, you can choose to shift your thoughts, feelings, and behaviors so they support the opening of your heart.

In my interview with Love Luminary Patricia Ellsberg, life coach and wife of *The Pentagon Papers* whistleblower Daniel Ellsberg, she shared a simple but effective heart-opening technique she does as part of her own daily Higher Love practice. Every morning when she first wakes up, Patricia lies in bed for five minutes or so, with one hand on her heart and the other on her stomach. With each inhale, she breathes in love through her heart, and with each exhale, she sends that love to any part of her body where she feels pain or tightness. She says every time she does this, she feels warmth in her heart and well-being throughout her body.

There's a scientific explanation for this. According to some experts, the act of placing your hand over your heart is a powerful way to start a "love reaction" in your own body: the warmth of your hand activates the parasympathetic system, triggers the release of oxytocin, and creates a calm and pleasant physiological state. Patricia told me that this technique helps her bring the experience of "being love" to the rest of her day.

Treat Yourself with Love

To change old habits, you have to become more aware of your thoughts and behavior, but be careful not to "beat yourself up" in the process. When you notice you're slipping into an old habit, instead of getting down on yourself, know that you're one step closer to positive change.

When you start to change a habit, at first you'll notice you've slipped into your old pattern of behavior *after* it happens. In that case, you just have to be aware of the error, make amends if necessary, and recommit to your goal. Soon you'll start catching yourself in the middle of the old behavior and will be able to make a midcourse correction. Over time you'll be able to choose how you want to behave *before* you act. And eventually the new desired behavior will become as natural and automatic as breathing.

No matter when you catch yourself, though, be loving to yourself. Many of us think we're only going to change by beating ourselves up, but harshness and self-hatred rarely lead to lasting change and never lead to more love. *Never.* They only weaken you and close your heart, hampering your progress. Being gentle with yourself will speed things up *and* improve your quality of life as you go.

Surround Yourself with People Who Support Your Commitment to Love

The people you spend time with have a huge influence on you. They can be a buoyant force for good in your life or they can be like an anchor dragging you down into negativity. One of the fastest ways to live a life of unconditional love is by harnessing the positive influence of other people. So set up a Love for No Reason support system by finding a "love buddy" and by joining (or starting) a support group.

A buddy is indispensable. Knowing you'll be reporting your Love for No Reason adventures to another person is highly motivating and makes the whole process much more fun. When you feel stuck, your buddy encourages you; he or she holds your vision for you when you lose your way. And when you have a Love for No Reason breakthrough, sharing it with your buddy boosts your enthusiasm.

The power of support is increased exponentially when you join what I call a love mastermind group or a "heart group." The group can be your family, your coworkers, your friends, or a group of "like-hearted" people dedicated to love. You can meet in person, by phone, or even online. I recommend that you go through the Love for No Reason program together, focusing on one Love Key each week and reporting your results. Sharing your unconditional love "challenges and wins" with others and hearing about theirs is inspiring. Being in a love mastermind group keeps your commitment to Higher Love lively.

Bonus Tip: Instant Booster for Love for No Reason

Another way to accelerate your experience of unconditional love in everyday life is by using aromatherapy. While I've always loved the essential oils prescribed in aromatherapy, I had no idea of the serious science behind the healing art of scent until I interviewed Love Luminary and aromatherapist Allison Stillman, whose anecdote you read in chapter 9. According to Allison, there's nothing that gets to our brain as quickly and affects it as directly as what we smell, which is why scents have such a powerful effect on our health and well-being.

When we smell something, the information is sent straight to the amygdala (a part of the midbrain involved with emotions and memory), and it affects our brain chemistry. In the following exercise, Allison has recommended a choice of two different oils for each of the energy centers that will help open up the corresponding doorway to Love for No Reason. You use the oils by applying them topically and/or by inhaling their aroma.

I've been using these oils every day and notice that they have a subtle but profound effect, helping me feel more open and loving.

Exercise

Aromatherapy for Opening the Energy Centers

Apply essential oils as part of your daily routine, either in the morning after bathing, or at night before bed. Each day, focus on one energy center you'd like to open. For maximum effect, apply the oils to the body *and* inhale the scent.

It's important to use high-quality pure essential oils. (For more information, see Allison's listing, Romancing the Divine, in the Resources section.) Also, essential oils are very potent, so it's best to dilute them by putting about thirty drops of an essential oil into one ounce of carrier oil, such as pure jojoba or almond oil. Or you can just mix the oils each time you use them by pouring a small amount of carrier oil—about the size of a dime—into your palm, adding a few drops of the essential oil, and blending with your finger. (A note of caution: Though it's rare to have an allergic reaction to pure essential oils, be aware that it's possible.)

1. Determine which energy center you'd like to work with. Apply one of the two essential oils recommended for that center to the areas specified below. Rub in.

2. Inhale by placing a few drops of your selected oil in one palm and rubbing your hands together. Cup your palms around your nose, and inhale deeply two or three times.

3. Stand or sit quietly for thirty seconds to allow the scent to be absorbed into your system.

   - Safety center: Apply patchouli oil or cedarwood oil to the soles of your feet and to your tailbone area.

   - Vitality center: Apply spruce oil or sweet orange oil to the area just below your navel and the corresponding area on your spine.

- Unconditional self-love center: Apply ginger oil or grapefruit oil (also good for digestion) to the area one inch above your navel, and the corresponding area on your spine.

- Openness center: Apply rose oil or ylang-ylang oil to the area around your heart and on the center of your back, right between your "wings."

- Communication center: Apply lavender oil or blue chamomile oil over the whole throat and jaw region and on the ears and around them.

- Vision center: Apply sandalwood oil or frankincense oil to the area between the eyebrows and on the back of the head.

- Oneness center: Apply angelica oil or neroli (orange blossom) oil to the top of the head.

Used by permission of Allison Stillman, www.RomancingtheDivine.com

Love for No Reason Applied— to Relationships and Work

In my interviews with the Love Luminaries, I not only asked how they developed the state of Love for No Reason, I also asked how it affected their relationships and their work—two of the most significant areas of everyday life. I could write another volume about their answers! Here's a sampling of what they said.

Love for No Reason in Relationships

When you *bring* unconditional love to your relationships, rather than trying to *get* love from them, you're free. You don't have to manipulate or control other people—or try to please or hide who you really are from them. You don't need their love or approval to be whole. All of your relationships change because *you* are different.

In my interview with world-renowned relationship expert, best-selling author of *Men Are from Mars, Women Are from Venus*, and Love Luminary Dr. John Gray, he told me about the transformational effect that living in unconditional love has on our relationships. "One of the reasons couples experience so much joy and passion in the first stages of relationship is they haven't begun to keep score; they give freely and unconditionally. But somewhere deep inside they unconsciously begin expecting to have love returned in a particular way. As they begin focusing on what they're *not* getting, an automatic resistance comes up to giving freely. Over time, that incredible feeling of giving unconditionally begins to diminish, and couples wonder why they've fallen out of love.

"The foundation of being able to give love unconditionally is to recognize that in the beginning of the relationship it was *you* who gave freely, and by learning to continue giving freely, you can sustain those good feelings. You have the power to bring out the best in your partner, over and over, when you come from that place of unconditional love. This is the secret to true and lasting love, a lifetime of passion and happiness."

Love Luminary Robb Sals is married to Sally, the woman you read about in chapter 6, who was able to heal her liver by learning to love the unlovable in herself. In our interview, Robb told me how bringing unconditional love to his relationship amplifies that love for both of them. "In Sally, I've found a mirror for the deepest love that's within me. As our love passes back and forth between us, it spirals upward, and we feel even more love for each other. It's like an energy vortex—a positive feedback loop. As a result of our relationship, we both feel a greater love for everybody else. It expands our love in all directions."

Love for No Reason at Work

Work is love made visible.

—Kahlil Gibran, twentieth-century Lebanese American author

For many of us there's an invisible wall that separates our work life from the rest of our life; we put our heart to the side when we walk through the door of "Money and Work." But what the Love Luminaries consistently told me was that true success comes when you bring your heart and its unconditional love to your workplace, whether it's a corporate boardroom, office cubicle, retail store, or restaurant.

Love Luminary Stewart Emery, one of the fathers of the Human Potential Movement and a best-selling author, said, "In the interviews for our book, *Success Built to Last*, we heard one statement over and over: 'You have to love the work that you do. If you don't, you'll lose your job to someone who does.' This came from four-star generals, Fortune 500 CEOs, scientists—people whom you might not expect to hear it from."

Stewart says that the best advice for success comes from Abraham Lincoln. "A little boy was sitting on Abraham Lincoln's lap, and looked up and said, 'Mr. President, what do you think I ought to be when I grow up?' And Lincoln responded, 'I don't know, lad, but whatever you are, be a good one.'"

Stewart continued, "When you're living in a state of love, it automatically brings the ability to 'be a good one' to whatever you're doing. It's love that causes that to happen. Without love for your work, you can't get good at it.

"What's interesting is that if you ask people who love their work *why* they love it, they'll invent reasons, because we're socialized to have reasons for everything, but the truth is that the love we're talking about 'passeth all understanding': it's beyond reasons. And it's this love that produces the greatest artistic, scientific, and business achievements."

Yet one of the things missing right now in the world of business is employee engagement. There's a well-known study showing that 80 percent of people aren't passionate about their work. When you love your work, you put your whole heart into it. My dear friends Chris Attwood and Janet Bray Attwood, radiant Love Luminaries and the coauthors of *The Passion Test,* are leading proponents of bringing love into the workplace through following your passion. In our interview, Chris explained what they mean by passion: "Your passions are the things that you love most, which matter most to you, and have the deepest meaning for your life. Passion is love made manifest. It's love in motion. It connects you to the deepest part of your own heart."

Janet told me that everyone can start to follow their passion at work with one simple step. "No matter what you do, you're faced with decisions, opportunities, and choices all day long. Whenever one comes up, choose in favor of that which has greatest meaning to you. In every moment, you're either moving towards what you love or you're moving away from it—by the choices or the decisions you make.

"Also, find a way to see your everyday work in a bigger context. Even the things you have to do that you don't love doing are satisfying if they're done in service of something that's meaningful to you."

When we think of work as an arduous thing, we shut down our hearts. But according to Love Luminary Matt Weinstein, there's an antidote: we can keep our hearts open and delight in our work through play. Matt is the founding president of Playfair, an international company that designs team-building programs for organizations. In our interview he told me, "Work and fun are not opposites. In fact, success comes from having fun and loving your work! Of course customers are going to buy with their minds; they're interested in price, in value, in service, but they also go by their feelings. What does it feel like to do business with this company or this individual? Being engaged and happy at work is a huge competitive advantage."

Matt advises employees and employers alike to open their hearts and minds through playful activities, games, and events at work. (His website is chock-full of examples; see the Resources section.) "Play is regenerative. Why is it that people take a play break and come back and have creative breakthroughs? It's partly because people don't let themselves rest. After play, people feel refreshed and rejuvenated and they have much more access to their intellect." In his more than thirty years of experience, Matt has found that love, play, creativity, delight, *and* a healthier bottom line go hand in hand.

I've experienced the power of play at work with Learning Strategies Corporation, a wonderful company that I've partnered with on various projects. This publishing and training company is a leader in the field of self-improvement, education, and health programs, incorporating accelerated learning technologies in their products.

Each year in March, Learning Strategies has their big "Einstein Day" to celebrate their anniversary and Einstein's birthday. Employees dress up as the famous physicist—white wigs, mustaches, and all—share their favorite Einstein quote (real or imagined), win mindless and mindful prizes, and receive their annual bonuses.

One year, I surprised everyone by showing up in full Einstein regalia. (There was one slight problem: no one recognized that it was me inside the costume, which dampened the surprise a bit.) Einstein Day is just one way that Learning Strategies brings delight into the workplace. Their commitment to love shows in the open-hearted atmosphere you feel the minute you walk in the door.

I knew it would be impossible to write a section about Love for No Reason at work without mentioning Café Gratitude, one of my favorite restaurants and an amazing example of combining heart, service, and business. Love Luminaries and successful entrepreneurs Matthew and Terces Engelhart are the founders and owners of Café Gratitude and of Be Love Farm, and the authors of *Sacred Commerce*. They have created a business model that's overflowing with unconditional love—for their customers, for their employees, and for the earth.

In our interview, Terces said, "We believe we're successful because we're doing more than just being engaged in a commercial endeavor; we're actually supporting people in their own transformations, and in the transformation of their families and their communities. We call it walking a spiritual path with practical feet. Something we engage in every day—work—can be made into an opportunity for people to wake up."

Clearly, sharing your Love for No Reason with others—at work and in your relationships—can have a profound effect on your own life and on people you care about. But the influence of your love is even greater than you know: there's a collective Love Movement happening around the globe, and you're an essential part of it.

In our next and final chapter, I'll share with you how love is transforming our world—and how your own commitment to Higher Love is contributing to a global shift of unprecedented magnitude.

CHAPTER 12

Supersize Your Heart:
Love on a Global Scale

There's an urgency on the planet today. We're living at a time on the earth when our great-great-grandchildren can't afford for us to move too slowly. Every place where we are weak, there is in the mind of God a blueprint where we become strong. Every place where we are sick, there is a blueprint in the mind of God where we become healthy.

—Marianne Williamson

There's a major shift happening on the planet *right now*. We're moving from a mind-dominated world obsessed with power, control, and survival to a love-dominated world that balances mind and heart and is committed to the flourishing of all sentient beings. You may have read about this shift, have heard about it from friends, or even feel it yourself. Or you may just look around and *hope* that it's happening, because in the words of that old Sammy Davis Jr. song, "something's gotta give."

If you focus on all the world's problems, it's easy to get discouraged. But I was cheered by what Love Luminary Gregg Braden had to say about our capacity as a world family to turn things around. Gregg, who is an author and pioneer in bridging science and spirituality, said, "In my book *The God Code*, I describe how over four hundred separate scientific studies, published in peer-reviewed journals, were done to determine the optimum amount of competition within species and whether or not violence is our true nature. The results of all these four hundred studies were unanimous: we are *not* a violent and competitive species by nature. At our core is a desire to cooperate and come together."

And it's our hearts—those portals of unconditional love—that are at the center of the shift.

Healing the World: One Heart at a Time

In his speeches and sermons, Martin Luther King Jr. often talked about the three primary words for love in the Greek language: *eros*, "romantic love with all of its beauty," *philia*, the "vital, valuable reciprocal love between friends," and *agape*, "an overflowing love which seeks nothing in return." He said that as important as the first two types of love are, the only one that can change the world is *agape*—the love for people that we don't even like. Though it's tempting to reject or even try to destroy the people we feel are hateful, Dr. King said that returning hate with hate "only intensifies the existence of hate and evil in the universe . . . It just never ends . . . The strong person is the person who can cut off the chain of hate, the chain of evil . . . and inject within the very structure of the universe that strong and powerful element of love."

Although those words were spoken more than fifty years ago, we still face the same challenge today: to love people we don't agree with and who don't see the world the same way we do.

Overcoming this love hurdle is the job of the heart center, supported by the other six energy centers. Your dedication to experiencing more Love for No Reason and becoming a conduit of love is the main way you can sail over that hurdle and help speed the shift on the planet.

My own experience of unconditional love—for myself and others—has taken a quantum leap during the writing of this book. But as Dr. King predicted, the real test comes when I feel someone has done something wrong. In the blink of an eye, my old judgmental/punitive self surfaces, and it takes self-compassion and some time spent "feeling my feelings" to move back to a space of love. So you'll understand why I found the following story that I heard from Love Luminary James Baraz so inspirational. James, the author of *Awakening Joy,* and teacher of a fantastic year-long course of the same name, quotes this story from Jack Kornfield's book *The Art of Forgiveness, Lovingkindness, and Peace:*

> In the Babemba tribe of South Africa, when a person acts irresponsibly or unjustly, he is placed in the center of the village, alone and unfettered. All work ceases, and every man, woman, and child in the village gathers in a large circle around the accused individual. Then each person in the tribe speaks to the accused, one at a time, each recalling the good things the person in the center of the circle has done in his lifetime. Every incident, every experience that can be recalled with any detail and accuracy is recounted. All his positive attributes, good deeds, strengths, and kindnesses are recited carefully and at length. This tribal ceremony often lasts for several days. At the end, the tribal circle is broken, a joyous celebration takes place, and the person is symbolically and literally welcomed back into the tribe.

The Babemba tribe's method of rehabilitation, which focuses on loving the person rather than punishing the misdeed, is a natural extension of living with an open heart.

The World Is My Family

Love the world as your own self; then you can truly care for all things.
—the Tao Te Ching

Perhaps the most quoted line in the Bible is the Golden Rule: "Do unto others as you would have them do unto you." When you care as much for others as you do for yourself, it's possible for love to flow unobstructed to everyone in the world.

This isn't as big a stretch as it sounds. In my interview with Love Luminary Dr. Art Aron, he said we've all had some experience caring about someone else as much as we care about ourselves. He told me, "When you have a close romantic relationship with someone, the other becomes part of yourself and you treat them, to some extent, like yourself. You're concerned with their welfare, because their welfare is your welfare. People can usually extend that care easily to their children, their family, and their friends. There's a great deal of research on including close others as part of the self."

This care even shows up on a physiological level. Dr. Aron told me that studies on the neural component of these feelings show that when you're very close to someone, if something happens to that person, your brain lights up in the same areas as it would if it had happened to you. Your brain actually considers the other person as part of your own body.

Dr. Aron's research has focused specifically on how entire groups of people—including those from other ethnic or religious groups—become included in the self. Dr. Aron and his team found that when you form a friendship with someone from another group, that person—*and* the group they belong to—become part of you. Your care and concern are extended via your friend to the friend's broader community.

What's really exciting—especially in the context of spreading love on the planet—is that this extending of concern can even work vicariously. "Any friend of yours is a friend of mine" appears literally to be true. Dr. Aron said, "We observed that if someone in your group has a friend in another group, much of that effect is transferred to you: you include the other group as part of yourself, even though you don't directly have a friend in that group." What this research suggests is that ultimately, if you feel that you're only one link away in the human chain from every other person in the world (one degree of separation), then you're going to have that feeling of inclusion with everyone. You truly feel the world is your family.

Loving Our Mother

When you live with an open heart, you treat the world as your family and the earth as your mother. Your unconditional love extends not just to people but to the planet too. Unfortunately, for some time now, we haven't been treating our mother very well, and the effects are endangering us all. If we want to preserve this beautiful blue ball that we live on, it's time to take action.

Many of us are already committed to living sustainably. We drive fuel-efficient cars, we buy organic, we recycle, we do everything we can to reduce our negative impact on the environment. These loving actions are important, yet what I learned from Love Luminary Jeddah Mali is that the most effective way to help *Mother Nature* is by fully experiencing your *inner nature*—the unconditional love at your core.

Jeddah, who is an international teacher and spiritual mentor, told me, "I'm not saying you don't take action, but when you act standing steady in the true nature of existence—which throughout history has been called love—then you don't need to apply as much effort to bring about your desired result. When you know from your own experience that harmony is the natural state of things, your attention shifts from trying to create harmony to allowing it."

I thought of Jeddah's point when I heard environmentalist Julia Butterfly Hill speak. Julia is best known for the two years she spent living on a platform 180 feet up in the canopy of a thousand-year-old redwood tree she called Luna. Her goal was to bring awareness to the destruction of the ancient forests. She was only twenty-six at the time, and though she faced strong, sometimes life-threatening opposition, she refused to give up.

Many times during her vigil, she sat listening as the trees around Luna were being cut down. Her fury and contempt for the loggers grew with each passing day. At one point, she knew that if she didn't find a way to deal with the rising tide of hatred she felt, she would drown in it. Overwhelmed and desperate, she prayed.

Her answer came in the form of a warm current of love that felt as though it were coming from Luna and from the earth itself; that love which—without condition—gives everything in the world life, flowed into her and dissolved her hatred.

This experience was a turning point for Julia in her life as an activist. From that moment forward, she was inspired by love, rather than motivated by anger and hatred. In the end, she managed to negotiate an agreement that permanently protected Luna and all the other redwoods in a three-acre buffer zone. Julia's story shows that the most environmentally conscious thing you can do is to allow your inner environment to blossom.

Love Luminary Lynne Twist is another beautiful example of someone who combines a radiant quality of inner unconditional love with focused love for Mother Earth. In 1995 she and her husband, Bill, founded the

Pachamama Alliance, an organization dedicated to protecting the earth's rainforests and the indigenous people who live there. (For more information, see the Giving Back section on page 338.) One of the Pachamama Alliance's programs is the Awakening the Dreamer Initiative, whose mission is to create an environmentally sustainable, spiritually fulfilling, and socially just human presence on Planet Earth by empowering individuals to take action in their own lives on a daily basis. This mission is based on the principle that experiencing unconditional love at our core is deeply connected to our care for the planet.

The Power of the Heart's Intention

The global transformation we're in the midst of today is being powered by love. What's unusual about this shift is that it's not coming from the top down; the world's established leaders aren't dictating laws that force people to live in love. Instead, this shift is coming from the hearts of a large number of people like you and me. Each day more of us are contributing our heart's energy to the giant wave of love that's enveloping the planet.

I know that might sound woo-woo and New Age, but it isn't just theory. With advances in modern technology, we're able to monitor the effects of group intention as never before. Love Luminary Lynne McTaggart has spent many years studying the power of our thoughts and feelings to change society and the physical world. In her book *The Intention Experiment* (and on its website), Lynne describes a series of scientifically controlled, web-based experiments she conducted, working with leading physicists and psychologists from distinguished academic centers around the world to measure the effects of group intention.

The most ambitious experiment to date was the Peace Intention Experiment carried out in September 2008. Lynne and a special team of scientists wanted to see if a large group intention would be powerful enough to lower violence and promote peace. The experiments chose an obscure target, the Wanni section of Sri Lanka, where civil war had been raging for over twenty-five years with no end in sight.

The group sending the intentions included more than fifteen thousand people from a total of sixty-five countries. The results were dramatic and compelling. During the week that the group sent their intentions for peace, there was a huge *increase* in violence, but within a few weeks after that, the level of violence dropped far below what it had been for years, and the civil war ended approximately eight months later. Furthermore, a time analysis carried out by an expert statistician revealed that after the experiment, violence remained far lower than predicted. Another scientist measuring the effect of group resonance through the use of certain sensitive equipment dotted all over the world discovered the biggest effect during the ten-minute window when the group intention was being sent. Nevertheless, until more experiments are conducted, there's no way to determine if the results were a coincidence or if the group intention actually accelerated the conclusion of the conflict.

While writing this book, I personally participated in one of Lynne's global intention experiments, conducted on March 21, 2010, to purify the polluted water of Japan's Lake Biwa, one of the world's oldest lakes. As I sat sending love and my intention, I felt wave after wave of warmth in my heart. The results were exciting: Russian physicist Konstantin Korotkov, who ran the study, collected data on two measures of pollution, the cluster structure of the water molecules and their pH, and found that they were both affected positively. I was delighted with the findings and loved the extraordinary experience of feeling connected to more than ten thousand other hearts around the globe.

Another research organization studying the power of a group's loving intention is the Institute of HeartMath's Global Coherence Initiative (GCI). GCI's groundbreaking mission is to shift global consciousness so that we experience greater peace in the world. Through the internet, they're bringing together people around the globe to send loving heart-focused intention to the planet at the same time. The theory is that the effect of people experiencing heart rhythm coherence simultaneously will be exponentially more powerful than individuals practicing by themselves.

One of the parameters the researchers are measuring is how love, in the form of directed heart rhythm coherence, influences the earth's magnetic field. The Institute of HeartMath is currently developing advanced sensing technology that will directly measure fluctuations in the magnetic fields generated by the earth and in the ionosphere. It's remarkable that science is getting to the point where it can show us how interconnected we are with each other and with our planet.

One World, One Heart

For years I've had a book on my shelf that I always reach for if I have a question about the chakras/energy centers. Its author, Love Luminary Anodea Judith, amazes me with the breadth and depth of her knowledge. When I interviewed her, I was also impressed by her wisdom about what's happening on the planet today. She calls this shift "waking the global heart," which is also the title of one of her books. In our interview, Anodea said that based on her understanding of the chakras, she believes that we're moving from a culture based largely on the third chakra, which is associated with power and the emergence of ego-based consciousness, to the fourth chakra, whose focus is love, relatedness, and a more transcendent consciousness. She speaks of this as our rite of passage from "the love of power to the power of love." This shift will uproot and transform every aspect of human civilization.

When each of us wakes up our own hearts, we're helping to awaken the global heart. A popular analogy for this collective transformation is the process of metamorphosis, the miraculous conversion of caterpillar into butterfly. In *Waking the Global Heart,* Anodea describes the similarities between the two shifts. She says that when a caterpillar encases itself in its cocoon, tiny cells called imaginal cells begin to appear within the chrysalis. They are entirely different from caterpillar cells, vibrating at a different frequency—the frequency of the developing butterfly. These imaginal cells keep multiplying, find each other, and cluster together. Eventually they create an entirely new structure and what emerges is the butterfly—a creature of exquisite beauty, grace, and freedom.

In the same way, as we open our hearts in unconditional love, we become the imaginal cells, building our love-bodies and bringing the energy of love to the world. Then, joining together, we create the new global heart—beating with love, compassion, and peace.

Jump on the Love Train

Every day, I see evidence that the tide of love is rising in the world. Though the bad news is still there, there are also points of light everywhere, like stars filling the night sky. It may have something to do with writing this book, but I've become highly attuned to anything Higher

Love–related. I've noticed that more and more people are posting videos on YouTube, writing blogs, creating a buzz about spreading love around the world. Wherever I go, I run into people who are helping to promote love in ways large and small.

You may be noticing the same phenomenon. To make it easy to find all the examples of this global love movement in one place, I'm collecting every one I come across and putting them on my website. For a dose of inspiration that will open your heart, visit www.TheLoveBook.com/global shift.

The global shift to living in the energy of unconditional love is a moving train. Having read this book, you're already on board. A world filled with Love for No Reason is a great destination. Let's enjoy the ride together.

Our Personal Journey Toward Love for No Reason

Writing *Love for No Reason* has felt like an epic journey: it's taken a long time, has involved an enormous amount and variety of material, and has touched on almost every aspect of human existence! Yet both Carol and I feel that this journey has been a huge gift from the universe to us.

Could there be any better topic to study? Love is the subject I've been most interested in for as long as I can remember. Spending the past three years interviewing extraordinary people about love has been beyond fulfilling. A spiritual teacher of mine used to say, "What you put your attention on grows stronger in your life," and I can't think of anything I'd rather have grow stronger in my life than unconditional love.

At each step of the project, Carol and I have felt a sense of being guided and helped. We were able to reach people we wanted to interview in often miraculous ways; just as we'd need to find a certain piece of information, the perfect book or email would appear. Even up until the last moments of writing, friends would call out of the blue and tell us stories that were the perfect illustrations of the points we were working on. It's felt as though the energy of love has led the way, leaving us humbled and filled with gratitude.

Carol has told me again and again that writing this book has been transformational for her. She says, "Life is so much sweeter now. I've always been a 'mind person.' I grew up in a loving and intellectually oriented family. And although I appreciate my intellect, while writing this book I've allowed my heart to come forward more—especially in areas where my mind used to shut it down. I feel softer, more open, more appreciative, and yet, at the same time, stronger inside.

"I've lost my edge, but that's a good thing. My husband says I'm nicer now. The sharpness that saw all the faults is mostly gone. I've started experiencing my life through the lens of love: the people I meet, the conversations I have, the view outside my window. The things that happen to me, good and even not so good—they all stir me in a new and beautiful way. I've discovered the joy of an open heart."

When I started this project, I certainly couldn't have imagined all the challenges that would happen in my life. I've already shared the major ones with you: the end of my marriage, the sale of our family home, and the death of my mother—each difficult in its own right and, taken together, a tsunami of difficulty. But what I also couldn't have imagined was how open and full my heart could feel even amid those challenges.

For most of my life, my heart, though sincere and caring, had also been crimped by judgment, jealousy, and fear. Today it feels as if those creases have been smoothed out; my heart is light, free, and expanded. I have greater love and compassion for myself and am able to love others more fully and deeply.

As I approached the conclusion of this writing project, a saying kept going through my head: "In the end, all there is, is love." It reminded me of my father's final days. Dad had just turned ninety-one and it was clear that he had very little time to live, so my whole family came to be with him. During the last week of his life, Dad spent his waking hours surrounded by his wife, children, and grandchildren, with a huge smile on his face. He'd look at each one of us and whisper, "I love you, I love you, I love you." That was all there was to say. The entire room was enveloped in love.

A few months ago, as I looked down at my mother's beautiful face for the last time, I had the same awareness: in the end, what really matters is love.

Thank you for joining me on this journey of love. I'm honored to be taking it with you. I hope that this book has the same effect on you that it's had on Carol and me—that you feel guided by the force of love and your heart remains open and free. My deepest wish for you is that you grow in

love, live in love, and flourish in love. In the fullness of love, I leave you
with this traditional Gaelic blessing:

> *May the long time sun shine upon you*
> *All love surround you*
> *And the pure light within you*
> *Guide your way home.*

RECOMMENDED RESOURCES

Programs to Help You Experience
Love for No Reason . . . Now!

Now you know it's possible to experience Love for No Reason and that there's nothing more important for the quality of your life and for life on the planet than having this experience grow day by day. To help speed your progress, I created the following programs that provide even greater support on your Love for No Reason journey.

Love for No Reason *Seminar*

In the Love for No Reason Seminar I will personally guide you in applying all the principles, habits, and tools in this book to immediately transform your life and lay the foundation for unconditional love. You will put into practice the fourteen Love Keys and strengthen your love-body so that unconditional love is your everyday experience.

Love for No Reason *Love Ambassador Program*

If you want to teach courses based on the material in *Love for No Reason*, you can become a certified Love Ambassador. This allows you to teach "The Love Course," a powerful program that offers students practical techniques for experiencing a lasting state of unconditional love. In this professional training, you'll get everything you need in order to teach two-hour presentations, half-day seminars, and full-day workshops, including PowerPoint presentations, course materials, and student handouts. Teaching this material is the fast track to enlivening it in your own life.

Love for No Reason *Coaching*

However grounded we are in the principles we've learned, life has a way of throwing curveballs that continually challenge us. This one-on-one coaching program is designed to help you integrate the Love Keys into your everyday life to make your experience of unconditional love truly unshakable. Coaching will help you develop new strategies for thinking, feeling, and acting that support this experience of love. It is the fastest and surest way to overcome old habits and begin living the life of your dreams.

Love for No Reason *Interview Series*

The knowledge in this book won't change your life until you make it an integral part of your daily reality. My in-depth interviews with the Love Luminaries will show you these concepts, habits, and tools in action, and bring them vividly alive. Seeing them applied in the context of people's varied real-life experiences will help you integrate them and inspire you with a vision of possibilities.

Love for No Reason *Yoga Program DVD*

The *Love for No Reason Yoga Program* DVD leads you through an easy but powerful process that helps you open the seven main energy centers in your body. Through movement, awareness, sound, and visualization you learn how to embody the unique qualities of each of the energy centers. You are guided step by step on a somatic journey to experience a more open heart and greater balance in your mind and body.

Love for No Reason *Keynote Presentations*

In my twenty-five years of delivering keynote addresses to countless corporations, associations, and professional and nonprofit organizations, I have learned that a keynote presentation can transform and galvanize individuals and organizations with measurable and often startlingly powerful results. It is my joy to offer my services in the inspiration and transformation of your audience or organization. Where individuals are experiencing unconditional love, any level of success is possible.

For more information on these and other programs, please visit
www.TheLoveBook.com/Programs.

Tools and Techniques

Access Consciousness—Gary Douglas

www.accessconsciousness.com

Access Consciousness offers a set of tools and techniques that allow you to create more conscious choices in life and quickly and easily change the parts of your life that cause unhappiness.

Adorata Meditation and Programs—Tiziana DellaRovere

www.adorata.org

The Adorata Meditation and Programs offer a unique method to directly connect with the love of the Divine within you. These programs can help you experience greater intimacy with others, feel deeply loved for who you are, and pursue your life's purpose with joy and ease.

Akashic Record Classes and Consultations

Ellena Lynn Lieberman, www.dynamicmanifestation.com

Ed Conmey, www.peacepath.org

Classes and consultations on the Akashic Record offer transformational insights for individuals from the soul level. Classes, accredited through Akashic Record Consultants International, are dedicated to the purity of this life-altering work.

American Buddha Spiritual Therapy—Stuart Mooney Jr., MA

www.americanbuddha.net

American Buddha Spiritual Therapy focuses on creating a "spiritual awakening" in each client. They provide professional guidance and support services to spiritual seekers from beginners to the most advanced levels.

The Anat Baniel Method—Anat Baniel

www.anatbanielmethod.com

The Anat Baniel Method is a revolutionary approach that awakens the remarkable capacities of the brain to create new connections leading to physical and mental breakthroughs bordering on the miraculous.

Angeles Arrien Workshops—Angeles Arrien

www.angelesarrien.com

Cultural anthropologist Angeles Arrien offers workshops that enhance personal and professional effectiveness. Her programs provide ancient and modern tools, practices, and resources that are perennial and relevant worldwide.

The Art of Living Foundation

www.artofliving.org

This international nonprofit educational and humanitarian organization offers workshops teaching meditation and breathing techniques that calm the mind, release stress, clear the body of toxins, and energize the whole system in minutes.

Awakening Coaching Training—Arjuna Ardagh

awakeningcoachingtraining.com

Awakening Coaching is a dynamic new modality that supports people as they wake up from the limiting confines of thought-based living. Coaches support their clients in discovering their unique gifts and in living from their natural state of clarity and resourcefulness in every arena of personal and professional life.

Awakening Joy Course—James Baraz

www.jamesbaraz.com

Led by James Baraz, founding teacher of Spirit Rock Meditation Center, Awakening Joy is a ten-month experiential course designed to develop your natural capacity for well-being and happiness.

Ayurvedic Healing—Drs. Suhas and Manisha Kshirsagar

www.AyurvedicHealing.net

Ayurvedic Healing is a wellness clinic with a consciousness-based approach to health. It offers mind/body consultations, yoga, beauty treatments, and various Ayurvedic programs and workshops.

Sergio Baroni

www.SergioBaroni.com

Sergio Baroni offers Love for No Reason coaching and personal intensives that will guide you in creating profound shifts in your life using the transformative power of unconditional love. A highly trained and gifted psychotherapist, coach, and healer. Sergio has been closely involved in developing the Love for No Reason programs. He provides a free introductory consultation for his one-on-one coaching or in-person intensives.

Dr. Bill Bauman

www.billbauman.net

Through workshops, mentoring, and consulting, Bill Bauman leads people to their destiny, which is becoming the *ultimate human* and *ultimate leader*. These programs focus on masterful living for the twenty-first century.

Best Life Design—Dr. Mollie Marti

www.bestlifedesign.com

Best Life Design provides tools to support a high-impact business as well as a healthy, wealthy, and meaningful lifestyle for success oriented entrepreneurs and professionals who are passionate about serving others.

The Bond—Lynne McTaggart

www.thebond.net

Lynne McTaggart offers a detailed tool kit of courses, teleseminars, and workshops growing out of her book *The Bond: Connecting through the Space between Us*, to help foster more holistic thinking, more cooperative relationships, and more unified social units.

The Boothby Institute—Bill Cumming

www.theboothbyinstitute.org

The institute offers programs for individuals and institutions that allow people to discover internal strength and the capacity to take charge of their own lives in a climate of lovingkindness.

Dr. Joan Borysenko

www.joanborysenko.com

Dr. Borysenko offers a premier resource for credible information on the intersection of mind/body science, positive psychology, and spiritual exploration, providing practical knowledge and inspiration for caring for your body, mind, and soul.

Brain Longevity—Dharma Singh Khalsa, MD

www.drdharma.com

Dr. Dharma Singh Khalsa offers cutting-edge programs to delay the onset of brain aging, reverse memory loss, prevent Alzheimer's disease, and improve the quality of your life.

Café Gratitude Cookbook and Workshops—Matthew and Terces Engelhart
www.cafegratitude.com
The *I Am Grateful* cookbook provides easy-to-follow recipes from the café's most popular items, making it easy for readers to prepare healthy foods at home. The Engelharts also offer workshops on relationship, abundance, and creating an awakening community at the workplace.

Calling In "The One"—Katherine Woodward Thomas and Claire Zammit
www.callingintheone.com
Calling In "The One": Spiritual Tools for Attracting Love offers a wide range of free resources, online programs, in-depth courses, and a coaching certification program for those seeking meaningful personal empowerment and authentic romantic connection.

The Canfield Training Group—Jack Canfield
www.jackcanfield.com
The Canfield Training Group offers life-changing live seminars, audio and video courses, and books that focus on inspiring and empowering people to live their highest dreams in a context of love and joy.

Celebrating Men, Satisfying Women Workshop—Alison Armstrong
www.understandmen.com
If you work with men or live with them, are in a relationship with one or want to be, this weekend workshop for women can help bring more satisfaction, happiness, and pleasure into your life.

The Center for Compassion and Altruism Research and Education at Stanford University (CCARE)—James R. Doty, MD
http://ccare.stanford.edu
CCARE uses the latest tools of neuroscience to understand the neural, social, and moral bases of compassion and altruism and how to potentiate such behaviors in individuals.

Changing the Paradigm of the Planet—Jeddah Mali
www.jeddahmali.com
Through her transformational courses and retreats, Jeddah Mali helps people experience greater inner peace, joy, and love.

The Compassionate Listening Project—Leah Green

www.compassionatelistening.org

The Compassionate Listening Project teaches heart-based skills to create powerful cultures of peace in our families and communities, in the workplace, and in the world. TCLP offers training, facilitator certification, and delegations to Israel and Palestine.

The Contemplative Society—Rev. Cynthia Bourgeault

www.contemplative.org

The Contemplative Society is a global group committed to recovering the ancient unitive Wisdom tradition and mystical heart of Christianity through contemplative teaching, retreats, and meditation.

The Creative Visions Foundation—Kathy and Amy Eldon

www.creativevisions.org

The Creative Visions Foundation supports "creative activists" who use media and the arts to create awareness of critical issues and catalyze positive change.

Katie Darling

www.theinfinitewave.com

Katie Darling is a brilliant teacher who combines science, spirit, and humor. She offers the iWAVE course, an accelerated awakening program for your body, emotions, mind, and soul.

The DaVinci Dilemma: Solutions for Multi-talented People—Liisa Kyle and Lisa Rothstein

www.davincidilemma.com

The DaVinci Dilemma provides creative people tools and resources to help discover, enjoy, and organize their many talents, and to deal with common challenges including fear, procrastination, lack of motivation, and guilt.

Difference Makers International—Helice "Sparky" Bridges

www.differencemakersinternational.org

Difference Makers International is a nonprofit international educational organization building better communities through leadership training, community programs, and acknowledgment products that help people make a difference where they live, work, and learn.

Divine Mother Guidance and Healing—Rev. Connie Huebner

www.DivineMotherOnline.net

Divine Mother Guidance and Healing facilitates a deeper connection to the Divine by healing blockages in the flow of your life energy, and by providing techniques to stay centered in your Self.

Dr. John Douillard's LifeSpa

www.lifespa.com

LifeSpa is a Boulder-based Ayurvedic panchakarma center and national educational resource providing current health news through video newsletters, individual consultations, and retreats. Dr. Douillard believes in self-sufficiency on the road to optimum health.

Dream University—Marcia Wieder

www.DreamUniversity.com

Founded by Marcia Wieder, this is the only university in the world with a world-class faculty that is solely dedicated to teaching people, via live events and an online campus, how to achieve their dreams.

Earth Spectrum Health—Lilli Botchis, PhD

www.earthspectrum.com

Earth Spectrum Health offers cutting-edge consciousness-based products, services, and technologies that vitalize and support the shift to high-energy, purposeful living.

Educating for Peace—Isha Judd

www.whywalkwhenyoucanfly.com

Isha's powerful system for the expansion of love-consciousness is explained in her book and movie, *Why Walk When You Can Fly?*

Patricia Ellsberg

http://PatriciaEllsberg.com/

Patricia Ellsberg helps women become a source of radiant love and find greater meaning and joy in their lives. Her website offers a beautiful free guided meditation.

Stewart Emery

www.stewartemery.com

Stewart Emery supports people and organizations in becoming world-class at doing things they love to do.

The Emotional Connection Program—Raphael Cushnir

www.cushnir.com

The Emotional Connection Program promotes healing, growth, well-being, and success. It clears out the blocked emotions that keep you stuck and allows you to meet new emotional challenges with freedom and equanimity.

Emotional Fitness—Barton Goldsmith, PhD

www.BartonGoldsmith.com

Through his writings and programs on emotional fitness, psychotherapist and NPR host Dr. Barton Goldsmith helps individuals, couples, families, and businesses reach their full potential.

Emotional Freedom Techniques (EFT)—The Tapping Solution

www.TheTappingSolution.com

The Tapping Solution is a breakthrough documentary (available on DVD) exploring the Emotional Freedom Techniques, a healing tool based on the body's subtle energy systems and meridians. Learn how to release pain or trauma and clear limiting beliefs.

The Enlightened Mom—Terri Amos-Britt

www.TheEnlightenedMom.com

The Enlightened Mom website offers various programs and a global community that gives *all* mothers the opportunity to release their burdens and become love overflowing. As a mom heals, a family heals—and the world heals.

Everything Is Energy—David and Kristin Morelli

www.Enwaken.com

David and Kristin Morelli create life-changing coaching programs. They utilize powerful energy practices to break through stubborn inner blocks, thus unleashing your greatest potential so you can live fully.

Feminine Power: The Essential Course for the Awakening Woman—Katherine Woodward Thomas and Claire Zammit

www.FemininePower.com

A program for women to awaken the power to create what they most yearn for: authenticity, love, higher creativity, and contribution to the world. Go to the website to download a free audio.

Focus on the Good Stuff—Mike Robbins

www.Mike-Robbins.com

Mike Robbins offers programs that focus on appreciation and authenticity, which are fundamental to the success and fulfillment of individuals, teams, and organizations. He is the best-selling author of *Focus on the Good Stuff* (Wiley) and *Be Yourself, Everyone Else Is Already Taken* (Wiley).

Foodlovers Workshops—Sherry Strong

www.sherrystrong.com

Foodlovers Workshops help people develop a healthier relationship with food, their body, and the planet so they can live the life they're meant to live.

Forgive for Good—Frederic Luskin, PhD

www.learningtoforgive.com

Dr. Fred Luskin offers a powerful method of forgiveness that emphasizes letting go of hurt, helplessness, and anger, while increasing confidence, hope, and happiness. This method has been validated by research conducted through the Stanford University Forgiveness Project.

Golden Heart Healing—Cathy Korson

www.goldenhearthealing.com

Golden Heart Healing uses pure gold foil from Burma. Applying it to the skin directly over the heart spiritually nourishes and illuminates the compassion in our hearts. All proceeds are donated to support various charitable projects in Burma.

Good Vibe Coaching—Jeannette Maw

www.goodvibecoach.com

Self-love practices and principles are the core of Good Vibe Coaching. The essence of this message is shared in the *Art of Self-Love* ebook and audio program.

Great Life Technologies, Inc.—Tom Stone

www.greatlifetechnologies.com

Based on Tom Stone's pioneering work in the new field of Human Software Engineering, Great Life Technologies offers simple and powerful techniques for "debugging" and "upgrading" your inner human software to remove the inner barriers to having the life you truly want.

Gregg Braden Programs—Gregg Braden

www.greggbraden.com

New York Times best-selling author Gregg Braden is building a new wisdom through science and spirituality. He offers seminars, events, and books that uncover the timeless secrets of wisdom traditions.

Rick Hanson, PhD

www.rickhanson.net

Dr. Hanson's website offers a wide range of resources, including step-by-step instructions for weaving good experiences into your brain and your self, talks and slide sets from his workshops, guided meditations, and key scientific papers.

Healing with Love—Dr. Leonard Laskow

www.laskow.net

Healing with Love seminars and consultations offer profound methods for coming into wholeness through love to heal the physical body, resolve emotional issues, enhance creativity, and support personal transformation and spiritual awakening.

Heartline Productions—Dr. Brenda Wade

www.docwade.com

Dr. Brenda brings a proven blend of science, spirituality, and psychology to seminars, retreats, coaching, and the International Love & Money Summit.

HeartMastery—Sheva Carr

www.heartmastery.com

This online training program, validated by cutting-edge science, gives you everything you need to create a life you truly love and a heart-based world.

The Hendricks Institute—Gay and Kathlyn Hendricks

www.hendricks.com

The Hendricks Institute teaches core skills for conscious living. Its focus is on assisting people in opening to more creativity, love, and vitality through the power of conscious relationship and whole-person learning.

HerFuture—Gabrielle Bernstein

www.herfuture.com

HerFuture.com is a community for women to find mentors and be mentors. This powerful network of like-minded women focuses on service, happiness, and releasing the blocks to the awareness of self-love.

Holosync

www.centerpointe.com

Holosync is a sophisticated form of neuro-audio technology that easily and effortlessly produces the electrical brainwave patterns of deep meditation every time. It's a scientifically proven brain technology that gives you all the benefits of meditation.

The Institute for Circlework—Jalaja Bonheim

www.instituteforcirclework.org

Circlework is the art of using circle gatherings to create a field of love powerful enough to heal us and our communities. Developed by author Jalaja Bonheim, it's now used around the world, including in Israel, Palestine, and Afghanistan.

Institute of HeartMath

www.heartmath.org

The HearthMath System consists of research, programs, products, and technologies to improve health and well-being while dramatically reducing stress and boosting performance and productivity. HeartMath research has demonstrated the critical links between emotions, heart function, and cognitive performance.

The Intention Experiment—Lynne McTaggart

www.theintentionexperiment.com

The Intention Experiment is a web-based "global laboratory" involving an international consortium of prestigious scientists and thousands of participants from around the world that tests the power of intention to heal the world. People in this community report a palpable feeling of oneness.

The Ison Method—David Ison

www.theisonmethod.com

The Ison Method helps people achieve physical well-being, emotional balance, and spiritual renewal through music, meditation, and the mind-body connection.

Kristine Carlson Programs—Kristine Carlson

www.kristinecarlson.com/healing/

Expanding on the phenomenal success of the work done by her late husband, Dr. Richard Carlson (the *Don't Sweat the Small Stuff* series), Kristine has continued to share her profound message of empowerment, success, emotional strength, and love.

The Lefkoe Institute: Making Change Easier—Morty and Shelly Lefkoe

http://recreateyourlife.com

The Lefkoe Institute helps individuals who want to make lasting changes in their behavior and/or emotions in a gentle yet effective way. Using the Lefkoe Method, people's unwanted beliefs are literally unwired for good.

Living Your Wow—Kute Blackson

www.kuteblackson.com

Living Your Wow and other programs offered by Kute Blackson provide transformation and empowerment of individuals, companies, and cultures. These programs reveal to people what they have to give by liberating who they are.

The Love Disc—Akhila Rosemary Bourne

www.colorpunctureusa.org/Colorpuncture_USA/Esogetic_Self_Care.html

The Love Disc, developed by Peter Mandel, is a mandala of crystals that helps clear patterns of negativity in our subtle bodies. It allows us to open to unconditional love beyond doubt or fear.

The Love Response—Eva M. Selhub, MD

www.theloveresponse.com

Dr. Selhub teaches individuals to find resilience, health, and balance through a unique program addressing the balance between stress and love.

Make Your Success Easy—Pamela Bruner

www.makeyoursuccesseasy.com

Using state-of-the-art mind-set tools, including meridian tapping techniques such as EFT, Pamela Bruner helps you remove the blocks, fears, or limiting beliefs that are keeping you from your success.

Peter Malakoff

www.petermalakoff.com

This website offers stories, poetry, videos, and articles on a variety of spiritual topics.

Mars Venus—John Gray, PhD

www.marsvenus.com

Mars Venus offers seminars, coaching, wellness retreats, and educational and nutritional products to support your relationships, your health, and your experience of unconditional love.

Master Your Workday Now—Michael Linenberger

www.masteryourworkday.com

The Master Your Workday Now program offers simple solutions to overcome workday overwhelm—giving you greater ease and relaxation and the ability to experience more unconditional love.

Meditation Instruction—Diana Lang

www.DianaLang.com

Diana Lang, author of *Opening to Meditation—A Gentle, Guided Approach*, offers seminars on meditation, body awareness, yoga, stress reduction, and relationship development.

Metatron Heart Opening Program (Free Software)—Ron Hall

www.GlobalCoherence.org

The Metatron Heart Opening Program free software, when downloaded onto your computer, creates a field conducive to inviting, encouraging, and allowing your heart to open.

Mind-Body-Spirit Medicine—Dean Shrock, PhD

www.DeanShrock.com

Dr. Shrock offers programs that focus on how to achieve self-love and stimulate the natural harmony that lies within you.

The Mirabai Devi Foundation—Mirabai Devi

www.mirabaidevi.org

The *Mirabai Devi* Foundation is dedicated to raising world consciousness through the awakening and healing of humanity. The foundation conducts, supports, and sponsors humanitarian projects, and promotes education to help people cultivate spiritual growth.

Morter Institute & HealthCenter—Dr. Sue Morter

www.suemorter.com

Morter Institute & HealthCenter bridges science, spirit, and human possibility through life-awakening seminars, home-study products, and personal development treatment and healing sessions designed to remove subconscious interferences in order to maximize human potential.

Ali Najafi, PhD

www.alinajafi.net

Dr. Najafi, a psychotherapist/counselor and founder of Self-Empowerment Training seminars, utilizes BEST (Bio-Energetic Synchronization Technique) to support clients in integrating emotional and physical health. He offers phone counseling and creates healing retreats for couples on the Garden Island of Kauai, Hawaii.

Nine Gates Mystery School—Deborah Jones

www.ninegates.org.

Nine Gates Mystery School offers spiritual training that challenges individuals to awaken to their fullest selves and undertake a radical interior transformation paralleling the essential changes needed in our world.

Notes from the Universe—Mike Dooley

www.tut.com

Fun, short, and sometimes humorous emails written to you from "the Universe" that will remind you of life's magic and your power.

The Option Method—Lenora Boyle

www.changelimitingbeliefs.com

Since 1991, Lenora Boyle has been helping people to be happier through her interactive seminars, private coaching practice, and teleclasses. She teaches seminars using the Option Method that specialize in going to the root of the problem—the limiting belief or past conditioning.

Paraliminals—Learning Strategies Corporation

www.learningstrategies.com/Paraliminal/Home.asp

Paraliminals are a neurolinguistic programming and whole-brain learning technology that increase your personal power by activating your "whole mind" with a precise blend of music and words. Each session is carefully scripted to give you life-changing results.

The Passion Test—Janet Bray Attwood and Chris Attwood
www.thepassiontest.com
The Passion Test provides a simple yet profound tool that has helped hundreds of thousands of people discover and live their passions. It's the perfect way to align yourself with those things that matter most in your life so you can share your special gifts.

Patanjali Kundalini Yoga Care
www.kundalinicare.com
Patanjali Kundalini Yoga Care is a spiritual guidance service for sincere seekers based on traditional kundalini science. It provides assessments, individual recommendations for spiritual practice, and follow-up support and guidance.

Pfeiffer Power Seminars—Janet Pfeiffer
www.PfeifferPowerSeminars.com
Pfeiffer Power Seminars provides innovative, exciting, and comprehensive workshops and seminars devoted to personal and professional growth, self-awareness, and life enrichment. They specialize in anger management techniques, conflict management, communication, and cooperation.

PhilosophersNotes—Brian Johnson
www.philosophersnotes.com
The most transformational big ideas from one hundred of the greatest personal growth books, which will inspire and empower you to live your deepest truths.

Playfair—Matt Weinstein
www.Playfair.com
Matt Weinstein is the nation's foremost authority on the use of fun and humor in team building. The Playfair organization travels internationally delivering leadership programs based on Matt's book, *Managing to Have Fun.*

Deva Premal
www.devapremal.com
World-renowned musician Deva Premal offers music, workshops, healing exercises, and concerts that open the heart.

Radiance Healing and Radiance Meditation—Deirdre Hade

www.deirdrehade.com

Radiance Healing and Radiance Meditation facilitate the self-healing of trauma, addictions, and pain, allowing you to easily receive the divine energy flow of life. You can download the Four Chambers of the Heart Radiance Meditation from www .deirdrehade.com.

Radical Compassion—Jori and Jim Manske

www.RadicalCompassion.com

Radical Compassion offers tools and practices for connecting more fully with yourself and others with presence, empathy, and authenticity. Through their training, mediation, coaching, and facilitation, you learn to compassionately influence the world.

Realization Process—Judith Blackstone

www.realizationcenter.com

Realization Process is an integrated approach to psychological healing, embodiment, and spiritual awakening. Unique body-centered meditative exercises release psychological patterns and awaken the clear light of unitive consciousness in the whole body.

Romancing the Divine— Allison Stillman

www.romancingthedivine.com

The Romancing the Divine website offers extraordinary tools and unprecedented techniques for awakening Divine consciousness through the ancient art of anointing. Learn more about personal sessions, pure essential oils, and workshops and retreats around the world.

Sacred Centers—Anodea Judith, PhD

www.sacredcenters.com

Sacred Centers offers life-changing events and classes in which Anodea Judith teaches about personal and global transformation.

Scheele Learning Systems—Paul Scheele

www.ScheeleLearning.com

Paul Scheele guides organizations and individuals to discover resources within. His expertise in transformative learning, leadership, and change provides everyone greater access to the full range of human intelligences and the achievement of extraordinary results.

The Sedona Method—Hale Dwoskin

www.sedona.com

The Sedona Method is a unique program for making positive changes in your life. The technique supports you in quickly shifting your state of consciousness from one of stress and resistance to one of relaxation and allowing. This method is featured in the movie *Letting Go*, www.LettingGo.tv.

The Self-Love 40-Day Practices—Christine Arylo

www.SelfLoveStudio.com

Self-Love Studio provides you with tangible, yet daring and fun practices and experiences that shift your self-sabotaging habits and beliefs into self-empowering and self-loving ones.

Sensorimotor Psychotherapy—Kekuni Minton, PhD

www.sensorimotorpsychotherapy.org

Sensorimotor psychotherapy is a mind/body/spirit approach to heal from trauma and develop deeper intimacy and connection.

Shaka Vansya Ayurveda—Dr. Rama K. Mishra

www.vaidyamishra.com

This website offers information about detox, Dr. Mishra's Transdermal Marma System, food as medicine, pulse diagnosis, herbology, and practical steps to increase love and bliss in daily life.

Bernie Siegel, MD

www.berniesiegelmd.com

Bernie Siegel, MD, teaches how reparenting oneself and finding self-love can lead to self-induced healing of the body, mind, and spirit.

Simple Brilliance—Raymond Powers

www.simplebrilliance.com

Transformational coach, spiritual mentor, and consultant for three decades, Raymond assists people in creating shifts of consciousness and training them in practical tools for everyday physical, emotional, and spiritual health.

Somatic Movement Education

www.livingsomatics.com

Somatic Movement Education teaches slow, gentle movements done with awareness. The practice improves the function of the neuromuscular system and energy centers, reduces pain, and increases ease and joy in the body.

The Soulmate Kit—Arielle Ford

www.soulmatekit.com

The Soulmate Kit is a step-by-step guide consisting of a DVD, three CDs, and a 104-page workbook designed for both men and women. It guides users through a deep and detailed program for clearing out the emotional baggage of the past while magnetizing Mr. or Ms. Right into your life.

Soul Medicine Institute—Dawson Church

www.soulmedicineinstitute.org

Soul Medicine Institute is dedicated to encouraging the understanding that a vibrant spiritual connection is essential to wellness. The institute facilitates training, education, and research into the role of intention, consciousness, and energy in healing.

Spirit of Now—Peter Russell

www.peterrussell.com

The Spirit of Now offers teachings about science and consciousness, spiritual awakening, and earth and the environment. Peter Russell distills the essence of the world's spiritual traditions and disseminates it in contemporary terms.

Spirit Repair—John Douglas

www.spirit-repair.com

John Douglas practices extraordinary spiritual healing using precise techniques/ processes to remove people's subconscious blocks. This speeds the healing of individuals and the earth on many levels.

Spring Forest Qigong—Chunyi Lin

www.springforestqigong.com

Spring Forest Qigong is a simple, efficient, and effective method for helping you experience your optimal health, wellness, and happiness, helping you heal physical and emotional pain, and enhancing the quality of your life and the lives of others.

Sutherland Communications, Inc.—Caroline Sutherland

www.carolinesutherland.com

Caroline Sutherland, medical intuitive and best-selling author of *The Body Knows*, offers health education products and seminars focused on healthy aging, hormone balancing, weight loss, and vital living.

Tapas Acupressure Technique (TAT)—Tapas Fleming

www.tatlife.com

TAT is a leading-edge energy meridian healing technique for ending stress, creating vibrant good health, and enjoying a happy life. At www.tatlife.com you can download a free how-to booklet.

The Taylor Method—Kenyon Taylor

www.kenyontaylor.com

The Taylor Method helps people release long-held stress or trauma in the body and reduce pain, creating deep ease and a renewal of joy.

Terri Tate, RN, MS

www.territate.com

Terri Tate offers consulting, workshops, retreats, and performances that help people overcome the obstacles in their lives with grace and humor.

Time Portal Publications—Janet Sussman

www.timeportalpubs.com

Janet Sussman offers intuitive consulting services to align you with your Higher Self. Time Portal publishes books and CDs that expand consciousness and reveal the nature of time and space.

Trust Your Vibes—Sonia Choquette

www.trustyourvibes.com

Trust Your Vibes offers revolutionary programs that assist you in activating your sixth sense, enable you to open your heart, and guide you to find the power of your spirit in a multitude of ways.

Unstoppable Giving—Cynthia Kersey

www.unstoppable.net

Best-selling author Cynthia Kersey shows why giving *must* be part of your overall life, love, and wealth-building strategy.

Vedic Behavior and Trend Analysis Systems—William R. Levacy

www.vedicsky.com

Vedic Behavior and Trend Analysis Systems helps analyze behavior and forecast events so you can anticipate good outcomes for your actions. It provides a road map for effective living, in tune with the laws of nature.

Voh'armic Institute—Fred Johnson

www.frejon.org

Using the power of the voice, Voh'armic healing techniques take you on a journey to loving yourself.

Walking Tall—Peggy O'Neill

www.YoPeggy.com

Peggy O'Neill offers programs for empowerment and healthy relationships. Her work helps people fulfill their purpose and enjoy life to the fullest.

Walking with God—James Keeley

www.howtowalkwithGod.com

Walking with God is a practical approach to spiritual healing that describes the process of creating a divinely inspired life of health, happiness, and fulfillment, regardless of your circumstances.

Wealth Mastery Success—Chaney Weiner

www.WealthMasterySuccessProgram.com

Chaney Weiner's Wealth Mastery Success program shows you how to overcome distracting emotions in order to break through challenges in your finances, career, and relationships so that you can have more money, more time, and more freedom in your life.

The Wisdom Connection—Karen Wilhelm Buckley
www.thewisdomconnection.com
Transformational leadership development for women shows you how to use feminine wisdom to fulfill your visions with passion, purpose, and high impact. The programs engender more effective leadership, build natural authority, and close the gap between desired and bottom-line results.

Women Food and God—Geneen Roth
www.GeneenRoth.com
Geneen Roth offers events, retreats, workshops, and a community based on her teachings highlighted in her best-selling book, *Women Food and God.*

The Work—Byron Katie
www.thework.com
The Work is a simple yet powerful process of inquiry that teaches you to identify and question the stressful thoughts that cause all the suffering in the world. People who do the Work faithfully report life-changing results.

Yes to Success—Debra Halperin Poneman
www.yestosuccess.com
Providing knowledge and inspiration about true success and the simple yet powerful techniques to achieve it, Yes to Success seminars help people transform their lives.

Zero Limits—Dr. Joe Vitale
www.zerolimits.info
Dr. Joe Vitale offers resources and programs on Ho'oponopono, an ancient Hawaiian method that allows you to "clean" the negativity in your unconscious mind so you can reconnect with the Divine and follow the path of pure inspiration.

ACKNOWLEDGMENTS

So many hearts and hands helped to write this book. Carol and I feel deeply grateful for the loving support and invaluable contributions of friends, family, colleagues, and the Love Luminaries. We want to thank all who have joined us on this journey of love.

From Marci

Carol, I am beyond grateful for you. Your extraordinary dedication, brilliant mind, profound insights, and superb writing talent have made this book what it is. Thank you for pouring your soul into this project and for living the message of unconditional love throughout the process. You've inspired me daily by how you've kept your heart open, no matter what. Above all, thank you for your loving devotion to our friendship of thirty-two years. Nobody else knows my mind, my heart, and my voice like you do. You are truly a sister of my heart.

The amazing family I've been blessed with: My mom and dad, whose unconditional love and belief in me have been the foundation of my life. May your loving spirits continue to live on in my words and actions. My sister Lynda, my brother Paul, and my sister-in-law, Susan, for your ongoing support and for carrying on the family legacy of love. My fabulous nephews and nieces, Aaron, Vickie, Jared and Lisa, and Tony; my "Latvian daughter" Maija Snepste; and my "little sister" Leah Basch, for all being my children in spirit.

Michael Linenberger, for being a wonderful partner on this journey of unconditional love. I am so grateful for your groundedness, support, and big heart, and for helping bring this message to my daily life.

Bonnie Solow, who continues to be a gift from the universe, as my literary agent extraordinaire and dear friend. I appreciate beyond words your impeccable guidance, steady support, and loving friendship. You are the fairy godmother of this book.

Sergio, for sharing a deep soul love no matter what form our relationship takes. You are always my ally on this journey of the heart.

Marianne Williamson, for continually inspiring me to "go deep." You are an amazing woman, a remarkable visionary, and a treasured sister. I am so grateful for your support and so blessed by your presence in my life.

Jack Canfield, for being a magnificent mentor and friend. You are a master at what you do, and I feel fortunate to have learned from the best. Inga Canfield, my magical friend, who is beautifully able to help me laugh and love through thick and thin. Patty Aubery, for being the most level-headed, wise woman around. Thank you for always being there.

Pete Bissonette, Bert Heaton, Shannon Mell, Janie Solarski, and the stellar team at Learning Strategies, for being my huge support and fabulous partners in spreading the message of love and happiness around the globe. You are my heroes.

My colleagues on the Transformational Leadership Council, I am constantly awed by your individual and collective brilliance, sheer goodness, and commitment to make a difference in the world. I so deeply appreciate your support.

Maharishi Mahesh Yogi, my first spiritual teacher, for giving me the gift of meditation, life-changing knowledge, and profound, ageless wisdom. My heart is full of gratitude.

Janet (Jani) Attwood, for your extraordinarily big heart. Thank you for always believing in me and for being the best kind of friend, who helps make the journey a joy. Chris Attwood, thank you for your unfailing kindness and unwavering support. Cindy Buck, for our enduring friendship that I cherish. I'm grateful for the way you are always there for me with love and just the right words. Debra Poneman, for getting me started in this world of speaking. I still want to be just like you when I grow up!

Bill Bauman, for being my personal guardian angel and spiritual mentor. Your expanded vision, deep love, and unique sense of humor are just a few of the reasons you are a constant blessing in my life. Tiziana Della-Rovere, for being my "enlovened" guide in helping me experience unconditional love from within. Deep thanks for your wise counsel. Deirdre Hade, for your radiant light, your exquisite support, and your practical spirituality. My heart is filled with gratitude.

Bill Levacy, for always inspiring me to move in the right direction and at the right time. You've guided me impeccably for the last eighteen years; you're a star! Nandu, for helping me stay on course and keeping the energy high. Michael Laughrin, for your steadiness and help in connecting me with cosmic support.

Dr. Suhas and Dr. Manisha Kshirsagar, for helping me stay strong, balanced, and healthy in body, mind, and soul. Thank you for being my gifted doctors.

Swami Chandrasekharanand Saraswati and Joan Shivarpita Harrigan for your brilliant teachings and practices that have made such a difference in my life.

Susan Burks, Shelly Roby, Gayatri Schriefer, Brian Siddhartha Ingle, and Jahavani Schriefer for bringing the spirit of this message to my home. I feel blessed to be around your great energy on a daily basis.

My extraordinary women's group, the Women of Marin: Shelly Lefkoe, Bonnie Gray, Lynne Twist, Joan Emery, Trisha Waldron, Alice Josephs, Dianne Morrison, Anat Baniel, Liza Ingrasci, Sydney Cresci, Maggie Weiss, Aimee Mandossian, Stephanie Wolf. You are my soul sisters, and I am so grateful for the sacred connection we have and for our group's being a beautiful container of love for me.

My phenomenal friends who have given me love and support throughout this journey: Lenora Boyle, Catherine Oxenberg, Jennifer Hawthorne, AlexSandra Leslie, Suzanne Lawlor, Mary Weiss, Sue Morter, Jill Lublin, Steve Lillo, Stewart and Joan Emery, Peggy O'Neill, Cynthia Kersey, Marcia Wieder, Elinor Hall, Ron Hall, Robert Kenyon, Renee Skop, Lynn Robertson, Arielle Ford, Brian Hilliard, Yakov Smirnoff, Amy Edwards and Hale Dwoskin, Donna Bauman, Diane Alabaster, Shanan Manuel, Angel Evans, Holly Moore, Lane Cole, Janice Peterson. And to all my friends who saw articles on unconditional love and sent them to me (you know who you are).

Judy O'Beirn, Peggy McColl, and the team at Hasmark Services, for your online marketing wizardry. I love working with you all. Bunmi Zalob, my social media goddess, for bringing me into the Facebook and Twitter world. Thank you for your wonderful dedication. Suzanna Gratz, for enthusiastically continuing to help promote this message throughout the world. Jennifer Geronimo, for joyfully bringing me the right speaking engagements.

The hundreds of people who have supported the happiness and love message by inviting me on their television or radio shows, teleseminars, or podcasts, or by blogging, tweeting, or otherwise getting the message out in a myriad of ways.

From Carol

Marci, my wonderful friend, soul sister, and "book co-mother"—we did it! Writing *Love for No Reason* has taken us places we've never gone before—together or alone. I am profoundly grateful for the opportunity you've given me to explore the subject of unconditional love in such depth. What I've learned has transformed my life—and my ability to love. You already know this, but I'll say it again: I am always here for you. Our friendship is one of my greatest treasures.

My dearest husband, Larry Kline. You are my rock. Thank you for your kindness, your humor, your spiritual depth: all these anchor me when I get too wired up on ideas, creativity, and deadlines. I'm so happy we're "doing life" together. My stepchildren, Lorin and McKenna—you are both amazing people. I am so grateful to know you and love you. My sister, Bobbie, author and all-around brilliant person, who is always so willing to help me out when I get stuck—personally and professionally. My sister-in-law, Pam, another skilled writer and editor, who listens so sympathetically to my complaints, challenges, and breakthroughs. My other sister-in-law, Diana, who provided me with her insightful thoughts on unconditional love at a crucial point in the book's evolution. Thank you for your encouragement and support. My other sibs and their spouses, Jim, Wilbur, Burt, Holly, and Charlie, who are each so talented at so many things and so dear to me. My niece Rachel and nephew-to-be Danny, for your enthusiasm and friendship while I was in the thick of the writing process. And my other nieces and nephews and their spouses, Sam and Steve, Jonathan and Lisa, Zach and Miriam, Michael and Monica, and Seth and Kerensa; I'm so lucky to have such a wonderful family. I love you all.

My spiritual teacher Sri Sri Ravi Shankar, who has given me true inner peace and joy. I am eternally grateful.

Cindy Buck, for being there for me whenever I needed you—and for being such a beautiful role model of holding on to the Self through the "fire." Your love and friendship mean the world to me. My women's group:

Karen Joost and Toni d'Orr, I admire your accomplishments, value your advice, and cherish your friendship. Thank you for everything; you know I love you. Alasdair Coyne, Catherine Gould-Stern, and Laurie Edgcomb, whose kindness and support came at just the right time. Thank you for looking out for me throughout this book process and beyond. John Lietz and Femke Van Velzen, my cheerleaders and marvelous companions— here's to adventures and the opposite of small talk. My dearly loved circle of friends, all radiantly wonderful (in alphabetical order): Patty Aubery, Ceci Balmer, Josie Batorski, Kathy Bennett, Ann and Jeff Beth, Lane Cole, Betsy Dockhorn, Nina Falk, Patti Gallagher, Stephanie Hewitt, Thom and Diana Krystofiak, Marcy Luikart, Wilma Melville, Hollie Moore, Georgia Nemkov, Peggy O'Neill, my co-mother Dia Osborn, Debbie Pogel (the OSR), Elizabeth Reynolds, Sheila Ross, Jerre Stetson, Allison Stillman, Kenyon Taylor, Kevin and Louisa Twohy, Elin and Stuart Valentine, Christian Wolfbrandt, Nick and Sarajane Woolf. You make me wealthy in all the ways that matter.

From Both of Us

Our amazing writing partners and editors: Amely Greeven, who is a warrior. Thank you for helping us put these complex ideas into coherent form. We are deeply grateful for your keen insights and dedicated support. Jennifer Hawthorne, who brought a loving presence as well as a clear, penetrating intelligence to the editing of these chapters. You were a lifesaver and we so enjoyed getting to work with you again. Cindy Buck, who has a magic touch when it comes to putting the heart into words. Thank you for always being there for us with your talent and love. Cynthia Lane, who combines the groundedness of Mother Earth with the expansiveness of the heavens. Your clear perception and guidance helped us stay on the right track, and your review of the interview transcripts was infinitely helpful. Danielle Dorman, your skillful editing was fabulous for the book and your calm, steadying influence was balm for our hearts. Divina Infusino, for your help in smoothing Part 1 and for your enthusiastic encouragement. Katie Darling, for your insightful feedback and suggestions for the manuscript.

Our main muses: Rick Hanson, we'll always be grateful for your important role during the conception stage of this book. You're a stellar human being with a wise brain and overflowing heart. Janet Sussman, who gave so generously of her time and amazing knowledge. We are transformed by our connection to you. Deirdre Hade, for your light and guidance. Thank you for helping nourish our souls.

Shelly Roby, Marci's marketing director, for her brilliance in everything she does. Huge thanks for running the business so flawlessly and for always bringing your giving heart, big smile, and infinite support to this book and to Marci's life. Kim Forcina for her dedication and enthusiasm in spreading the message of love and for keeping Marci's life in the flow. Thank you for being the great heart of the Love Ambassador Program. Suzanne Lawlor for her brilliant coaching and teaching skills and her loving service to the highest good. Thank you for being the divine mother of the Love Ambassador Program. Sue Penberthy, Marci's steadfast friend and bookkeeper, who is the epitome of "mother love."

Courtney Paulson, for her excellent help reviewing and processing the Love for No Reason survey results. Mary Weiss, for doing such a good job of "harvesting" the interview transcripts to make them more accessible. And D'ette, our permissions queen, who skillfully managed this daunting process with humor, effectiveness, and grace.

Sarah Clarehart, for your dedication and beautiful graphic design help. Joe Burull and Jerry Downs, for being photographic geniuses and producing photos of Marci she really likes—no easy feat! Susan Burks, for translating our vision into clear and useful diagrams. Thank you also for your valuable feedback on the manuscript and for your support of us throughout the birth of *Love for No Reason*. Jerry Teplitz and Amsheva Malani, for energetically uplifting this book. Deena Fettner and Abigail Paladin, for diligently transcribing hundreds of hours of interviews.

Our publishing team at Free Press, whom we love for *every* reason. It's a pleasure to be able to work with such talented and kind human beings. Dominick Anfuso, for being the most supportive, unflappable, and delightful editor we could ask for. Martha Levin, for your continued confidence in us and belief in the importance of this topic. Maura O'Brien, for your thoughtful editing and for being so on top of all the details that ensure a high-quality book. Leah Miller, for being a fabulous resource and handling all our requests with great competence, grace, and speed. You're a joy. Suzanne Donahue, for being our marketing queen, generating innovative approaches, and supporting the creative ideas we suggest. Carisa Hayes, our publicity champion, whose charming persistence ensures that our message is broadcast loud and clear. And Heidi Metcalfe and Jill Siegel, our PR superwomen, who leave no stone unturned to find every possible media opportunity. We love working with you. Jennifer Weidman, for your superb legal counsel. Eric Fuentecilla, for your work on another great cover.

The Love Luminaries, for so openly sharing your experiences, wisdom, and expertise to help others lead a life of unconditional love. You've blazed a beautiful trail. Also, to the many people who responded to the Love for No Reason survey and offered your great input and ideas. Your contributions to the Love for No Reason Program were invaluable.

Doc Childre, Deborah Rozman, Howard Martin, Dr. Rollin McCraty, Sheva Carr, and the rest of the extraordinary HeartMath team, for being global leaders in the science and application of the heart's intelligence. Your support of us and this project is a beautiful expression of your own developed hearts.

Jack Canfield, Mark Victor Hansen, Patty Aubery, and the rest of the *Chicken Soup for the Soul* family for providing the foundation of our writing careers. We feel so fortunate to have walked this path with you.

Because of the size and scope of this project, we may have left out the names of some people who contributed along the way. If so, please forgive us, and know that we really do appreciate you very much.

We are so grateful and love you all!

GIVING BACK

In the spirit of giving back, we are delighted to donate a portion of the author proceeds from *Love for No Reason* to the following worthy nonprofit organizations:

The Global Coherence Initiative (GCI) is a science-based, cocreative project to unite people in heart-focused care and intention, to facilitate the shift in global consciousness from instability and discord to balance, cooperation, and enduring peace. GCI's goals are to

- empower our ability to navigate through global changes with less stress and more ease.
- build a Global Coherence Monitoring System to test the hypothesis that groups of people in heart coherence can positively affect the earth's energetic fields.
- correlate coherence-level data collected from the GCI global community with changes in the earth's fields, along with changes in social, environmental, and health outcomes.

Global Coherence Initiative (sponsored by the Institute of HeartMath)
14700 West Park Avenue, Boulder Creek, CA 95006
(866) 221-6339
www.glcoherence.org

One World Children's Fund (OWCF) is a community of people committed to supporting children around the world who lack the most basic necessities. They do this by empowering people living in the United States to champion grassroots organizations that are building sustainable solutions to local problems affecting children and their caregivers. One World Children's Fund is a force of love in the world to help all children live in peace, prosperity, and equality.

One World Children's Fund
1012 Torney Avenue, San Francisco, CA 94129
(415) 255-3014
www.oneworldchildrensfund.org

The Pachamama Alliance is dedicated to empowering indigenous people to preserve their territories and way of life and thereby protect the natural world for the entire human family. Their main strategy includes supplying rainforest peoples with the tools and resources necessary to support the continued strength and vitality of their communities and culture. The indigenous people offer a new way of seeing and living in the world that is inherently interconnected and sustainable. The Pachamama Alliance is a reciprocal partnership working to bring forth an environmentally sustainable, spiritually fulfilling, and socially just human presence on this planet.

The Pachamama Alliance
1009 General Kennedy Avenue, PO Box 29191, San Francisco, CA 94129
(415) 561-4522
www.pachamama.org

The Wellspring Institute for Neuroscience and Contemplative Wisdom offers skillful means for changing the brain to benefit the whole person. It draws on psychology, neurology, and the great contemplative traditions for tools that anyone can use in daily life for greater happiness, love, and wisdom. The Wellspring Institute collects, organizes, and distributes resources for psychological and spiritual growth, actively supporting the work of others aligned with its mission. It sponsors focused research activities, including pilot studies of peak states.

Wellspring Institute for Neuroscience and Contemplative Wisdom
25 Mitchell Boulevard, Suite 3, San Rafael, CA 94903
(415) 491-4900
www.wisebrain.org

ABOUT MARCI SHIMOFF

*M*arci Shimoff is a celebrated transformational leader and an expert on unconditional love and happiness. She has inspired millions of people around the world with her message of the infinite possibilities that life holds. As a top-rated professional speaker, she has delivered speeches and programs for a large variety of audiences and organizations, including numerous Fortune 500 companies. For over twenty-five years, she has received wide acclaim for sharing her breakthrough methods for personal fulfillment and professional success.

Marci is the author of the *New York Times* best seller *Happy for No Reason: 7 Steps to Being Happy from the Inside Out*, which has been translated into thirty-one languages worldwide. She is the host of the national PBS television special called *Happy for No Reason*. She's also the woman's face of the biggest self-help book phenomenon in history, *Chicken Soup for the Soul*, as coauthor of six of the top-selling titles in the series, including *Chicken Soup for the Woman's Soul* and *Chicken Soup for the Mother's Soul*. Her books have sold more than 14 million copies worldwide, have been on the *New York Times* best seller list for a total of 118 weeks, and have been #1 on the *USA Today*, Amazon, Barnes and Noble.com, and *Publishers Weekly* best seller lists. Marci is one of the best-selling nonfiction authors of all time.

In addition, Marci is a featured teacher in the international movie and book phenomenon *The Secret*, offering her insights on the key principles to creating lasting success and fulfillment. A popular and engaging media personality, Marci has appeared on more than six hundred national and regional television and radio shows and has been interviewed for more than a hundred newspaper articles throughout North America. Her work has been published in national women's magazines, including *Ladies' Home Journal, Self, Body and Soul,* and *Woman's World*.

President and cofounder of the Esteem Group, Marci delivers keynote addresses and seminars on success, happiness, love, and the law of attraction to corporations, women's associations, and professional and nonprofit organizations. She received her MBA in organizational behavior from UCLA and also completed a one-year advanced certification program to become a stress management consultant.

Marci is a founding member and serves on the executive committee of the Transformational Leadership Council, a group of one hundred top leaders serving over 10 million people in the self-development market. Marci is dedicated to fulfilling her vision and life's purpose of helping people to live more empowered and joy-filled lives.

To find out more about Marci's keynote presentations, books, or seminar programs, you can contact her at

The Esteem Group
57 Bayview Drive
San Rafael, CA 94901
Phone: 415-789-1300
Fax: 415-789-1309
www.MarciShimoff.com
www.TheLoveBook.com

ABOUT CAROL KLINE

Carol Kline is the coauthor with Marci Shimoff of *Happy for No Reason: 7 Steps to Being Happy from the Inside Out*. She also coauthored five books—with over 5 million sold—in the best-selling *Chicken Soup for the Soul* series, including *Chicken Soup for the Dog Lover's Soul* and *Chicken Soup for the Cat Lover's Soul*, and the #1 New York Times best-selling *Chicken Soup for the Mother's Soul 2*. She is also the coautheor of *The Ultimate Dog Lover* and *The Ultimate Cat Lover*. In 2006 she cowrote *You've Got to Read this Book: 55 People Tell the Story of the Book That Changed Their Life* with Jack Canfield and Gay Hendricks.

A freelance writer/editor for over thirty years, Carol, who has a BA in literature, specializes in narrative nonfiction and self-help. Carol is also a speaker, self-esteem facilitator, and animal welfare advocate. In addition, she has taught stress-management systems to the general public since 1975. At present she is at work on several writing projects on a variety of topics.

To write to Carol or to inquire about her writing or speaking services, please use the following contact information:

Carol Kline
Carol Kline, Inc.
P.O. Box 521
Ojai, California 93024
Email: carol@thelovebook.com

BIOGRAPHIES OF THE LOVE LUMINARIES WHOSE STORIES APPEAR IN *LOVE FOR NO REASON*

Johnny Barnes is a happy Christian gentleman who has endeared himself to thousands of Bermudians and tourists alike with his simple gestures of greeting. Monday through Friday, Johnny waves and calls out happy wishes to the commuters as they pass him on the Crow Lane roundabout in the city of Hamilton in Bermuda.

Bill Bauman, PhD, is a noted trainer, speaker, and empowerer of people—as a psychotherapist, seminar leader, entrepreneur, peace advocate, spiritual teacher, and visionary of life's possibilities. Bill's books include *Oz Power* and *Soul Vision: A Modern Mystic Looks at Life through the Eyes of the Soul.* www.billbauman.net

Russell Bishop possesses an uncommon ability to inspire clarity and provoke transformational change. Russell created Insight Seminars in 1978 with well over 1 million graduates in thirty-four countries, is the author of *Workarounds That Work* (January 2011), and founded Bishop and Bishop, a management consulting firm specializing in the implementation of strategy. www.BishopandBishop.com

Sheva Carr speaks to people around the world on how to access heart intelligence and how to receive the benefits of the heart's impact on consciousness, health, performance, and creativity. At heart she is a stand for impossible good made real every day through the power of love. www.sheva carr.com

Mirabai Devi is an international spiritual teacher, a conduit for healing, an author, and the founder of the Mirabai Devi Foundation. Her programs include guided meditations, transformational healing, and the transmission of Divine Light. To order one of her meditation or knowledge CDs, her book *Samadhi,* or for additional information about Mirabai's work, please visit www.mirabaidevi.org.

Melissa Etheridge is an award-winning singer/songwriter and musician who has sold more than 27 million albums worldwide and has received two Grammy awards and one Academy award. She is also a breast cancer survivor and an author. www.MelissaEtheridge.com

Amely Greeven is a writer and teacher who specializes in delivering messages of change and transformation—both inner and outer. She has cowritten books including *Clean* with Dr. Alejandro Junger and Mariel Hemingway's *Healthy Living from the Inside Out.* She also teaches meditation around the world and writes about it at www.twentyminutemeditation.com.

Deirdre Hade is a spiritual teacher, healer, and mother who guides people to live a life of "Radiance." A master of mystical teachings and energy work, she is the founder of Radiance Healing and Radiance Meditation, a healing modality and spiritual practice created from her own experience of awakening in Kabbalah. www.deirdrehade.com

Gay Hendricks has served for more than thirty years as one of the major contributors to the fields of relationship transformation and body/mind therapies. Along with his wife, Dr. Kathlyn Hendricks, Gay is the author of many best sellers, including *Conscious Loving, At the Speed Of Life,* and *Five Wishes.* www.hendricks.com

Kathlyn Hendricks has been the CEO and director of training for the Hendricks Institute for over twenty years. A board-certified dance/movement therapist since 1975, she has coauthored ten books with her husband Gay and has led seminars in their somatic approach to relationship transformation all over the world. www.hendricks.com

James Keeley, author of *Walking with God: How to Achieve Health, Happiness, and Fulfillment through Spiritual Healing,* has had the privilege to facilitate healing for individuals, couples, and organizations throughout the world. Download hours of free audio lectures and discover how to create a Divinely inspired life at www.howtowalkwithGod.com.

Morty Lefkoe, president and founder of the Lefkoe Institute, is the creator of a series of psychological processes (the Lefkoe Method) that result in profound personal and organizational change, quickly and permanently. He is also the author of *Re-create Your Life: Transforming Yourself and Your World.* www.recreateyourlife.com

Jim and Jori Manske share their passion for compassion, offering training, coaching, and mediation inspired by decades of spiritual practice. As certified trainers with the Center for Nonviolent Communication, they offer NVC around the world. www.radicalcompassion.com

Dr. Sue Morter is an authority and master of the Bio-Energetic Synchronization Technique (BEST), a neuroemotional process that addresses the mind, body, and spirit, and their influence on health. In 1987 she founded Morter HealthCenter, which teaches patients how to tap into the healing force of body, mind, and spirit naturally. www.suemorter.com

Janet Pfeiffer, motivational speaker, award-winning author, and corporate consultant, specializes in healing anger. A TV host, a columnist, and an instructor at a battered women's shelter, Janet is a frequent guest on radio and TV, including Lifetime, NBC News, and Fox. Her book, *The Secret Side of Anger*, is endorsed by best-selling author Dr. Bernie Siegel. www.PfeifferPowerSeminars.com

Yvonne Pointer is a community activist, philanthropist, humanitarian, author, and international speaker. The recipient of numerous awards such as the 908th Point of Light (from former President George H. W. Bush), a 2001 Essence Award, and induction into the Ohio Women's Hall of Fame. Yvonne has written books including *Behind the Death of a Child* and *Two Dollars In My Pocket*. www.yvonnepointer.com

Debra Halperin Poneman began in 1981 to teach cutting-edge knowledge about true success and simple yet effective techniques to achieve it. Having "retired" for nineteen years to be a mom at home to son Daniel and daughter Deanna, she has now returned, with deeper wisdom and greater insight into the human spirit. www.YesToSuccess.com

Geneen Roth has written eight best-selling books, including *Women Food*

and God, that teach that what you believe about life, love, change, joy, and possibility is revealed in how, when, and what you eat. www.GeneenRoth.com

Sally Sals's occupation is loving people. She also writes poetry and children's stories, paints, does art therapy with children, and does inner child work with adults. She lives in deep gratitude for the magic and sacredness of life. Sally and her beloved husband, Robb, reside in Isla Mujeres, Mexico. sallysals@ymail.com

David Spangler has been a spiritual teacher since 1964. He was codirector of the Findhorn Foundation Community, cofounded the Lorian Association, a spiritual educational foundation, and is a director of the Lorian Center for Incarnational Spirituality. His books include *Blessing: The Art and the Practice* and *Facing the Future.* www.Lorian.org

Allison Stillman is a renowned aromatic alchemist, author, and expert on the historical use of essential oils in religious and spiritual ceremonies. Her book *The Sacred Art of Anointing* is a result of her thirty years of research and practical experience with essential oils and anointing. www.romancingthedivine.com

Terri Tate, RN, MS, is a speaker/humorist who thrives in the wake of disfiguring oral cancer from which she had a 2 percent chance of survival. Her hilarious solo show, *Shopping as a Spiritual Path,* and her upcoming book chronicle that journey. Terri also gives presentations on *Humor, Resilience, and Hope in the Face of Unwanted Change.* www.territate.com

Rosemary Trible is an author, speaker, and activist for those caught in the cycle of fear, especially from sexual assault. Having been raped at gunpoint, she shares her book, *Fear to Freedom,* to help heal others. Today, she and her husband, a former U.S. senator, partner to inspire leaders with compassion to change the world. www.feartofreedomjourney.com

THE LOVE LUMINARIES

Terri Amos-Britt, www.enlightenedfamilyinstitute.com

Arjuna Ardagh, arjunaardagh.com

Alison Armstrong, www.understandmen.com

Constance Arnold, www.fulfillingyourpurpose.com

Dr. Art Aron, www.psychology.stonybrook.edu/aronlab-/

Angeles Arrien, www.angelesarrien.com

Christine Arylo, www.daretoliveyou.com

Chris Attwood and Janet Bray Attwood, www.thepassiontest.com

Anat Baniel, www.anatbanielmethod.com

James Baraz, www.jamesbaraz.com

Johnny Barnes

Sergio Baroni, www.sergiobaroni.com

Bill Bauman, www.billbauman.net

Gabrielle Bernstein, www.herfuture.com

Trudy Siewert Bhaerman, trudy@truehearttransformations.com

Russell Bishop, www.BishopandBishop.com

Kute Blackson, www.kuteblackson.com

Judith Blackstone, www.realizationcenter.com

Jalaja Bonheim, www.instituteforcirclework.org

Dr. Lilli Botchis, www.earthspectrum.com

Reverend Cynthia Bourgeault, www.contemplative.org

Lenora Boyle, www.changelimitingbeliefs.com

Gregg Braden, www.greggbraden.com

Helice "Sparky" Bridges, www.differencemakersinternational.org

Dr. Wilma Bronkey, www.enchantedacres.org

Pamela Bruner, www.makeyoursuccesseasy.com

Karen Wilhelm Buckley, www.thewisdomconnection.com

Jack Canfield, www.jackcanfield.com

Kristine Carlson, www.kristinecarlson.com/healing/

Sheva Carr, www.shevacarr.com

Beth Nielsen Chapman, www.bethnielsenchapman.com

Doc Childre, www.heartmath.com

Sonia Choquette, www.soniachoquette.com

Ed Conmey, www.peacepath.org

Bill Cumming, www.theboothbyinstitute.org

Raphael Cushnir, www.cushnir.com

His Holiness the Dalai Lama, www.dalailama.com

Deanna Davis, www.deannadavis.net

Michael Dean

Tiziana dellaRovere, www.enlovement.com

Mirabai Devi, www.mirabaidevi.org

Dr. James Doty, http://ccare.stanford.edu

Patrick Dougherty, www.awholeheartedembrace.com

Gary Douglas, www.accessconsciousness.com

John Douglas, www.spirit-repair.com

Dr. John Douillard, www.lifespa.com

Hale Dwoskin, www.sedona.com

Kathleen Eldon, www.creativevisions.org

Patricia Ellsberg, http://PatriciaEllsberg.com/

Stewart Emery, www.stewartemery.com

Matthew and Terces Engelhart, www.cafegratitude.com

Fariba Enteshari, www.rumiedu.com

Melissa Etheridge, www.melissaetheridge.com

Nina Falk, www.NinaFalkglass.com

Tapas Fleming, www.tatlife.com

Arielle Ford, www.arielleford.com

Dr. Barton Goldsmith, www.BartonGoldsmith.com

Dr. John Gray, www.marsvenus.com

Leah Green, www.compassionatelistening.org

Amely Greeven, www.twentyminutemeditation.com

Deirdre Hade, www.deirdrehade.com

Ron Hall, www.GlobalCoherence.org

Jim Hamilton, www.VisionariesLab.com

Dr. Rick Hanson, www.rickhanson.net

Gay and Kathlyn Hendricks, www.hendricks.com

Brian Hilliard, www.soulmatesecret.com

Connie Huebner, www.DivineMotherOnline.net

David Ison, www.theisonmethod.com

Fred Johnson, www.frejon.org

Deborah Jones, www.ninegates.org

Dr. Zoran Josipovic, http://homepages.nyu.edu/~zj232/

Isha Judd, www.whywalkwhenyoucanfly.com

Dr. Anodea Judith, www.sacredcenters.com

James Keeley, www.howtowalkwithGod.com

Cynthia Kersey, www.unstoppable.net

Dr. Dharma Singh Khalsa, www.drdharma.com

Kaho Koinuma, www.mandalasoftheheart.com

Cathy Korson, Shao6123@aol.com

Norberto Krug, www.johnofgod.com

Drs. Suhas and Manisha Kshirsagar, www.AyurvedicHealing.net

Dr. Liisa Kyle, www.liisakyle.com

Cynthia Lane, www.firstlighttransformations.com

Diana Lang, www.DianaLang.com

Morty Lefkoe, www.mortylefkoe.com

Shelly Lefkoe, www.thelefkoeway.com

Ellena Lieberman, www.dynamicmanifestation.com

Chunyi Lin, www.springforestqigong.com

Michael Lindfield, www.meditationmount.org

Dr. Frederic Luskin, www.learningtoforgive.com

Peter Malakoff, www.petermalakoff.com

Jeddah Mali, www.jeddahmali.com

Jori and Jim Manske, www.RadicalCompassion.com

Dr. Mollie Marti, http://bestlifedesign.com

Jeannette Maw, www.goodvibecoach.com

Dr. Rollin McCraty, www.heartmath.org

Lynne McTaggart, www.lynnemctaggart.com

Jim Mikesell

Dr. Kekuni Minton, www.kekuniminton.com

Vaidya R. K. Mishra, www.vaidyamishra.com

Stuart Mooney Jr., www.stuartmooney.com

David and Kristin Morelli, www.Enwaken.com

Dr. Sue Morter, www.suemorter.com

Laura W. Murphy, www.lwmurphy.com

Ali Najafi, www.alinajafi.net

Sweet Medicine Nation, www.fwfoundation.com

OmaKayuel

Peggy O'Neill, www.YoPeggy.com

Judy Palumbo, Judy.Palumbo@yahoo.com

Janet Pfeiffer, www.PfeifferPowerSeminars.com

Yvonne Pointer, www.yvonnepointer.com

Debra Halperin Poneman, www.yestosuccess.com

Dr. Stephen G. Post, www.stephengpost.com

Raymond Powers, www.simplebrilliance.com

Deva Premal, www.devapremal.com

Bill Psillas, billpsillas@gmail.com

Leslie Robarge

Mike Robbins, www.Mike-Robbins.com

Sherry Rogers, www.magicdoeshappen.com

Barry Ross, barryross@lisco.com

Geneen Roth, www.GeneenRoth.com

Peter Russell, www.peterrussell.com

Scott Rutherford

Robb and Sally Sals, robbsals@sbcglobal.net, sallysals@ymail.com

Paul Scheele, www.ScheeleLearning.com

Dr. Eva Selhub, www.theloveresponse.com

Dr. Dean Shrock, www.DeanShrock.com

Dr. Bernie Siegel, www.berniesiegelmd.com

David Spangler, www.Lorian.org

Temba Spirit

Allison Stillman, www.romancingthedivine.com

Tom Stone, www.greatlifetechnologies.com

Sherry Strong, www.sherrystrong.com

Janet Sussman, www.timeportalpubs.com

Caroline Sutherland, www.carolinesutherland.com

Terri Tate, www.territate.com

Kenyon Taylor, www.kenyontaylor.com

Rabbi David Thomas, www.bethelsudbury.org/

Katherine Woodard Thomas, www.FemininePower.com

Rosemary Dunaway Trible, www.feartofreedomjourney.com

Amy Eldon Turteltaub, www.creativevisions.org

Lynne Twist, www.soulofmoney.org

Colin Ude-Lewis, www.wisdomnote.com

Joe Vitale, www.mrfire.com

Bob Votruba, www.onemillionactsofkindness.com

Doug Waagen

Dr. Brenda Wade, www.docwade.com

Chaney Weiner, www.WealthMasterySuccessProgram.com

Matt Weinstein, www.Playfair.com

Marcia Wieder, www.marciawieder.com

Marianne Williamson, www.marianne.com

PERMISSIONS

We are grateful to the various people who shared with us their compelling and uplifting stories for inclusion in this book. In addition, we thank the following individuals and organizations who have given us permission to reprint their material:

Pg. 15   *The Monk and the Samurai story.* Adapted with permission from John Porcino, contributor and coeditor of *Spinning Tales, Weaving Hope: Stories of Peace, Justice & the Environment,* edited by Ed Brody, Jay Goldspinner, Katie Green, Rona Leventhal, and John Porcino, New Society Publishers, 1992.

Pg. 75   *The Realization Process—Embodiment.* Printed by permission of Judith Blackstone.

Pg. 78   *From Fear to Freedom.* Adapted from *Fear to Freedom: What If You Did Not Have to Be So Afraid?* by Rosemary Trible, published by VMI Publishers, February 2010, ISBN: 978-1935265092.

Pg. 85   *Circles of Support Process.* Printed by permission of Rick Hanson.

Pg. 102   *Free Your* Hara—*Awaken Your Vitality Exercise.* Printed by permission of Anat Baniel Method.

Pg. 107   *"The Deeper Song" by Geneen Roth.* © 2011. Printed by permission of Geneen Roth & Associates, Inc. All rights reserved.

Pg. 115   *The CORE (Center of Remaining Energy) Technique.* Printed by permission of Tom Stone and Great Life Technologies.

Pg. 138   *An EFT Tapping Exercise for Loving the Unlovable in Yourself.* Printed by permission of Pamela Bruner. "Emotional Freedom Techniques EFT" is a registered trademark of Gary H. Craig.

Pg. 150   *The Self-Empowerment Questions.* Printed by permission of Jack Canfield.

Pg. 179   *HeartMath Inner-Ease Technique.* Printed by permission of the Institute of HeartMath.

Pg. 186   *Lyrics from "Fearless Love."* Reprinted by permission of Melissa Etheridge.

Pg. 211   *Nonviolent Communication: Speaking Exercise.* www.NonViolentCommunication.com

Pg. 213   *NVC Listening story.* Adapted from *Nonviolent Communication: A Language of Life,* by Marshall B. Rosenberg, PhD, published by PuddleDancer Press. www.NonViolentCommunication.com

Pg. 220 *Compassionate Listening Exercise.* Printed by permission of Leah Green.

Pg. 237 *Dissolving Limiting Beliefs with the Option Method.* Printed by permission of Deborah Mendel and Lenora Boyle.

Pg. 248 *Inner Chamber—The Heart of Intuition Exercise.* Printed by permission of David and Kristin Morelli.

Pg. 267 *Meditation for Oneness.* Printed by permission of John Douglas.

Pg. 277 *Invitation to Divine Grace: Grace Points and Divine Grace Prayer.* Grace Points printed by permission of Edward Conmey. Excerpt of Divine Grace Prayer printed by permission of Connie Huebner.

Enjoy more unconditional love day by day . . .

Claim Your FREE
LOVE FOR NO REASON TOOLS at
www.TheLoveBook.com/bookgifts

Congratulations! You're on the Love for No Reason journey, and you'll continue to grow in the experience of unconditional love every day if you put the knowledge you've gained in this book into practice. To help speed you on your way, I've created the following gifts for you:

Free Audio Recording: *Highlights of the Love Luminary Interviews*

Listen to some of the most inspiring and enlightening excerpts from my interviews with the Love Luminaries. There's a special power in hearing these people share their remarkable stories and insights about creating a life of unconditional love.

Free *Love for No Reason Workbook*

This downloadable 20-page workbook includes the *Love for No Reason* Questionnaire, all 14 of the Love Key Exercises, and special bonus material.

Free *Love for No Reason eZine*

Every few weeks I will send you an inspiring and practical ezine that includes valuable tips and the latest breakthroughs and ideas on unconditional love.

BONUS: Free *Love Keys Miniposter*

This beautiful one-page summary of the 14 Love Keys is perfect to hang on your vision board or display in a special place where you will see it daily as a reminder.

For these and other free gifts, visit
www.TheLoveBook.com/bookgifts.

To access free gifts, users must register by providing their first name and email address. Offer subject to availability.